WHO KILLED CHANNEL 9?

WHO KILLED CHANNEL 9?

The death of Kerry Packer's mighty TV dream machine

GERALD STONE

MACMILLAN
Pan Macmillan Australia

First published 2007 in Macmillan by Pan Macmillan Australia Pty Limited
1 Market Street, Sydney

National Library of Australia
Cataloguing-in-Publication data:

Stone, Gerald (Gerald Louis).
Who killed Channel 9? : the death of Kerry Packer's mighty TV
dream machine.

ISBN 9781405038157 (hbk.).

1. Packer, Kerry, 1937-2005 - Influence. 2. National Nine
Network (Australia). 3. National Nine Network (Australia) -
History. 4. Television stations - Australia. 5.
Television broadcasting - Australia. I. Title. II. Title :
Who killed Channel nine?

384.550650994

Typeset in 12/16 pt Minion by Midland Typesetters
Printed in Australia by McPherson's Printing Group

In memory of Richard Carleton

Contents

Acknowledgements

This is a book bound to be short on acknowledgements. While there are dozens of contributors who deserve my utmost thanks, most prefer not to be mentioned by name for obvious reasons. They are professionals working in a relatively small industry, wary of triggering reprisals from the powers that be. That's bitterly ironical, indeed, since their only motive for agreeing to speak to me was the intense loyalty they still feel towards a television network that once meant so much to their lives. The best way to express my gratitude to each and every one of them is through the pages to follow, helping others to understand their heartfelt sense of loss.

Meanwhile, a word of explanation about the title. In the early 1980s, America's CBS network – renowned for the news service pioneered by the legendary Edward R. Murrow – was torn asunder by a purge strikingly similar to the campaign of cultural cleansing that was to befall the Nine Network of Australia twenty years later. A new management team, determined to reap maximum profits, set out to rid the organisation of its old 'Murrow men', contemptuously dismissing the traditional values they stood for as far too costly and inefficient. The devastating repercussions were powerfully portrayed in Peter J. Boyer's *Who Killed CBS?* I found the comparison with the spiritual demise of Kerry Packer's Channel 9 simply too compelling to resist.

Requiem

Who says you can't take it with you? When Kerry Packer died he took along a whole fucking era. The Golden Age of Australian television faded to black with the fabulous character who created it.

CHAPTER 1

Packer unexpurgated

'Am I still here? How fucking long is this going to take?'
Kerry Packer on his deathbed, 26 December, 2005.

As billionaires go, Kerry Francis Bullmore Packer may not have been as reclusive as Howard Hughes but he was every bit as secretive about his private life. He would not have taken kindly to what I intend to reveal about him now. Yet, it would be impossible to tell the story of the unmaking of Kerry's beloved Channel 9 without a total understanding of the man who ran it with an iron hand: his flair, his flaws and, ultimately, his failing health. Well before his death, the destabilising impact of his prolonged illnesses would tip the nation's number one network into a downward spiral of mismanagement and disarray.

For Packer, Nine was never just a business. It was a living, breathing part of him – an extension of his gargantuan ego, a TV station with soul. It reigned as the dominant force in Australian television not only because it topped the ratings year after year but because in all of the industry, it was the best place to be, a mecca for men and women of talent prepared to work their hearts out for high reward. To get an inkling of the scale of disaster that overwhelmed it, think Pompeii: a thriving, high-spirited, artistic-minded community happily getting on with life, oblivious to the dark, volcanic forces building up a poisonous head of steam nearby. That was the sorry fate about to engulf the Nine Network in the last days of Kerry Packer.

By mid-December, 2005, Australia's wealthiest and most powerful businessman knew he had only days to live. But if Kerry was about to cross over to the other side after several previous near misses he was determined to do it in classic Packer style – an exit worthy of a living legend. Right to the death knock, he had been keeping a jet on standby to fly him to Las Vegas, the mighty whale eager to return to his northern hunting grounds for a massive farewell plunge. It wasn't quite the trip his doctors had in mind when they warned him that his famous transplanted kidney was failing and he'd be lucky to see in the new year. Then again, the belligerent media magnate had beaten the medical odds countless times before and delighted in defying the eminent specialists to whom he paid tens of millions of dollars to try to save him from himself.

Of all the Packer anecdotes, those involving his running battles with his doctors are among the most outlandish but, for obvious reasons of patient confidentiality, least known. After one serious heart scare, he even bullied a cardiologist into doing the unthink-able. 'Light my cigarette, son,' he taunted, setting his price for agreeing to submit to the required course of intensive follow-up treatment. A specialist at the internationally acclaimed Cornell Medical Centre in New York was so appalled by Kerry's non-chalant attitude towards his own survival that he threatened to quit the case. 'This is ridiculous to expect us to look after you,' he proceeded to berate the bemused Australian as he lay in bed waiting for a critical series of operations. 'It's like teaching a grown man to use toothpaste.' Kerry listened quietly throughout the tirade, then suddenly reared up, whipped off his oxygen mask and pointed a quivering finger at one of the few people in the world deemed capable at that moment of snatching him from the jaws of death. 'All right, son, you've given me the fucking lecture. I've listened to it. Now are you going to fucking fix me up or aren't you?'

That was the patient from hell before surgery. At his impatient worst, recovering from one of his numerous operations, he could terrorise an entire hospital wing.

'You'd see the eyelids start to flicker, the bottom lip start to drop, you knew the conversation had about twenty seconds to go,' recalled a veteran member of Packer's personal MASH unit. '"Call a car, I'm off!",' he'd shout at a nurse. 'Then he would do this absolute runner where he would yank off his monitors, yank off his oxygen mask; even worse than that, he'd literally be yanking out drains and cannulas with all sorts of luckless people running behind him trying to cap and dress wounds as he disappeared out the door and into the car. He did that on a number of occasions.' One such tantrum, a walkout from an emergency ward in Columbus, Ohio, led to a hilarious pursuit reminiscent of the O.J. Simpson car chase – Kerry's getaway limousine being trailed by a caravan of ambulances sent after him by exasperated hospital officials.

Kerry hated any public discussion of his long and tortuous medical history lest it spook the share market, but his health problems are inseparably entwined with the troubles besetting Channel 9. It helps, then, to get at least a rough idea of what he had to cope with during his last years while still trying to guide his flagship into the twenty-first century, with its many challenges for free-to-air TV. Apart from full-scale heart attacks in 1990 and

1999, Packer had gone on to endure: a coronary artery bypass; a mitral valve replacement; the implanting of various heart regulating devices (like a pacemaker and defibrillator); six angioplasties in three sessions to various blocked coronary arteries; two angioplasties to kidney arteries; then his renal transplant, donated by his friend and helicopter pilot Nick Ross in November 2000.

The transplant certainly extended his life but opened a Pandora's box of new ailments. The anti-rejection drugs needed after the surgery, particularly the steroid prednisone, left him more vulnerable to lung infections, disfiguring skin lesions and other gruesome side effects, the worst of which was a virulent onslaught of diabetes. The diabetes, in turn, would put added stress on already badly weakened heart muscles: all that in a classic, hyper tense 'A'-type personality who refused to stop smoking or cut down on his intake of junk food. The powerful steroids, meanwhile, could only have aggravated his explosive mood swings.

Kerry himself dictated the terms of his own demise shortly before he reached his sixty-eighth birthday on 17 December, 2005. It had become obvious by then that the transplanted kidney had deteriorated beyond repair. Packer insisted, however, that there would be no more hospitals, no major surgical intervention. 'Don't mention the "D" word – don't go near dialysis, it's not on,' he growled. That made it anybody's guess how long he might have left. The trip to Las Vegas was, sadly, not to be, though the final scenes in his extraordinary time upon the stage would still be the stuff that great dramas are made of, bristling with suspense and intrigue.

In recent months the media magnate had been spending fewer nights at his sprawling family estate in Sydney's Bellevue Hill. He had set himself up in an apartment closer to the city. He and his wife, Ros, as occasionally happened in their more than 40 years together, were going through a difficult patch. Most couples could relate to that, though the Packers were hardly an ordinary family.

By chance of birth Kerry was as close as an Australian could ever get to living the life of a feudal lord; and Cairnton at Bellevue Hill was less a home than his castle – a symbol of his onerous obligations as head of a fabled media dynasty and business leader of world renown. For him, too, the place must have still reeked of unhappy childhood memories: a father who bullied him mercilessly and a mother who called him stupid. There were periods, then, when he felt the pressing need to escape and seek refuge in a less demanding parallel life; understandable, perhaps, though no less difficult for a proud woman like Ros to learn to accept. Theirs was perhaps best described as a European marriage, with Kerry's outside adventures tolerated so long as they were discreet. Emotional entanglements, though, aren't always easy to control.

When Packer was still in his thirties he found himself falling madly in love with magazine editor Ita Buttrose, then hailed as Australia's most admired woman. It was easy enough to see why he might. The two had worked closely together in the launching of *Cleo* magazine and the relaunching of the *Australian Women's Weekly* – key projects that had set Kerry free at last from living in the shadow of his dictatorial father, Sir Frank. Sharing the heady thrill of success was a natural catalyst for a torrid office romance. Given time and public exposure, the relationship of two such strong personalities might well have developed into the kind of high-voltage match reminiscent of a Richard Burton and Elizabeth Taylor. As it happened, their association became a talking point in London well before there were any whispers about it back home. During his lengthy stays in his suite at the Dorchester, a besotted Packer made no attempt to hide his feelings for Ita from close British friends like financier Jimmy Goldsmith, and John Aspinall, the gambling czar. At one point he even talked of marriage. Ita, though, displayed far more common sense and remained focused on her soaring career. A blazing row would eventually send them on their separate ways.

The heart-wrenching experience did nothing to curb his amorous pursuits. Perhaps, though, it at least taught him to grow up enough to stop acting like a lovesick schoolboy. All future involvements would be relatively short-lived, save one. Julie Trethowan, a slim brunette with the build and grace of a ballerina, was destined to assume a permanent role in Packer's parallel life. She was twenty years younger, but their relationship would mature and evolve over the years into a comfortable companionship. Julie effectively became the head of a second household where Kerry could seek temporary sanctuary when he felt overpowered by his inner demons. For all his bull-elephant antics, Packer had been weighed down throughout his life by a nagging sense of unworthiness and inadequacy, the likely legacy of growing up with parents who treated him as if he were a constant disappointment. Julie would prove a steadying influence, encouraging him to relax, as much as he was capable of relaxing, and begin to like himself a lot better.

So it was that Kerry's fast-approaching finale confronted him with a cruel dilemma. He knew he would be leaving two devoted women to struggle with the shock and grief associated with premature widowhood, each, in their own way, deserving of his loyalty and attention in his final hours. It no doubt would have been a lot easier for him to die in an in-between world: what better place than on a jet airliner bound for Las Vegas?

On Thursday, 22 December, Kerry felt well enough to show up at his office in Sydney's Park Street, headquarters of Publishing and Broadcasting Limited, mother company of the Nine Network. There he would put his signature to a record bid for television rights to the AFL, worth a staggering $150 million a year by the time the PBL boss ordered his advisers to top it up with millions of dollars worth of free advertising and other frills. The press, at the time, described the offer as Packer at his aggressive best: setting out to inflict maximum pain on his arch-rival,

Kerry Stokes, should the Seven Network exercise its option to match Nine's terms. This, however, was not the Kerry Packer as most ordinary viewers might remember him, the pugnacious jut-jawed giant putting a bunch of uppity federal politicians in their place during a televised parliamentary hearing in 1991. 'If anybody in this country doesn't minimise their tax they want their head read, because, as a government, I can tell you, you're not spending it that well that we should be donating extra,' he declared then, to the resounding cheers of his fellow Australians. Those same viewers would have been shocked to see him that Thursday, pitifully frail and waxen-faced, his skin stretched thin and translucent as vellum, so taut it sometimes bled spontaneously through the pores.

That evening, when Kerry went 'home' from a hard day at the office, it would be to the apartment rather than Bellevue Hill. Over the next two days his ravaged body began sending out enough alarms to light up a dozen intensive care wards. It must have been clear to him that he had reached the end game but even then he was reluctant to spoil James's holidays in the far-off Maldives by summoning him home. On Christmas Day at 4 pm Kerry Packer arrived back at Cairnton in an ambulance. The guests who had been attending the Packer family's traditional Christmas Day lunch were asked to leave before Kerry got there – by then there was no doubt about the finality of the crisis. There was real doubt, however, about whether James could make it back from his Indian Ocean resort in time. He immediately set out on a near-impossible dash from one airline transfer to another, a journey covering more than 9700 kilometres. At each critical point, he telephoned home or had messages relayed to report his progress – leaving the Maldives, arriving in Singapore, crossing the Australian coast to pass close by Newcastle Waters, the family's giant outback spread where he spent time as a jackeroo. He finally walked through the door at 9 pm on that fateful Boxing Day, his mother Ros and sister Gretel embracing him with tears of relief. From that point on the story deserves to be told in the present tense, the way it would be forever frozen in the minds of those who participated in the final, poignant scene.

Kerry Packer lies suspended in a twilight zone, a team of doctors and nurses silently attending to their duties around him like performers in an intricate mime. They have been working around the clock to keep their patient sedated with just enough medication to ease the pain, yet leave him within reach of consciousness should he still have the chance to say his goodbyes to James. Gaily wrapped Christmas presents are strewn around the spacious bedroom, lending a touch of bittersweet irony to the sombre occasion. The respectful hush surrounding the dying man gives no hint of the battle raging within him, the swarming toxins over-running the last of his bodily defences cell by cell. On a microscopic level it's much like one of the blockbuster war movies Kerry enjoyed so much, this time with the bad guys winning, but he's floating far above the fray. With the most delicate of adjustments the painkillers are reduced enough to bring him back to reality. He can see James bending over to hug him. Everyone else leaves the room to allow them their moment of privacy, the emotion fairly crackling in the atmosphere like so much static electricity.

What Kerry says to his son is strictly between them, but we do know the simple but moving words he used during a medical crisis a few years earlier when he had every reason to believe he was on the verge of death. 'I'm ready to die if it happens,' Kerry said, then, 'but you know, I've had a really great privilege in life that a lot of fathers don't get. I've been able to work closely with my son, James. I really think that was something special.'

'Dad made us all know that he loved us,' is all that James will say about that farewell.

When James finally leaves the room, the doctors step in to ease Kerry into unconsciousness once more. Then it's only a matter of waiting for his ravaged body to find its own peace. He closes his eyes, consigning himself to the outgoing tide of sleep everlasting. Incredibly, though, he's soon enough back again. This, after all, is a man notorious for his impatience. As in life, so in death. 'Am I still here?' he mumbles plaintively. 'How fucking long is this going to take?' But with that, he plunges back into the void he's visited several times before. And an eternity beyond.

'It was eerie to be there after he died,' James confided later, 'to be there with a body that was so different to his character. Kerry was such a large character, so full of life. All our lives are less full and interesting without him.' Those were the feelings of a loving son, not quite able to grasp how someone overflowing with so much energy and passion could now just lie there so white and still. But that same feeling of stunned disbelief would be shared by many of us who worked under Kerry Packer in those exhilarating glory years. Each of us had our own special image of Kerry imprinted in our brains, and there was no way it could ever be reconciled with the stark reality of a dead man in a bed. For my part, I still have fifteen words ringing in my ears from long ago – Kerry's succinct instructions when he called me into his office to appoint me as founding executive producer of a new Sunday night public affairs program to be called *60 Minutes*.

'I don't give a fuck what it takes,' he ordered. 'Just do it and get it right.'

It was the golden rule for the Golden Age, the win-at-any-cost credo that would drive the Nine Network to success after success for years to come.

*

The Golden Age of Australian television. You could say it began the first moment viewers spotted the rich yellow hue glinting in their TV screens. With the introduction of colour transmission in March, 1975, audiences blossomed and advertising skyrocketed, bringing the nation's three commercial networks an unexpected windfall, more than enough to happily share around. Seven and Ten duly proceeded to maximise their soaring profits and minimise their expenditures, as properly run companies do. Kerry Packer, though, had not the slightest interest in sharing anything. His natural instincts told him to break free of the pack and set out to be first and best whatever the price. The profits might be a lot less to begin with, but if he could establish Nine as the industry's undisputed leader, advertisers would flock to his door begging for air time, willing, even, to pay a handsome premium on top of the prevailing ad rates. *Let us be the one.* That was where the real riches lay.

Kerry took charge of the network, then consisting of TCN 9 in Sydney and GTV 9 in Melbourne, upon the death of his father, Sir Frank, in May, 1974. He knew little about the visual medium – his older brother Clyde had run the TV side of the business while Kerry focused on magazines. Clyde, though, was gone from the scene, off to make his own fortune by the time Kerry took over. He struggled for a year or so to attune his instincts to the special magic of the small screen; but when he felt he was finally ready for lift-off, he did it with a bang. By the start of the 1977 ratings season he had set his sights on turning Nine into a role model for the entire industry, creating Australia's own little Hollywood, a galaxy ablaze with charismatic stars and whiz-kid producers. Comedian Paul Hogan, the future Crocodile Dundee, was among the first of the big prime time names recruited, along with daytime host Mike Walsh – both pinched from other networks.

From then on the list of Nine's Golden Age personalities reads like a trip down Nostalgia Lane: Lorraine Bayly as the compassionate Grace Sullivan; ringmaster Richie Benaud and his circus of World Series cricketers; Ray Martin, George Negus, Jana Wendt; Brian Henderson in Sydney and Brian Naylor in Melbourne; Daryl Somers and Ozzie Ostrich; Bert Newton and the perennial favourite, Graham Kennedy.

Each of them was far more than a performer or presenter. Together, they became part of an extended family and for nearly three decades the Nine Network could claim a special place in Australian life. It wasn't always the first and certainly not always the best, but whatever it did, it did with a passion that couldn't be matched by its commercial rivals, no matter how hard they tried. With Nine there were times when viewers got sucked so deep into a program they could almost feel the hot breath and the pulse beat. Perhaps they really could. The proprietor spurred his staff on to heights they never dreamed possible. 'You can do better, son,' he constantly prodded them. And he gave them the resources to make it happen, most notably in sports, news and current affairs, as well as the special event programming – celebrity concerts and other spectaculars – that Nine did as well as any network in the world.

This, then, was Kerry Packer's unbeatable dream machine, dominating an era when 85 per cent of Australian living rooms were lit by the flickering glow of a TV set and sewer levels rose measurably with the end of the Sunday night movie. How quickly that cosy picture would change amid a veritable explosion of competing entertainment formats. With the dawning of a new century, Nine, as leader of the 'old media' free-to-air broad-casters, would have been in serious trouble in any case. For a start, it was an exceptionally expensive operation to maintain, not only because of the hefty amounts poured into Channel 9 programs but the tens of millions of additional dollars spent on buying up extra overseas news feeds and entertainment output deals simply to keep them out of reach of the opposition. That's how bloody-minded Kerry was in his determination to stay number one in the ratings.

Financial issues, though, were only a part of the problem. The impact of a harsher economic climate was compounded many times over by the magnate's deteriorating medical condition and the distraction that inevitably caused. Within the hierarchy of the Packer-controlled media and gaming corporation, it was well understood that no one, not even son James, messed with Kerry's 'baby', the TV arm of the company, without his approval. Even during his frequent absences in hospital, urgently needed decisions were left hanging lest they be rescinded as soon as the big man was on his feet again. So it was that a network that had once gained so much advantage through Packer's extraordinary vision suddenly found itself hostage to his whims, ever more erratic as he plunged from one health crisis to another.

Of course, it wasn't just Nine confronting the challenge of an entirely new communications landscape. The free-to-air industry as a whole was under threat, with pay TV just beginning to turn its first profit and advertising on the Internet soaring towards the billion-dollar mark. Faced with shrinking audiences and ad revenues, no network was in a position to avoid one painful round after another of job cuts and other forms of cost-slashing. Yet Nine had always managed in the past to distinguish itself from its rivals by its willingness to put people before profit. It's almost too corny to say it, but every viewer knew it to be true, and every key player in the Australian TV industry knew it, too. Packer's Channel 9 had always been considered something special: a network with heart. Wasn't there a way to survive as a business and still keep that pumping, too? Kerry, to his last breath, kept insisting that there was; but that was seen as merely confirming how out of touch he was in terms of modern management techniques, a sickly old man unable or unwilling to begin treating television like any other commercial enterprise. Still, Kerry was not a lone voice in seeking to hold on to Nine's traditional values. He would find a soul-mate and ally, someone as passionate about the network as himself; but by then he no longer had the strength to give that eager young executive the support he needed to resist the new circle of advisers settling into power at 54 Park Street in anticipation of James's ascendancy.

Kerry Packer wasn't the kind of man to say sorry about anything he did, but he's known to have died with two profound regrets. The first was the way he had let down his good friend and helicopter pilot, Nick Ross, by abusing the most precious gift one can give another. Almost from the day of the transplant, he reverted to his perverse old habits, smoking away and cramming in junk food from one medical setback to the next. 'He feels he let Nick Ross down badly by doing that,' one of his long-suffering medical advisers later acknowledged. 'I know he feels that.'

The second regret would follow on from the first. As Kerry's health steadily waned, so too did his finely honed gambler's instincts for making the right calls under extreme pressure: separating risks worth taking from the sucker bets. The extra five years that his kidney transplant gave him were no doubt precious to him and his loved ones, but they would turn out to have dire consequences for Channel 9 in terms of some of the more impetuous and ill-considered decisions he made. One of those would trigger a long-smouldering management crisis destined to reduce the once mighty network to little more than a shadow of its former glory.

What man can bear to see his proudest achievement unravelling before his eyes? Well before that fateful deathbed scene, the creator of television's Golden Age was forced to acknowledge that he had made one of the most disastrous mistakes of his life.

'They stuffed the place up.' That was the phrase Kerry Packer used in a lament shared with one of his most trusted advisers – his own succinct epitaph for the old Channel 9 spoken shortly before his death. Who 'they' were and what they did to warrant their boss's stinging disapproval is precisely what this book is all about.

CHAPTER 2

Malice in Wonderland

As anchor of the Nine Network's *A Current Affair*, Mike Munro sat in television's hottest of hot seats. Not only did he have Channel 7's *Today Tonight* snapping at his heels, but his show was taking a beating from the press critics, accused of 'dumbing down' in a desperate bid to keep ahead in the ratings. Here was a program that once prided itself on a nightly menu filled with hard-hitting interviews, sensational crime investigations and the inside dope on the latest titillating celebrity scandal. More and more it had begun to dwell on diet fads and shopping tips, topped up with melodramatic ambushes of small-time con men, or the inevitable tear-jerkers about battling families who can't pay their rent.

No one would have preferred to return to the good old days of *ACA* than Munro. He had first made his name as its fearless, foot-in-the-door investigative reporter, working with veteran newsman Mike Willesee to come up with some of the most memorable moments of the Golden Age of TV. But he was now the face of the show as seen in its more banal, lifestyle format and he was about to pay a heavy personal price. Among the stars at Nine, Mike Munro would be first to feel the chill winds of change as Kerry Packer slowly faded from the scene. On the morning of 24 November, 2002, he opened his Sunday newspapers to find a report of his imminent demise.

> Channel 9 is set to axe Mike Munro as compere of *A Current Affair* in a major revamp of the program designed to take it upmarket. Former *ACA* host Ray Martin is expected to be sitting in Munro's chair as soon as December 2.

TV careers, glamorous as they might appear, are built on quick-sand. Munro was well aware of the growing concern over his program's diminishing lead in the vital 6.30 pm time slot. With *ACA* still finishing the 2002 ratings season in front, however, he felt sure his job was safe until at least well into the new year. He had no way of knowing that his fate had been sealed months before. Since the beginning of the year Channel 9 had been struggling to adjust to a major management shake-up, with the ailing Packer appointing a special deputy at Park Street to keep close watch over the network, pushing for whatever improvements he saw fit. That included programming as well as day-to-day administration, and *ACA* would be singled out as a symbolic battleground, pitting the old regime against the new.

Ironically, Munro, with his brashness and vitality, happened to be one of Packer's favourites. As a crime reporter he had showed the kind of derring-do Kerry so admired, whether bluffing his way through police lines to get to the action or chasing a suspected villain down five flights of stairs. But there was also a more endearing side to Munro's on-camera persona that his Shrekish-looking boss may well have envied. He exuded a cheeky, boyish charm that allowed him to get away with asking women the most outrageous questions. 'How big are they?' is one he put to the buxom Dolly Parton without getting a slap in the face. In television terms that was known as a *hey Martha!*, a husband gasping in disbelief at what he's just seen on his set and calling for his wife to come rushing to watch what might happen next. Just the kind of riveting TV that would have had Kerry slapping his knee in delight. No one was better at delivering *hey Martha!*s than Mike Munro, not the most prominent or highest paid of Nine's celebrity presenters but a thoroughly professional all-rounder who also doubled as presenter for the ever-popular *This Is Your Life*.

The man Kerry chose to supervise his TV network, by contrast, was not at all impressed with Munro's somewhat rough-edged image and regarded him as an impediment to progress. He envisaged *ACA* featuring far more serious coverage and analysis, more like the feature pages of a quality newspaper. That was understandable enough since he had impeccable newspaper credentials himself; indeed, had served with distinction in the senior managerial ranks of the *Sydney Morning Herald*. The story of his ascension to power over the nation's number one network has much to reveal about the inherent differences between the medium of print and the medium of television and, in particular, how managerial techniques of proven success in one realm can so easily wreak havoc within the other. Kerry Packer should have known that better than anyone else, which makes it all the more important to try to understand how he ever came to put his proudest possession in such untried hands.

Australia's wealthiest man may have been the total sceptic when it came to religious notions like the afterlife but in his secret heart of hearts he still believed in miracles and was constantly on the lookout for those who could make them happen. Despite the millions he paid for expert medical advice, for example, he still had his personal staff scouring the world for a miracle diet that would allow him to eat the hamburgers and other junk food he craved without worrying about gaining weight and further damaging his heart. Told about a macrobiotic guru who was supposedly achieving wondrous results in America, he immediately arranged to fly him to Sydney along with the special ingredients needed to prepare him a meal. 'I can't eat this shit,' he snarled after a bite or two. He endured those kinds of bitter disappointments time and time again but that didn't stop his obsessive quest for the magic recipe.

So, too, when it came to his business affairs, Packer was capable of great leaps of faith – pinning his hopes on the most unlikely people to pull off some near-impossible feat for him. Perhaps as the son of an overpowering father he was prone to doubt his own abilities and naturally drawn to those he saw as more disciplined or clever than himself. After his famous polo-ground heart attack in 1990, in a period when he was feeling particularly vulnerable, he sought the help of one of America's most controversial corporate figures, the notorious Al 'Chainsaw' Dunlap, to take charge of Australian Consolidated Press, the Packer company that would later evolve into PBL. Kerry relied on him to impose the large-scale job cuts he simply couldn't bring himself to carry out. The two quick-tempered alpha males lasted barely a year and a half together, but before Chainsaw was sent packing he at least fulfilled Kerry's brief by trying to indoctrinate James in his pet theories about how to run a successful business. 'If you worry about whose feelings you will hurt, you will fail,' was his farewell message to Packer's son and heir.

It's no coincidence, then, that within a year or so of Kerry's kidney transplant, when nagging complications were making him feel more fragile than ever before, he should put all his trust in another miracle man of similar mould. In this case he discovered his new superhero right under his nose: an executive within PBL's magazine division who had managed to double profits through his sharp eye for cost-cutting. John Alexander's brief from Kerry would be simple enough: to produce the same kind of miraculous turnaround in TV.

Alexander – J.A. as he's commonly known – had first joined PBL's magazine arm in 1998, his reputation somewhat under a cloud after being dismissed from the Fairfax group for his allegedly disruptive dabbling in office politics. Whatever the truth of that allegation, he quickly managed to redeem himself in the eyes of the Packers, father and son, and by the relatively young age of 50 had become the talk of the Australian print world. His success was all the more impressive considering where he started from – a Housing Commission estate on the northern fringes of Sydney. Though his family was by no means impoverished, they faced a struggle to get by, particularly after the mother fell ill. Any chance of young John having a carefree childhood was cut short by his need to help care for his younger siblings and virtually support himself from the age of nine or ten by doing odd jobs such as caddying at a nearby golf course.

With that humble background, he could hardly have gone on to reach such heights in his chosen profession without exceptional drive and talent. At his best, operating in a field like print journalism that he knew and loved, he could be an inspiration to his staff – constantly prodding them to lift their games. 'He might be a bastard but he's our bastard,' one critic conceded. His undoubted attributes, however, make it all the more difficult to understand his reputed propensity for mischief-making as described in various newspaper articles about him: playing his staff off against one another, subverting those he saw as rivals, double-crossing his own lieutenants by deciding things behind their backs. It's fascinating to see his former press colleagues struggling to find the word that best sums him up, short of outright slander. 'Machiavellian' ranks high on the list, suggesting his preference for behind-the-scenes manipulation rather than direct confrontation. 'Cruel', 'cold', 'meticulous' and 'imperious' all feature prominently. Such descriptions happen to be a perfect fit for the classic character known as the *courtier,* ingratiating to all above him, an object of terror to those below.

In January, 2002, John Alexander would be appointed to the newly created position of head of PBL Media, giving him extraordinary power over both the magazine division and the Nine Network, at that point still the veritable jewel in the Packer crown. Before that could happen, however, one formidable obstacle had to be removed from his path.

David Leckie had been Nine's chief executive officer for eleven years, leading it from one triumphant season to the next, including a phenomenal stretch of 113 winning weeks in a row. One might have thought with such feats to his name he would have been elevated to Olympian heights, regarded at PBL headquarters as a kind of demigod. His long record of success, in fact, was part of his problem. Leckie had become far too dominant a figure for Kerry's liking. Even his imposing height may well have become a psychological factor in their increasingly abrasive relationship. Within the organisation, David Leckie was the only one tall enough to stare Kerry down during their tempestuous confrontations and he had the granite resolve to go with his stature. Time and time again he demonstrated his preparedness to stand firm against one of his boss's lightning-bolt edicts if he thought it unnecessarily disruptive of day-to-day operations. One of their more spectacular clashes occurred in September, 1992, a couple of years after Kerry bought back Nine from the bankrupt Alan Bond. The network had just begun airing an hour-long show called *Australia's Naughtiest Home Videos*, rife with bare bottoms and off-colour jokes, when Packer called up to demand it be taken off air immediately. This was how I described their exchange in *Compulsive Viewing*, my unofficial history of the Nine Network, published in 2000.

'Take that shit off the air,' Kerry orders TCN managing director David Leckie only 5 minutes into the program. Leckie refuses, insisting the program has been passed by the censor and at any rate he's not going to throw the channel into chaos by interrupting its schedules only partially through a half-hour. Like the Monty Python knight defending the bridge despite being chopped apart bit by bit, he continues to stall through several increasingly ferocious phone calls. He assumes his career is finished. All he wants, as his last bequest to the station, is to at least delay replacing the show until the half-hour commercial break so the next half-hour will start cleanly.

'You fucking well do as I say or I'll fucking well do it myself,' Packer finally tells him. Which he does, phoning directly to the station's on-air co-ordinator. She can still see the mushroom cloud rising from the earpiece as she turns in catatonic shock to cue in a laugh-filled edition of *Cheers*.

Leckie somehow managed to survive that episode but their relationship hardly got any easier over the next decade. He continued to try to shield his department heads from Kerry's outbursts. 'If I sacked everyone that he told me to, there would be no one there,' he once observed. Inevitably, though, that loyalty to those below him was interpreted as 'obstructionist' by those above. In Kerry's eyes, and there was none at PBL headquarters to disagree with him, Leckie was merely out to protect his own turf and growing more surly by the day.

So long as the network performed well on all fronts – ratings, advertising share and profit – the proprietor had little choice but to put up with his CEO's independent-minded nature. The medical setbacks that followed his transplant, however, hardly improved his ability to cope with constant confrontation, while the steroid drugs he was taking added fuel to his blast furnace rages. During 2001 he found good reason to be furious: the introduction of a new system of measuring viewership appeared to be showing Nine in a less favourable light than the old Nielsen ratings. The change had been approved by the commercial television industry as a whole – Leckie reluctantly agreeing to go along with the majority – but Packer blamed him directly for the unfavourable survey results and the issue finally gave the magnate a tangible reason to demand the CEO's head.

In the second week of January, 2002, Leckie received a fateful phone call at his holiday home at Palm Beach. 'Kerry really wants to see you,' he was told. But when he showed up at Park Street in jeans and tee-shirt, Kerry was nowhere to be seen. Instead, James Packer was waiting for him, along with Peter Yates, then overall head of PBL operations, to pass on a message all the more hurtful for the euphemistic terms in which it was couched. 'Kerry doesn't want you to be here anymore.'

By any standard, Packer's sudden dismissal of David Leckie was an extraordinarily risky move, thrusting Australia's leading broadcaster towards the most dangerous turning point in its history. While there were worrying signs that Nine's prolonged dominance of the commercial TV industry might be beginning to slip, it was still pulling in the largest audiences and raking in the biggest slice of the revenue pie. To dump its long-serving CEO in the mere hope that someone else could do better was adventuristic to say the least. If Kerry hadn't been so desperate to rid himself of Leckie, he might have at least thought twice before turning his network over to someone with no experience whatsoever in such a highly complex industry. Leckie and his legendary predecessor, Sam Chisholm, had both come up through TV sales, the very heart of the business,

combining intimate knowledge of the interaction of program place-
ment, ratings, marketing and advertising. Alexander, by comparison, had spent his career working as a journalist, editor and senior
manager on papers like the *Sydney Morning Herald* and *Australian
Financial Review*. In his spare time he was a devout aesthete who
studied the fine arts and collected rare books and antiques. He was
hardly likely to know much about the tastes of a typical television
viewer – certainly no match for Kerry Packer, noted for watching the
small screen up to seven or eight hours a day.

Not unexpectedly, James had shown early signs of sharing his
father's passion for the visual medium and would later serve a
successful stint presiding over TV executive meetings during the
last part of David Leckie's reign. 'James has got a young, bright
view of what works on television and what doesn't,' Leckie
observed back then, 'and he's always on the phone suggesting
things.' The younger Packer, however, would soon switch much of
his focus to overseeing PBL's rapid expansion into the gaming and
technology areas, leaving him precious little time to deal directly
with network issues in any detail. With television contributing an
ever smaller percentage of the corporation's revenues, James's
main interest was in making sure Nine at least pulled its own
weight like any other business. Considering Alexander's outstanding success in magazines, he had every reason to feel confident
that the print executive, assisted by the inner circle of advisers
available to him at Park Street, would see that it did.

Kerry, for his part, appeared to react a bit defensively when a
long-time associate expressed amazement at the decision to
appoint someone without any expertise in the industry to fill the
gap left by Leckie. 'You know,' he explained, offering this almost
childish rationalisation, 'John's wife [Alice Pagliano, internationally known photographer] lives overseas more often than in
Australia. That means he must watch a lot of television, and he
would probably be quite good at the job.'

Given his inexperience, Alexander might well have been expected to set out on a crash course to learn as much about the visual medium as possible. Instead he appears to have convinced himself that most of what went on within the TV industry was so much self-serving mumbo jumbo, an excuse for TV executives to justify their overblown salaries. During his first months as PBL Media's chief executive officer he naturally enough took his cues from Kerry and James as to any specific changes they wanted implemented – not exactly easy because, as we're about to see, father and son had totally different priorities for reorganising the network.

But Alexander, too, soon came to have his own private agenda. As a point of personal pride he wanted Nine's top-rating news and current affairs division – 'newscaff' as it's known in the industry – to break from the pack and start emulating the kind of journalistic excellence associated with the broadsheet newspapers on which he had built his reputation. In seeking to fulfil that ambition, however, he automatically set himself on a collision course with perhaps the single most formidable executive at Channel 9, Peter Meakin, the network's feisty newscaff director. 'Upmarket is a lovely way to go but first of all we've got to identify what it means,' Meakin argued. 'I don't mind going upmarket as long as we don't go upmarket to oblivion. And they can be one and the same. If we get too serious-minded we could do so at our peril.'

The visual medium, as veterans like Meakin had traditionally interpreted it, was more about feelings than facts: resistant to the kind of detailed explanation that might appear in a newspaper feature page. Television was at its powerful best as a visceral experience, strumming the emotional chords, stimulating the senses, encouraging those watching to come to their own instinctual conclusions about the right or wrong of any situation. The difference between viewers and readers could be summed up in five words. *Don't tell me. Show me.*

Alexander might dismiss such explanations as a fanciful excuse for lazy journalism, but Meakin spoke from the perspective of a battle-scarred survivor of the ratings wars. Exactly what could one expect from an *ACA* going 'upmarket', as the Park Street executive demanded? Would audiences who tuned in to see cellulite cures and quarrelling neighbours stick around for a fact-filled inquiry into foreign trade kickbacks? That was no mere theoretical question. The producers of both *ACA* and *Today Tonight* were able to analyse each evening's ratings minute by minute, and the evidence was inescapable. Any segment involving a more cerebral type of journalism – a political interview or in-depth investigation – was met with an instant turn-off. Far from 'dumbing down', then, the two current affairs shows were being as smart as free-to-air television can get – keeping in close touch with the changing nature of the available audience, giving the great majority of viewers precisely what they wanted. With mums cooking dinner, the kids playing up, the father coming home grumpy after a tough day at work, the last thing they needed at 6.30 at night was a TV show that demanded extra concentration. In an increasingly complicated world, they sought information immediately relevant to their own lifestyles and they were perfectly happy to look at a program filled with useful shopping tips or stories about families very much like themselves embroiled in the same kinds of problems they were struggling to get through.

Meakin, then, foresaw a ratings disaster if *ACA* began straying too far from its tabloid roots, surrendering more and more air time to 'worthier' topics that might suit an ABC viewer but threatened to send its traditional audience rushing to change channels. His resistance must have been doubly frustrating for the PBL Media boss since Ray Martin, Alexander's choice to replace Munro, was not likely to agree to return to the program without the guarantee of a substantial change of format. During Martin's previous time fronting *ACA*, in 1994 to 1998, his 'good guy' image had taken some bruising knocks, including an angry public outcry over the suicide of a supposedly shonky tradesman the program had been pursuing.

Martin had made his feelings clear enough during secret negotiations that began in September, 2002 and stretched on for more than four anxious months. His first concern had been the loyalty he felt he owed to a colleague. 'I'm not prepared to discuss anything behind Mike's back,' he declared, only to be assured that Munro was 'going in any case'. After that, he sought tangible proof that the network was genuinely determined to set *ACA* on a bold course to lift its sights. 'Are you serious about this?' he asked time and time again. 'Will you sustain some ratings body-blows to augment your image?' Alexander went a long way towards reassuring him by revealing that he was also attempting to sign the highly respected investigative reporter Paul Barry and former *60 Minutes* presenter Ellen Fanning to beef up *ACA*'s on-camera line-up.

From the very start of these covert discussions Alexander had enlisted the support of David Gyngell, then the network's deputy CEO, to help him swing Martin around. Peter Meakin, though informed of what was happening, was left largely out of the loop. He reluctantly agreed to accept the change of hosts but only on condition the program format not be transformed too radically. As far as he was concerned his debate with Alexander on the proper balance between lighter and heavier stories was still in full swing. The leaked *Sun-Herald* report of 24 November, making the upmarket change seem a fait accompli, came as almost as much of a shock to him as it did to Munro.

Remarkably, Mike Munro had not the slightest inkling about the intensive manoeuvring that had been going on for so long behind his back. When he saw the newspaper story, he naturally went around the station trying to find out if it was correct. Gyngell, like Meakin, had been upset by the leak and mystified about its source, but even then, he gave Munro no hint of how close to the truth it was. 'I will be the one who will look you in the eye and tell you whether you are or are not doing *A Current Affair*,' the deputy CEO equivocated, 'and I'm telling you, at this moment, that you are.' Technically, it was an honest answer because Kerry Packer, even at that late stage, was still wavering on the wisdom of sacking a front man whose show was winning its time slot. So it was, despite mounting press speculation about his imminent axing, that Munro was hung out to dry by the network he had served so well for nearly two decades – left to sweat it out through December and even into mid-January amid nothing but ominous silence from senior executives. Considering the relatively short time in which John Alexander had been in charge, the episode marked a seismic shift in managerial style for an organisation that had always gone out of its way to protect its high-profile personalities from harmful or embarrassing publicity. Finally, with just days to go before the launch of the new ratings season, Meakin phoned Munro at home and asked if he could drop by for a chat.

'Look, it's no surprise,' the newscaff director declared upon his arrival, coming right to the point. 'We've been reading about it for weeks. You're no longer on *ACA*.'

We've been reading about it for weeks. That remark goes a long way towards explaining the possible motive behind that first leak. Clearly, by that date, no firm agreement had yet been reached on replacing Munro, otherwise there would have been an official announcement. Exposing the secret plans in cold, hard print then, appeared to mark the beginning of a softening up process, a whispering campaign aimed at encouraging the various interested parties to agree to the desired conclusion.

Where had such a well-informed story come from, if not from within Channel 9 itself? John Alexander is known to have told a newspaper colleague about his decision to dump Munro as early as July, 2002. He went on from there to speak to others along similar lines. The *Sun-Herald* revelation certainly seemed to suit his purposes though that in itself didn't necessarily constitute an intentional leak. Considering Alexander's widespread friendships within press circles, it was natural to exchange confidences on the basis of mutual trust – a bond that wasn't always treated with the respect it deserved. The PBL Media chief could always raise the defence made famous by the twelfth-century King Henry II in trying to explain away his role in the assassination of the Archbishop of Canterbury, Thomas Becket. The king, it seems, was overheard lamenting, 'Will no one rid me of this turbulent priest?' That indiscreet remark, if the monarch was to be believed, would lead to totally unintended consequences – a fawning admirer setting out on his own initiative to fulfil his wish. J.A., perhaps, had any number of fawning admirers within the press corps more than happy to undermine someone on his behalf.

The one point beyond dispute, however, is that with the dawning of the Alexander era at Channel 9, such painful and humiliating press leaks would become an everyday fact of life. From then on, any presenter, producer or channel executive singled out for dismissal or demotion was likely to suffer the added indignity of having to read about it first in the newspapers.

Meanwhile, J.A.'s grand design for an upmarket *A Current Affair* produced just the kind of viewer backlash Peter Meakin had predicted. On 10 February, the start of the 2003 ratings season, the show unveiled its worthier image by featuring an exclusive interview with the Federal Treasurer, Peter Costello. Ray Martin took a hammering from Channel 7's *Today Tonight*. Never had the long-running show suffered such an embarrassing loss on such a symbolic occasion as opening night of the year. Worse, much worse, was to follow over coming months as the rival program – steady and predictable in its populist format –

relentlessly closed the gap and eventually overtook the Nine Network's schizophrenic part tabloid, part high-minded contribution to nightly current affairs.

Mike Munro, for his part, somehow managed to emerge from his ordeal virtually unscathed compared to so many sad stories to follow. Though dumped as *ACA* anchor, his career continued to thrive as presenter of the top-rating *This Is Your Life*. It was a role that would lead him at one point to a most dramatic encounter. In the second week of August, 2003, the surprise 'guest' for the night was the venerable *Australian Women's Weekly*, and as part of that show Munro did a feature interview with Kerry Packer, whose father founded the magazine. After completing the videotape session in Packer's office, the two men had an emotion-charged reunion, with a conversation that went something along these lines.

'Kerry, this is the first time I've come face to face with you since you fired me. Why?'

'I don't know why,' the proprietor responded. 'It got out of hand. I mean, basically, it became a life of its own, the fact that you were going; and really there was no decision made. It became a fact we just kept reading about.'

Munro ventured another question. 'Do you know where all that came from?'

'I have my ideas,' Kerry told him. 'But I'm not sure.'

Munro pressed his luck a third and final time. 'Well, what do you think about it?'

'We made a major mistake. The program is not doing nearly as well as we would have hoped. And I'm sorry for you.' With that they shook hands warmly, almost like father and son, Kerry putting his other hand affectionately over the top of Mike's.

By that stage – the middle of 2003 – Kerry Packer was already admitting to having grave misgivings about the miracle man to whom he had so impetuously entrusted the precious results of his life's work. To understand how and when the rot began to set in, it's necessary to go back to the very start of John Alexander's reign at Channel 9 a year and a half before.

CHAPTER 3

Cultural cleansing

There was a list of those to be eliminated. There always is when it comes to bloody political purges. *Political* may seem a strange word to use when one is talking about a major public company dealing with a subsidiary. In the eyes of some at 54 Park Street, however, the Nine Network had effectively ceased to be an integral part of the corporate family. It had come to be regarded more as a rebellious colony – enemy territory under the command of a rogue feudal chieftain and his renegade band. They were well beyond reach of trendy new management techniques like incentivising and downsizing. They needed to be brought ruthlessly to heel. Us versus Them. It couldn't get more political than that. As John Alexander would later complain, Channel 9 'is in a time warp'. The station executives 'treat me like I know nothing'. The newsroom 'regards me like a total idiot'. No one there 'shows me any loyalty'. Almost everyone is 'out to get me'. Alexander said all that to a respected TV presenter he was trying to hire without the knowledge of the relevant department head at Channel 9. God only knows what he must have been saying to Kerry Packer and his son James.

For a lot more people than Mike Munro, then, 2002 proved to be the year of living dangerously. Before it was over, eight executive heads would roll. Two others, industry stalwarts whose names had been most closely identified with Channel 9's unparalleled ratings success, would resign in disgust in the first weeks of 2003. 'A thousand years of experience gone in a flash,' one of the hit-list victims observed – hyperbole, perhaps, but in light of subsequent events not all that much of an exaggeration.

Immediately after David Leckie's abrupt dismissal, Kerry and James both hit the phones to try to explain the move to Leckie's executive team and hose down any sign of protest.

'I've just fired your mate, Leckie,' Kerry told Peter Meakin, responsible not just for news and current affairs but a top-rating group of lifestyle and reality programs.

'Oh, I'm sorry to hear that,' Meakin responded with typical bluntness. 'Why?'

'Because I'm sick of the roadblocks,' the big boss snapped back. That, with its martial overtones, was a telling analogy. With Leckie gone, there would be no stopping the tanks rumbling in from Park Street. James Packer soon arrived at the Sydney station with an ultimatum that left no room for misinterpretation.

'This business,' James told the assembled Nine executives, 'can't sustain having anything less than a 40 per cent share of the advertising market. We haven't got that in the last years under David and that's why Leckie had to go. So, I'm saying it here in front of everyone. If you feel an allegiance to him, then come and see me and we can talk about how we can get you out of your contract.'

At that point he introduced John Alexander, who delivered a brief but conciliatory message. 'It's going to be all right,' he reassured the assembled managers. 'We'll work as a team and go forward together.' There was nothing remarkable in his words but a department head who happened to be sitting behind him will never forget what he saw that day. As the new boss of PBL Media rose to speak, his hands began to shake so violently that he held them behind his back to keep others in the room from noticing. It was not something one expected to see of a high-flyer with the reputation for impeccable sangfroid. Of course, it could just have been a touch of stage fright in a room full of strangers, but a Freudian psychoanalyst steeped in the workings of the subconscious mind might well have offered a more intriguing explanation. One sure sign of how badly someone wants to get his hands on something is the way they start to tremble in anticipation.

Did Alexander actively lobby for control of the network? A former member of the PBL hierarchy offers this insider's view. 'When I was there, I would do anything to avoid having a conversation with Kerry, because you could get grilled within an inch of your life. There was only one person who actively sought Kerry out – and his name was John Alexander.' Among veteran Packer executives from other parts of the business, Channel 9 had traditionally been regarded as an absolute no-go area, as dangerous as a nuclear testing ground. It was, after all, Kerry's most jealously guarded possession and he could turn on someone in instant fury for offering a well-meaning comment that he judged to be stupid or irrelevant – which he invariably did. In one infamous incident from the Golden Age, he invited suggestions for the kind of program needed for a given time slot. Though he seemed to be in good humour at the time, a program manager who was silly enough to venture an answer got a cricket ball hurled straight at his head.

The dawn of the twenty-first century had hardly made Kerry any less difficult to deal with when it came to the medium he knew and loved the best. As his son James led the push to develop new areas of the empire like gaming and IT, Packer senior began to spend even more of his time fussing over the network with his constant nitpicking, glad to be free of Leckie's stubborn resistance. The new position of CEO of PBL Media was obviously not for the faint-hearted, riddled as it was with more booby traps than Indiana Jones's Temple of Doom. Still, no one ever suggested John Alexander didn't have the survival skills to match his ambition. A run-of-the-mill courtier constantly walks the razor's edge, desperately trying to second-guess what his king is thinking so he can be sure to agree with it. The really clever one puts forward his own ideas but knows how to make the king believe he thought of them first.

Even with Alexander placed in strategic command, the network still required its own management structure to guide it through day-to-day operations. Ian Johnson, a trusted adviser within the Packer group, was brought up from Melbourne to steady the ship as its chief executive officer, but only on a short-term, transitional basis. He had previously served in top management positions at GTV 9 and later at Crown Casino, a congenial and well-liked administrator who had no pretensions of being another David Leckie. The appointment of Johnson's deputy would be far more significant in the turbulent events to follow.

Both Kerry and James had great faith in the potential of David Gyngell to become a true force within the network, though they felt he needed a period of apprenticeship before becoming a fully-fledged CEO. If a talent for television ran in the blood then Gyngell couldn't miss. His father, Bruce Gyngell, was not only the first face on Australian TV back in 1956 but he had gone on to establish an international reputation as a true programming genius, with an uncanny knack for picking both watchable shows and charismatic talent. David, as a little boy, remembered his father bringing home American hits like *Mr Ed*, *Happy Days* and *Starsky & Hutch* to test out on his family, trying to calculate how well they would rate here. At first he was so intimidated by his dad's towering reputation that he was determined to avoid the TV industry altogether, going on instead to start a chain of surf shops. However, he and James had always been as close as brothers and Kerry was like a second father. James coaxed him into joining PBL in 1999, with a special brief to develop new revenue opportunities for the network, while improving cross-promotion between the TV and magazine arms. After Leckie's dismissal, the Packers convinced him to take on the deputy's job under Johnson while he learned more about the business. The younger Gyngell, very much like Bruce, believed great TV sprang from gut instinct, pure and simple. Some people could be in the industry all their lives and never get a feel for it, while a newcomer with the right vibes could soon have a faltering channel pulsing with creative energy. He was eager to take over the reins at Channel 9 but agreed, at Kerry's urging, to be patient a while longer.

Apart from Johnson and Gyngell, each key area of operations had its own department manager – from heads of specific program areas like sport, drama or light entertainment on up to the chief programmer, ultimately responsible for selecting the ideal mix of shows and scheduling them in the most effective time slots. At Nine that was John Stephens, long recognised as one of the best in the industry, the man who delivered that record-breaking streak of 113 straight weeks of ratings wins covering almost three full ratings seasons. To mark the occasion, 'Stevo' was presented with a Rolex watch but considering who he worked for, he deserved the TV equivalent of the Victoria Cross. Day after day, early morning or late at night, the head of programming at the Nine Network could expect to be bombarded by phone calls from Kerry Packer challenging his every decision. Winning was hardly a defence since Kerry came armed with an irrefutable rebuttal. 'Yes, but couldn't we do a little better if . . .' Putting your career on the line on the basis of daily, minute-by-minute ratings was nerve-wracking enough – in earlier days they at least only came out once a week. With that kind of pressure and the 'KP' factor, too, Stephens could hardly have managed to last more than a decade in the job without the tolerance of a saint.

'Kerry called me virtually every morning at 9.15 for the ratings,' Stephens recalls, 'and those phone calls could last for 5 minutes or all morning; or I'd be called over to his office. On numerous occasions, too, I'd be home late at night, eleven or midnight, and the phone would ring and it would be Kerry. I'd say, "Oh, Kerry, do you know what time it is?" He'd say, "Oh, sorry, son, did I get you out of bed? I just want you to think about this, that or the other thing." Deep down he was a pretty lonely sort of guy. I think he just liked to chew the fat about what he loved most dearly. He loved the Nine Network and he loved programming.'

Each of the different branches of prime time entertainment fell under Stephens's umbrella jurisdiction, but there was one department head who was virtually autonomous in his day-to-day decision making and undoubtedly ranked as the most powerful of all. Nine's traditional emphasis on news and current affairs meant that Peter Meakin controlled a massive amount of air time, notable not only for its audience numbers but its critical role in defining the network's prestigious image, the one most Australians turned to in periods of crisis or disaster. Apart from the ABC, no broadcasting organisation came close to challenging that distinctive status or producing anything approaching the same number of newscaff programs. The network spanned the entire 'hard' information spectrum, boasting top-rating local news services in Sydney, Melbourne and Brisbane, along with national shows like *60 Minutes*, *ACA*, *Sunday*, *Business Sunday*, *Today* and *Nightline*. Meakin not only acted as chief co-ordinator for the lot but extended his influence into the 'soft' information area as well, overseeing the development or subsequent evolution of numerous lifestyle and reality programs. *Money*, *Good*

Medicine, Our House, RPA, Animal Hospital and *Getaway* all came under his broad supervision.

By any standard, Meakin and Stephens could be credited with major contributions to Nine's success over the years; but that long record of achievement actually worked against them as Alexander set out to impose his authority over a network seen to be underperforming and resistant to change. They were regarded, in effect, as yesterday's men – Meakin approaching 60 and Stephens in his midfifties, pushing the limits for an occupation as stressful as programming. They were tarnished by their association with David Leckie, viewed as part of the old Nine 'culture', pampered professionals attempting to maintain production standards far too costly to be tolerated in a time of shrinking audiences and ad revenues.

Meakin, in particular, stood out as the virtual personification of Nine's independent, stand-alone spirit, determined to prevent his newscaff resources being misused for promotional purposes, refusing to tone down coverage that might reflect adversely on PBL's broader commercial interests. Stephens, too, was considered overly protective, loyally sticking by department heads who failed to live up to Park Street expectations. As a TV professional, Stephens was well aware that even the most brilliant head of drama or light entertainment could hit a bad patch of failing shows and deserved to be allowed his share of rotten luck – a philosophy that Kerry, with his impatient nature, could never accept and Alexander, with his inbuilt contempt for television, was even less likely to appreciate.

For the moment, however, the network's two most highly decorated front-line commanders could count themselves beyond Alexander's reach. Kerry didn't want to lose either Meakin or Stephens so soon after Leckie's dismissal and he certainly didn't want to see them turning up at a rival network. Yet, if the head of PBL Media found himself temporarily barred from getting rid of the two most venerable symbols of the old Nine culture, he could certainly go around them – a tactic he would develop into a finely honed art. It's not clear how much Kerry knew of Alexander's subversive manoeuvring but we know what he thought about the repercussions. He would later acknowledge them to have been disastrous.

With Leckie out of the picture, the first months of 2002 saw the PBL blowtorch applied mainly to the middle layers of management. Packer proceeded to cut through the chain of command to call department heads directly into his office for unrelenting interrogation, with Alexander often sitting by his side, saying little but clearly making mental notes. It turned out to be a culling process, as surely as park rangers decide upon the animals to survive or die.

The final selections couldn't have been made in a more fitting locale. One brisk autumn morning about nine o'clock, a large helicopter settled upon the landing pad at Ellerston, Kerry's fabled Hunter Valley retreat. Along with the polo grounds and golf course, Packer, a keen big-game hunter in his youth, used the property for target practice, riding around with a rifle to hunt down feral cats. The chopper, though, was filled with larger prey, a contingent of Nine Network executives summoned to an all-day harangue about falling ratings and rising program expenses. John Alexander's presence on the flight did nothing to calm their nerves. He spent the hour or so avoiding any eye contact, staring out the window, remaining ominously silent.

The eight or nine TV managers found themselves ushered into a huge study, then seated in a wide semicircle with the big man behind his desk, slouched across a chair, in the middle. For the next six hours they would not be offered a cup of tea or even a chance to take a leak. There was to be no introductory pep talk or any attempt to exchange pleasantries. Packer turned on them one by one to commence his grilling. Each confrontation would prove a riveting little drama in its own right – a Grand Guignol of inquisitorial terror – but two stand out as the most memorable of the day.

Rory Callaghan, as head of light entertainment, was responsible for overseeing quiz and game shows, as well as one-off spectaculars like the hugely successful *National IQ Test*. At the time of the Ellerston grilling, though, that big hit was yet to go to air and meanwhile, his name was associated with several flops, including a quiz show called *Shafted*, a short-lived replacement to the long-lasting *Sale of the Century*, and *Fear Factor*, a format in which contestants are asked to perform daredevil feats. When Kerry finally got around to him, he opened with a totally unexpected question, a zinger plucked out of nowhere.

'So where are the figures I asked you to get for the last ten years of *Sale of the Century*?'

Callaghan was left absolutely stunned. 'You never asked me for those figures,' he replied.

Packer glared at him with total disdain, turned to look around the arena as a triumphant gladiator might before lopping off a head, and then turned back to Callaghan himself, staring him straight in the eye.

'I fucking well did,' he snarled.

'No you didn't,' Callaghan bravely persisted.

'Right,' Packer retorted, 'let's fix this once and for all.' With that he picked up the phone to his personal assistant back at Park Street, Di Stone, and barked into the mouthpiece. 'Di, who's the fucking idiot I spoke to about getting all those statistics for *Sale of the Century* – you know, so we could discuss the seven o'clock slot?' He listened a moment, then Callaghan could almost sniff the brimstone on the dragon's breath. 'Rory Callaghan! That's exactly what I fucking thought!'

After that Callaghan could probably count himself lucky that he lapsed into a state of shock, aware of Kerry proceeding to slice him to ribbons but too numb to feel anything. All he could think about was who it might have been back at the station who took Packer's message and failed to pass it on.

Kris Noble, head of drama, faced an even more ferocious mauling, as everyone knew he would. Kerry, in the first place, had no feel for drama whatsoever, which explained why it had traditionally been the least successful area of programming in all of Nine's repertoire. There had been a few notable exceptions – *The Sullivans* and the *Flying Doctors* series – but until Noble took on the poisoned chalice in 1992, Nine lagged far behind Seven and even Channel 10 in providing the kinds of dramas and soaps that people talked about the next day. Noble was determined to set out in an entirely new direction, turning his back on Nine's macho, bully-boy approach to everything it did and selecting themes much more appealing to women. Even in the crime genre, the emphasis was still on relationships. The renaissance began with a series of telemovies starring Rebecca Gibney under the *Halifax f.p.* banner, proceeded to *Water Rats* and *Stingers* and reached its zenith with *McLeod's Daughters*. Still, Noble had a voracious tiger by the tail, with the costs of a polished drama, shot on film rather than videotape, escalating by the year. An hour-long episode made for $200,000 to $250,000 in the 1990s might be double that for twenty-first century productions. Noble tried to argue that the best way to offset these costs, strange as it might sound, was to produce dramas of the highest possible quality, since they had the best chance of picking up overseas distribution. Packer dismissed him as an artistic wanker and Ellerston was to be their final showdown, though Noble had no way of knowing that as his turn came up for the ritual excoriation.

'Why is all this stuff so fucking expensive?' Packer accosted him, thumbing through a handful of budgets. 'Your job is to make dramas for $200,000.'

'I can't do that,' Noble told him.

'Well, that's your job. Why do you make everything on fucking film?'

'Because it's the only way we can afford it, to sell it overseas.'

'No it's not. You're just a fucking film snob.'

Noble tried to explain he was anything but that, having spent most of his career in comedy and light entertainment, trained to keep production costs to a minimum with scenes turned around quickly and shot on video. Packer then came up with what must have been the most startling question of the day, considering it was about a much-loved series renowned throughout the world for its stunning photography of Australia's great outback.

'Why aren't you shooting *McLeod's Daughters* in the studio?'

Noble fought hard to stifle a gasp of outright disbelief.

'Because it's about girls on horseback,' he tried to explain. 'It's about making this country look amazing. It's about making viewers think, Wow! What a thrill it must be to live in wide-open country like that, out of the hustle and bustle of the city. That's why we sell it. We sold it to Hallmark [a leading US cable network]. They've put a lot of money in. Isn't it great we can sell it?'

Packer simply changed the subject.

'What about *Stingers*? It costs way too much money. I want you to drop the price.'

Noble was the last to be interviewed, forced to sweat it out until three o'clock before being served up by Kerry as the closest thing to dessert. Though they hadn't eaten all day, no one really cared that much – they just wanted to get out of that torture chamber. There was an immediate rush for the toilets and Rory Callaghan was about to find himself in trouble again. He was the last one in the queue and when he went outside to pick up a lift to the helipad he and one other of the Nine team, chief program-mer John Stephens, ended up in the second of two Toyota HiLuxes. His mates had all piled into the first one. This one had Kerry Packer in the driver's seat. Callaghan noticed a rifle lying across the top of the dashboard.

'Loaded?' he asked cautiously.

'Yeah, there's one in the spout and one in the magazine,' Packer smirked, with enough of a devilish curve on his lips to make the two executives squirm.

As they drove over a hill Callaghan spotted a glorious golf green and decided he would try to lighten the mood. 'Oh, Mr Packer, that's a lovely looking golf course,' he enthused.

'That's a fucking practice green, you idiot!' Kerry snapped.

Once back in Sydney, Callaghan, in a mounting rage, set out to find out who might have let him down so badly by forgetting to pass on Packer's message about the *Sale of the Century* ratings data. Before he could confront anyone, though, he needed to know which day it was that Kerry rang up his office. He phoned Packer's personal assistant, Di Stone, to find out.

'Di,' he said, 'you know when you were talking to Kerry this morning . . .'

'I haven't spoken to Mr Packer all day,' she corrected him.

Kerry, he realised in a flash, had made up the whole bloody scenario just to give him a fright and shake up everyone else in the room – a dazzling display of theatrics to pound home his message that their jobs were well and truly on the line. 'That prick!' Callaghan thought at the time, though he can laugh about it now.

Within his inner circle, Packer, in one of his more sombre moods, occasionally referred to a sad flaw in his character, a trait he was ashamed of in himself. 'I don't know any other way to manage people than through fear, to scare the fucking shit out of them,' he admitted. He was being a bit too hard on himself, of course, because he could also be charming and witty when he wanted to be. As much as that dark side was true, however, he had been extremely fortunate during his reign over Nine. Whatever inadequacy he had in dealing with people was more than compensated for by his reliance on two of the most forceful, energetic and knowledgeable chief executives in the history of the Australian television industry.

Back in the 1970s and 1980s he and Sam Chisholm seemed as interdependent as Siamese twins: Packer's obsessive, win-at-any-cost ethos pumping Chisholm's extraordinary ability to motivate and inspire. While they were entirely different personalities, Packer as introspective and brooding as Chisholm was bright and gregarious, they both knew the television business inside and out and together were able to infuse the Channel 9 team with an exhilarating sense of esprit de corps.

David Leckie took over in far leaner times, the early 1990s, when the network was starved of cash. However, he, and his chief financial adviser, Nick Falloon, managed to keep morale on a high by closely consulting with executive producers and department managers about how they themselves would choose to reduce their own budgets. Much of the necessary cost-cutting, then, was done voluntarily rather than having impractical reductions forced upon the staff from the outside. Leckie soon managed to rebuild the operation into the powerhouse it used to be, encouraging Kerry to spend the necessary development money when and where it was needed most. For all their friction, the two continued to share a fierce sense of pride in Nine and loved to see their competitors choking in its dust.

In turning to John Alexander, however, Packer senior no longer had a second-in-command who shared his love of the television business and could make up for the negative impact of his ill-tempered, bullying management style. Why should Alexander bother when he looked upon the network, at best, as a kind of hermit kingdom locked in the past, filled with a bunch of self-indulgent has-beens allowed to get away with squandering PBL money for far too long? The new team of Packer and Alexander was a far, far cry from the inspirational, symbiotic relationship of the Packer–Chisholm days. As Siamese twins, the only thing they shared was the same bile duct.

After that traumatic day at Ellerston, there was no doubt that

Kerry and Alexander had proceeded to make a final selection of the executive scalps they aimed to collect before the year was out. During senior management meetings, Ian Johnson, the interim CEO, soon began to hear the same names mentioned over and over again in such an adverse light that he had no doubt they were targeted for termination. 'Whether it was an actual written list I don't know for sure,' he concedes, 'but for all practical purposes, it might as well have been.'

In August, after the *National IQ Test* had proved to be a major triumph for the network, Rory Callaghan remembers marching into Johnson's office at the station on a Rocky Mountain high. His contract was coming up for renewal and he was confident he would be able to wangle a healthy rise. Earlier in the year, he had actually been on the verge of resigning after receiving a tempting job offer to join a prestigious international production company. Nevertheless, he felt a great loyalty to Nine, having started out there as a mere researcher in the early 1990s, and his success with the *National IQ Test* led him to believe he might still be able to carve out a promising future despite his misgivings about all that had happened at the network following the dismissal of David Leckie.

'Now, Johnno,' he started off brightly. 'About my contract, can we talk about some more money, because . . . '

Johnson cut him short with a wave of his hand.

'As a friend I suggest you try to look for another job because you're going to get nailed if you stay here,' he confided. 'Your name's on the list.'

Callaghan, along with a couple of others, was able to leave with a little dignity before he felt the cold, sharp edge of the axe.

Kris Noble wasn't so lucky. His execution would prove to be one of the messiest of them all.

CHAPTER 4

High drama: the *McLeod's* debacle

Claire and Tess. They're two hard-driving, highly competitive women, half-sisters sired by the same father, but otherwise worlds apart in their backgrounds and aspirations. A twist of fate brings them together to save a heavily mortgaged outback cattle station left to them in the old man's will. There you have the plot of *McLeod's Daughters*, the most successful quality drama series ever produced in Australia, sold to more than 200 territories world-wide.

It's with no little irony, then, that two hard-driving, highly competitive female producers connected to that show should find themselves drawn into a real-life plot pitting one against the other. John Alexander made secret overtures to each of them to take over Kris Noble's job at the network well before Noble had any inkling he was going to be sacked. The PBL Media chief's meddling in a specialised area he knew so little about would turn out to have an almost farcical ring to it, though it obviously wasn't all that funny to those who had to suffer the repercussions. Before the bizarre episode was over, *McLeod's Daughters* itself would come close to imploding from the recriminations and ill will ignited by his antics. The names of the key characters in this steamy little drama-within-a-drama are Posie and Susan. They make Claire and Tess look like wimps.

It's easy enough to see how Posie Graeme-Evans came to be included in a world-wide list of twenty significant women in television and film, as compiled by *Variety* in late 2002. From concept to reality, she battled for close to ten years to bring *McLeod's Daughters* into Australian homes as a television series. The idea first came to her in 1992 inspired by a single photograph, a bunch of high-spirited young Aussie 'jilleroos' hanging out in the heat and dust of a cattle yard showing off their Akubra hats. For Posie it had all the makings of an exciting ongoing saga of feminine pluck in the face of adversity – women teaming together to run a remote outback station, taking on any obstacle man or nature could throw in their path. Under her constant needling, Nine finally cleared the way for her to make a two-hour TV movie. When it eventually appeared on Mother's Day 1996, it turned out to be a smash hit. Even then, however, Nine's programming executives weren't convinced the concept could sustain a weekly series.

Great passion and great patience are qualities rarely found within the same personality, but they're the essential qualifications for a successful drama producer. Graeme-Evans kept plugging away until one unforgettable evening in September, 2000, she joined hundreds of millions of others around the world in watching the opening ceremony of the Sydney Olympics. The stunning sight of the Snowy River horsemen galloping into the arena gave her all the ammunition she needed to get her series launched at long last. In an impassioned pitch to David Leckie and John Stephens in the Nine boardroom, Posie Graeme-Evans generated enough electricity to light the entire Olympic stadium.

'Why wouldn't you do this?' she challenged Leckie. 'When that first Man from Snowy came out into the arena and then all those others, the whole world was watching and it spoke to the hearts of them all. I am telling the other side of the story, a story that's not been told before. That's half of your fucking audience – they're the people who make you your money . . . '

McLeod's, the series, made its highly successful debut in August, 2001, and from then on, there was no stopping it. Not only did Posie have her name on the credits as executive producer and co-creator, but she had also shared the co-creator honours in pioneering *Hi-5,* a lively children's show format that quickly caught on in the United States and around the world. With her long experience in the industry, including running her own independent production company, Millennium Pictures, Graeme-Evans might well have seemed a most promising candidate for the prestigious position of head of drama. Yet, surprisingly, she wasn't the first *McLeod's* team member John Alexander decided to approach when he set out on his clandestine hunt for Kris Noble's replacement.

Susan Bower was a relatively late starter in drama production, having spent twenty years as a nurse before getting her first job as a researcher on Channel 7's *A Country Practice.* What she lacked in experience she quickly made up for in hard work and dedication, moving up through the ranks to work on successful shows like *All Saints.* She originally joined *McLeod's* as a script producer, a considerable step below Graeme-Evans, though within a year she would take on broader responsibilities as supervising producer. She and Posie, superficially, at least, had much in common: both nudging into their fifties, both known to their workmates as tough, ambitious professionals, well able to hold their own in a dog-eat-dog industry.

When it came to catching John Alexander's eye, however, Bower had one notable advantage over Graeme-Evans. She belonged to a meditation group that included Alice Pagliano, wife of the PBL Media boss. During breaks between relaxation routines the group members naturally chatted to each other about their professional lives. Bower not only stood out for the interesting line of work she was in but her impassioned criticism of the TV networks for failing to provide viewers with enough well-made Australian drama. She insists that at the time she didn't know of Pagliano's relationship with Alexander. However, the woman who ran these group meetings happened to be a close friend of the Italian-born photographer and her influential husband, mixing with them socially. One day in September, 2002, Bower received a phone call from the group leader suggesting she get in touch with Alexander. Not quite understanding that he was actually wanting to speak to her, Bower did nothing about it until the woman approached her again, saying Alexander was wondering why she hadn't phoned him yet. When Bower finally got up the nerve to call Alexander's personal assistant, she was immediately put through.

'I'd really like to meet you if you have time for a cup of coffee,' he told her. As supervising producer of *McLeod's*, Bower's main job was to oversee filming on location in South Australia's Barossa Valley; but she flew up to Sydney every eleven days for program meetings. The two soon got together for what would turn out to be the first of a number of confidential discussions.

'I found him totally fascinating, even mesmerising,' Bower recalls. 'He asked me my opinion of Australian drama – some things that were working, some things that weren't. I'm passionate about Australian drama and once somebody asks me what I think, I just go for it.'

Alexander obviously liked what he heard. 'He asked me to go away and do an analysis for him, a stream of consciousness about what I thought was working, why it was working, why things weren't working, what I thought might help.' The producer sent him a document of several pages, which impressed Alexander enough to request another meeting. This one, though, would be like no other Bower had ever attended. She was a bit annoyed when Alexander's PA tried to schedule her in for 11 am, since she had previously warned that she had other business in Sydney around that time. When Bower protested that she needed an earlier appointment, however, she was stunned at the reply.

'Oh, but Mr Packer doesn't have meetings before 11 am.' It was the first she had heard she was being called in to meet Kerry himself. 'I'm seeing Mr Packer?' she asked incredulously. 'Yes,' the assistant replied. 'Didn't John tell you?' Thinking, 'Oh my God!', Bower asked to be put through to Alexander to see what he could possibly be thinking.

'Yes, I really liked what you sent me,' he congratulated her. 'I found it very interesting and I'd like you to say the same things you said in your e-mail to Kerry Packer.'

And so it came to pass that a member of Posie Graeme-Evans's production team at *McLeod's Daughters* – someone less senior, less experienced and far less famous within the industry – should be summoned to Packer's office at John Alexander's urging to audition for the prestigious role of Nine's next head of drama. Bower is undoubtedly a thorough professional, but one can only marvel at the serendipitous way in which she was so suddenly singled out to walk through Kerry's door. According to the *Encore* directory, bible of the Screen Producers Association of Australia (SPAA), there are well over 500 film and television producers Alexander could have chosen from, not the least of which was SPAA's Independent Producer of the Year for 2001, Posie Graeme-Evans. It's possible, of course, that he knew enough about all of them to decide no one else was worth interviewing in his secret quest to find Noble's replacement. Or did he know of just one, the interesting woman in his wife's meditation group who spoke with such enthusiasm about Australian television drama in between her transcendental chanting? Ummm. That's a question well worth pondering.

Although Bower was understandably nervous about meeting Packer, the two clicked almost immediately with a topic of mutual interest that was totally up her alley. The media magnate had started off by politely asking if she minded if he put his feet up on his desk. As an experienced nurse she was quick to recognise the medical implications. 'Oh,' she asked him, 'have you got oedema from your kidney transplant?' During the subsequent discussion about his various health problems she relaxed enough to be at her forceful best when the conversation inevitably got around to TV drama.

'What do you think of Kris Noble?' Kerry quizzed her. Bower protested that it was an unfair question considering Noble, in his overriding supervision of *McLeod's Daughters*, was technically her boss.

'But you're obviously very passionate about drama,' Kerry persisted. 'Not that I'm necessarily offering you the job, but do you think you could do it?'

'Yes, I do,' she replied, determined to be as straightforward as possible.

Though Alexander had been in the room to start with, he left on a number of occasions to attend to other business. Bower's conversation with Kerry stretched on for an hour and a half as she discussed her ideas for reorganising Nine's approach to drama to make it more competitive with Seven's highly successful output. That meant investing in more extensive audience research, allowing more time for shows to settle in, creating pilots to test the mood of the market, and giving the network a healthy injection of in-house productions. At the end, Packer bade her a warm farewell, saying how much he had enjoyed their time together.

As Alexander escorted her to the lift, however, the producer expressed misgivings about how well she had performed. 'I was scared shitless,' Susan admitted. J.A. assured her that from what he had seen, she had gone 'very, very well'. Then he left her with words she will never forget. 'No matter what happens, always remember this – very few people in the world have had an hour and a half of Kerry Packer's time.'

It was a highly revealing remark, coming as it did from the man who had gone out of his way to set up the appointment. Of course, it was meant to flatter her, to remind her how fortunate she had been to be considered worthy of such an opportunity. At the same time, however, it provided an extraordinary insight into how Alexander viewed his own relationship with Kerry. He seemed to see himself as Packer's gatekeeper, protecting the magnate from wasting his precious time, making sure he saw only the people who mattered. In this case, he clearly believed he had brought Packer a rare gem he had discovered all on his own – a drama guru no one else in the entire Nine Network knew anything about or would have the imagination to recognise even if they did. That presumably explains why he never bothered to run Bower's name past his three most senior TV advisers – Ian Johnson, David Gyngell, or programmer John Stephens – to see what they might think of her. Instead, he was determined to follow his own star and proudly deliver unto his boss a gift of truly magian proportions.

By the time of that meeting in Kerry's office in the spring of 2002, Alexander had formally taken over from Ian Johnson as CEO of the network, while remaining head of PBL Media. David Gyngell continued in his role as deputy CEO, but on the understanding that he would begin assuming more control over day-to-day operations at the network, with Alexander focusing on broader strategic issues. Still, Alexander had yet to confide in Gyngell about his keen interest in Susan Bower as the new head of drama. Matters came to a head towards the end of November. Bower herself suggested she submit a business plan outlining her ideas for a major reorganisation of the network's drama department. Alexander, again, was so impressed, that he told her it was time he introduced her to Gyngell.

'I've got this Susan Bower coming to see me,' he explained to his deputy CEO over the phone. 'Will you come in and meet with her?' Gyngell reluctantly agreed to go to Park Street to listen to Bower's presentation, but he was privately appalled that negotiations with her had been allowed to go so far down the track without his knowledge. Gyngell, like John Stephens, still considered Kris Noble a valuable asset to the network and thought it a shame that Kerry Packer had developed such a mindset against him. However, if there was to be a new head of drama, the network's second-in-command had no doubt who that should be. He was a big fan of Posie Graeme-Evans, with her proven ability to put together major production deals not only locally but internationally. She also generated tons of favourable press coverage, the recognition of her achievements culminating in the *Variety* article of 18 November naming her as a world-class operator. Though he was polite enough to hear Bower out that day, he set his mind on making an immediate approach to Graeme-Evans, with Alexander's consent if possible, but going over his head directly to Kerry Packer if necessary.

Bower was certainly alert to the bad vibrations from that first meeting with Gyngell. 'I got a very strong feeling,' she recalls, 'that David had no confidence in me, a very strong feeling.' Yet that same afternoon, after Gyngell returned to the station, Alexander virtually promised her Noble's job. His proposal was that she begin working to reorganise the drama department while

Noble was still serving out the last six months or so of his contract. That, in his view, would lead to a smoother transition. Bower refused point-blank, instinctively recognising the proposal as a recipe for disaster. If Noble didn't like her plan – and he was not likely to – she could easily find herself bogged down in a prolonged clash of wills. Alexander was totally taken aback by her rejection.

'You won't do it?' he challenged, with the steely edge of ultimatum in his voice.

'No, it simply won't work,' she insisted. 'If you want to consider bringing me in in six months' time after Kris is gone, maybe we can talk about it then.'

To Bower's amazement, Alexander almost immediately caved in. 'Then, you have forced my hand,' she remembers him saying. 'Within the next 24 hours I will have to speak with Kris Noble, and within the next 24 hours we will make an announcement.'

'I was taken aback by that,' Bower concedes today, 'because I honestly thought that he would say no, we're not doing it then.'

Alexander walked her to the lifts of 54 Park Street for what would turn out to be the last time. There was no phone call from him in the next 24 hours, and certainly no announcement about Kris Noble's demise. When Bower eventually phoned to find out what was happening, Alexander told her: 'Something else has happened and we need more time to think about it. I can't tell you any more.'

'Now you are making me extremely nervous,' she replied. And she certainly had good reason to be. What she couldn't possibly know is that the prospect of her imminent appointment had spurred Gyngell on to a direct confrontation with his network CEO.

Bower, he tried to explain, was a 'show-runner' – a producer – not the creator of a major drama series, like Posie Graeme-Evans. 'She does a good job on *McLeod's Daughters*, but why take her out of that role and possibly damage the show? If we're going to get rid of Kris Noble, I want to go after a creator, someone like Posie.'

Alexander may not have liked what he was hearing but he was not prepared to see the matter brought to Kerry in a showdown. Bowing to the inevitable, he agreed to Gyngell phoning Graeme-Evans to set up an urgent meeting, which subsequently took place at the network offices in suburban Willoughby on Tuesday, 3 December. Posie, to this point, had not heard the slightest whisper about Alexander's intensive wooing of one of her producers. She had never met him before and was intrigued to know why he should want to see her without Kris Noble being there as well. Noble had always been her main point of contact for any other functions at the station. She felt uneasy enough having to wait outside Alexander's office at the station – David Leckie's old office – knowing word was bound to get back to Kris. As soon as she walked in, she got the shock of her life.

'I hear you're the queen of drama,' Alexander told her. 'How would you like to be the head of drama in this place?'

David Gyngell was also in the room, looking at her with an encouraging smile. Posie, though, was almost too staggered to come up with a coherent response, even as the two men continued to press her. What did she think of the idea? Would she be at all interested? Would she at least agree to discuss the matter further with David?

'I was enormously flattered,' Graeme-Evans recalls, 'but I was completely stunned. I didn't know what to say. I walked out of the place reeling, thinking, "What was that all about?"' She was also concerned about going behind Noble's back; but Alexander and Gyngell had made her swear to secrecy, assuring her that his contract would not be renewed in any circumstances.

Never before in her career as a TV producer had she thought of herself striding down the corridors of power at Australia's number one network. That image, once imprinted in her brain, was hard to erase despite her grave misgivings about the radical change it would mean for both her professional and private life. She still carried the emotional scars of losing her first marriage to the pressures of working herself to a frazzle day and night – she didn't intend to lose another. As a producer over the years she was well used to suffering last-minute rejections and disappointments. She may well have hoped, in her heart of hearts, that the job prospect at Nine would just vanish by itself. Instead, it suddenly got a lot more serious.

Posie came back to Gyngell with a list of conditions that needed to be agreed upon before she could even begin to consider the appointment seriously, and was surprised to find that nothing appeared to be in the too-hard basket. Just the opposite: Gyngell soon contacted her again to ask her if she was prepared to meet with Kerry Packer for lunch in Park Street's legendary fifth-floor dining room. That put her a long way ahead of Bower's morning meeting in his office. Kerry's dining room was a sanctum strictly reserved for the anointed, or those soon to be.

Anyone else might have felt thoroughly intimidated. Graeme-Evans probably did as well, though she was damned if she was going to show it. To understand what makes her tick, it's best to begin with how she describes herself. 'I'm not blonde, you know, I'm not 5 foot 9 and leggy, so I don't give a rat's arse.' Clearly, she finds it easier to say what she's not rather than to try to define the volatile mix of all the things she is, the kind of compact but highly complex little bundle of energy they dropped on Nagasaki. She and Kerry hit it off fabulously, laughing and shouting at each other as if they were long-lost mates. Alexander was there, flattering her profusely, but Kerry had the running and he made his feelings known almost at once: the job is yours, are you going to take it or not?

'And I said, "No! My life is too short. I'm prepared to work all the hours God gives me, but I'm just not sure about this. When I die one day you're not going to be there, helping me into the next world; but I hope my husband is.'" The truth was, she didn't really need the job. Years of struggle had finally started coming good for her, with *Hi-5* a big hit around the world, *McLeod's Daughters* reaping rave reviews as well as undreamed of ratings, her name as lyricist on a best-selling album of music from that series, a new career just beginning for her as author of a string of historical novels. If all that wasn't enough, she couldn't have wished for a happier second marriage – her husband, Andrew Blaxland, also a program maker, sharing in the running of Millennium Pictures. Packer might be the closest thing to an emperor she had ever met, she told him, but she, too, was a general in her own way, very much in command of her own loyal regiments. Kerry had a good chuckle at the analogy, the giant listening to such cheeki-ness coming from someone who barely reached up to his navel, a sugarplum fairy he could have swallowed in a bite. Still, Australia's most powerful businessman was nothing if not the grand master of persuasion, the greatest mind game of them all. With just a few well-chosen words, he implanted a thought that threatened to haunt her the rest of her life.

'You realise if you don't take this job,' he warned, 'you will never know if you could have measured up.'

'The bastard, he nailed me!' Graeme-Evans admits.

Her recollection of Kerry at that lunch is a vivid portrait of the charismatic businessman at the very top of his form. 'My God, I've never met a more powerful bloke, a silverback gorilla, the apotheosis of masculinity, courageous and frightening, funny and charming, clever and witty and world-weary – just a wonderful bunch of things. He was extraordinary, I was dazzled.'

Graeme-Evans continued to hold out, however, refusing to give Packer the firm commitment he demanded. Alexander knew that after the lunch she was due to fly to South Australia for talks with her field producers. That meant Posie coming face to face with Susan Bower, whom he had left dangling within a microdot of a formal offer for the job he was now promising to her boss. He was like a juggler trying to keep two time bombs in the air, both set to go off about 6.30 pm Adelaide time. There was only one way to try to defuse the situation.

'You should know that we've already talked to Susan Bower about this position,' he confessed.

'Then what the fuck am I doing here?' Posie erupted, slamming her knife and fork down on the table, barely able to stop herself from bolting out the door and into history as the first fifth-floor luncheon guest ever to walk out on Kerry Packer. There was so much to be furious about she didn't know where to begin. It was hard enough to deal with the revelation that a producer she had promoted and nurtured could dare keep such a secret from her. She was even more mortified to think that Nine's bosses could consider dishonouring her in such a way, as if her ratings successes counted for nothing. What would have happened had Bower actually become head of drama – how would Posie have been expected to feel, having to come cap in hand to her to beg for more resources for *McLeod's*? Most upsetting of all, though, was the potential threat to her precious baby – the offspring of her creative soul. What network in its right mind would risk destroying a highly regarded drama series by playing off one of its producers against another? Graeme-Evans fought to control her emotions, but she wasn't about to let Alexander get off the hook entirely.

'So how would you expect me to go on working with Susan after this?' she demanded to know.

The Nine CEO stumbled over himself with apologies but it was Kerry who finally managed to save the day by giving Posie a remarkable glimpse into his closely guarded private life. It concerned his feelings of deep distress during the Goanna saga, when almost all the media was abuzz with rumours about his connection to drug smuggling and murder. He was particularly hurt when he saw a prominent reporter who had made his fame and fortune at Nine featuring among the pack in pursuing the allegations against him.

'I kept on working with Mike Willesee,' Packer said quietly. 'If I could do that, you can do this.'

The lunch ended with Posie's mind in turmoil. She still refused to give a definite yes to the offer, but she had at least agreed to talk it over with her husband, Andrew, who was in South Australia awaiting her arrival. 'Look, you may still change your mind; give me a call,' Alexander told her.

As soon as she left, he got on the phone to Susan Bower. If it was a difficult conversation for him, it was devastating for her, his every word resounding like another shovelful of dirt on her professional grave.

'I told you the other day that something else had happened and a wild card had been thrown into the ring,' he began. 'We have just finished interviewing Posie Graeme-Evans and we have decided to go with her.'

There was only one reaction possible. 'Fuck!'

'But I've protected you,' the Nine boss tried to reassure her, 'by telling Posie what has been going on.'

'You haven't protected me,' Bower challenged him. 'I'm going to lose my job.'

Alexander, stung by her icy disdain, struggled to find something he could say to appease her enough to bring this excruciating ordeal to an end. What he came up with was one of the most far-fetched propositions in this whole sorry saga of seduction and betrayal. Her future was secure, he promised, 'because I really want you to work at Channel 9 with Posie. That's the plan.' It was an idea never even hinted at during his lunch with Kerry and Graeme-Evans and never to be heard of again.

'You didn't discuss it with me, John,' Bower rebuked him,

dismissing his 'plan' as the absurdity it was, 'and it won't work after what's happened, not for the network, not for Posie or for me.'

'Well, now you've changed everything,' he accused her.

'No, John,' she interrupted. 'You've changed everything. You've cost me my job.'

Susan hung up, resigned to her fate, certain she would be fired as soon as Posie walked through the door. Of course, she was distraught at being passed over for the Nine job at the very last minute, still confident she could have made a worthwhile contribution. At the same time, however, she held no hard feelings whatsoever towards Graeme-Evans, accepting that she had the kind of track record bound to appeal to a network looking for a drama head with just the right image. The two women might have fought tooth and nail over creative differences but they still admired and respected one another as devoted program makers.

'Well, yesterday I had two jobs and now I've got none,' Bower thought to herself as she strolled off to a local pub to buy a Scotch and a pack of cigarettes while she waited for Posie to fly in from Sydney. Graeme-Evans stormed into her Barossa Valley office around 6.30 pm 'like a galleon in full sail,' as Bower remembers it. 'I've just spoken to Alexander, I know what's going on,' was her opening salvo. Bower, as a nurse of twenty years, was used to dealing with many a bloodied trauma victim. If she was about to become one herself, she intended to survive the ordeal with all the dignity she could muster. 'Okay, Posie,' she began, 'I just want a chance to tell you my side of the story.' At that point, though, Graeme-Evans had a far bigger issue on her mind – whether to accept Kerry Packer's challenge and take the job or live out the rest of her days always wondering if she could have handled it. She needed to speak to Andrew, to make sure she had his blessing. Her confrontation with Sue Bower could wait until the next day.

And then something miraculous happened, as it tends to do in good, heart-warming television dramas, the ones that bring tears to your eyes and make you believe that mankind – and womankind, too – is capable of the most incredible acts of forgiveness and understanding. Bower walked into Posie's office with a bottle of French champagne she had been saving for herself, to celebrate what was supposed to have been her new career. Instead, she popped the cork and poured them both a glass, raising a toast of congratulations to the queen of Australian drama, long may she reign at Channel 9.

'If the shoe had been on the other foot,' Posie conceded, 'I might not have been as generous.' And that brought the laughter that cleared the air between them like a fresh Barossa breeze. Perhaps they weren't cut out to be bosom buddies, but they realised, then and there, that it was sheer common sense to keep working together – like Claire and Tess – to save a treasured property from foreclosure. Susan Bower would go on to replace Posie as executive producer of *McLeod's Daughters*. In that capacity she was directly responsible to Nine's new drama boss, who didn't hesitate to give her hell about sticking to her budgets and sharpening up her story lines. And the two hard-driving, highly competitive female producers continued to annoy each other happily ever after, or at least until they eventually went their separate ways.

Kris Noble, meanwhile, was about to spend the most miserable festive season of his life. He knew nothing of the weeks Alexander had spent plotting his downfall, nor was he aware of the behind-the-scenes upheaval at *McLeod's Daughters*. Even after Graeme-Evans accepted the offer to replace him, there was not even a hint that his contract was about to be terminated. It was a particularly invidious humiliation for the drama head, since he worked so closely with the *McLeod's* team. Indeed, he was due to give a rousing speech at the *McLeod's* Christmas party to congratulate everyone on a second successful season and urge them on to even greater heights under his command in 2003. Posie Graeme-Evans felt sicker and sicker at heart as the date for that function approached, with the network doing nothing to inform Noble of his fate.

'It all got weirder and weirder,' she recalls. 'I was making three phone calls a day to David Gyngell but no one would talk to Kris.' From the network's viewpoint, it was still negotiating with Posie over various clauses in her contract and was adamant no official announcement should be made until the document received Park Street's final stamp of approval. Graeme-Evans, for her part, felt obliged to honour her promise of confidentiality. Nevertheless, the community of drama makers within Australia is close-knit and gossipy, and rumours inevitably began to spread about Posie Graeme-Evans moving into Nine's third-floor executive suite. John Stephens, alerted to the buzz, couldn't take it seriously.

'I just thought it was press gossip and really took no notice,' Stephens says, 'because I assumed I would have been consulted if anything was happening.' One day, though, he happened to run into Posie at the birthday party of a mutual friend and got the chance to ask her directly. 'A funny rumour is going around that you're coming to Nine to be head of drama. Is that true or not?' He raised the matter only half-jokingly, but was amazed to hear her response.

'And she said, "Well, Stevo, it's true,"' Stephens recalls. 'I took a couple of steps back and said, "What? What do you mean it's true?" And she said: "Oh, I've been having discussions with John Alexander and Kerry Packer and David Gyngell. They want me to come and run drama – and I think I'm going to take it."'

Graeme-Evans remembers their encounter, though in a slightly different version. Flustered by Stephens's direct question, she recalls beating a fast retreat, advising the programmer: 'Look, I can't say anything, you've really got to talk to David Gyngell or John Alexander.' The next day the chief programmer did try to get through to them both, but neither returned his phone calls.

'They wouldn't take my call because they obviously knew what it was about,' Stephens says. He had no choice but to leave the issue simmering as he flew off on holidays. Posie, by the evening of the *McLeod's* Christmas party, was almost beside herself with self-recrimination. When Kris Noble arrived at the gathering, he immediately sensed the tension in the air. He remembers Posie coming up to him, visibly upset and struggling to find the right words. 'Kris, look, I think you've got to speak to David Gyngell as soon as you can.'

'Straight away I thought to myself, "Oh fuck, so this is it."' Even today Noble's voice reflects the shattering impact of that moment. While he was well aware of Park Street's hostility towards him, he had felt relatively secure knowing he had several important projects on the boil and months still to run on his contract. It was so close to Christmas, he thought he could count himself safe at least until some time in the new year. Posie's warning, though, reminded him of how many other executives had been purged from the system during 2002. The head of sport, Gary Burns, the head of light entertainment, Rory Callaghan, the senior business manager, Hugh Marks, the managing director of GTV 9, Graeme Yarwood, the chief of production in Melbourne, Graham Tripid, GTV's finance director, Brian Tucker – all had either been pushed out or had opted to bail out voluntarily. As he walked up to give his pep talk to the *McLeod's* mob, he did his best to keep things bright and breezy. All he could think of, though, was: 'Shit, is this really going to happen to me?'

Then he went home to break the bad news to his wife and children, expecting a call from Gyngell or Alexander at any moment. 'So I wait Saturday and Sunday and no one calls. On Monday morning I go into work as usual and Gyngell walks into my office about 8.30. I said, "David, are you going to talk to me or what?" He said, "Yeah, yeah, mate. It wasn't my idea, it really wasn't."'

Gyngell, at least, arranged to pay him out of his contract in full. It was a kindly gesture that would become less and less common in the turbulent months to come.

Programmer John Stephens, meanwhile, would have the entire holiday period to brood over how shabbily he had been treated, left totally out of the loop in a decision affecting drama – one of the most crucial areas of his administration. If he felt bad for himself he felt even worse for Kris Noble, a long-time friend, as well as a colleague, and one who, in Stephens's view, had been most unfairly dismissed considering his valuable contribution during the previous decade. Here, then, was a key executive left to stew for several weeks over the high-handed actions of Park Street and – unfortunately for Nine – with a new contract lying on his desk back at Willoughby still waiting for his signature.

The basic terms of the program chief's new agreement had been worked out with David Gyngell before he flew off to North Queensland, providing for a substantial increase in salary and bonuses. There were a few minor points yet to be settled, however, which meant that as of 31 December he was no longer legally bound to the network and technically free to leave as he pleased. Channel 7 was obviously aware of when his contract was due to expire, because by 1 January they were right onto his case with a tempting offer to become head of programming strategy, a newly created position in which he would effectively serve as senior adviser to a younger team that was just settling in. The pay was less than he would have received at Nine but, considering his wounded pride, respect was far more important than money.

'I just thought, there's no point going back there, I was so bloody pissed off.' On the night before he signed with Seven, he returned to his office to clear out all his personal effects, assuming that once he handed in his letter of resignation, it wasn't likely Alexander would invite him to linger.

'I went in next morning and straight to Gyngell's office, and as it happens, John Alexander was sitting there with him,' he recalls. Both executives were obviously hoping to gloss over the fact that, a few weeks before, they had refused to return his phone calls demanding to know what the hell was happening with Kris Noble and Posie Graeme-Evans.

'Hi, Stevo, season's greetings to you, how are you? Did you have a great break? Good to have you back,' they tried to jolly him along. The programmer, though, was not exactly brimming over with the Christmas spirit.

'Well, guys, it's probably not the time to do all that,' he interrupted them, 'because I am pretty pissed off about what happened while I was away – the fact that there was no communication from either of you about letting Kris go or who his replacement was going to be.'

'Oh, it wasn't our fault,' they replied as one, resorting to the Nuremberg defence, 'it was really Kerry who wanted to drive the situation. We had no choice.'

Stephens was having none of it. 'Well, at least I could have been consulted if you knew this was going on before I went on holidays,' he admonished them.

John Stephens is usually a calm man, as programmers need to be in the heat of the ratings battle, but their response couldn't have made him angrier if they had tried. 'Oh, we knew you were close to Kris,' one or the other tried to explain, 'and we didn't really want to upset the apple cart when we were in the midst of renegotiating your contract.'

'Well, you can forget about that,' Stevo corrected them. 'I'm leaving.'

David Gyngell was stunned by the announcement and desperate to make amends. 'We thought it might upset you but not as bad as this. Let's just sit down and talk it over.' However, when Stephens revealed he was going to another network, the room fell deathly silent, immersed in a morgue-like chill. Here was the mastermind of the Nine Network's programming strategy for the coming ratings season about to defect to a competitor. When he finally told them which network, their reaction was straight out of a horror flick, like two Transylvanians frantically making a sign of the cross or waving garlic in the face of Count Dracula. 'We want you out of here instantly!'

Stephens was well prepared for an abrupt departure. He immediately handed over his keys to the company car and his mobile phone, said a quick goodbye to his teary-eyed staff and walked out of the building that had been his second home for thirteen years, ten of them as the guiding force behind the Nine Network's incredible run of winning ratings seasons.

Soon enough there would be an even bigger bombshell to follow.

CHAPTER 5

Double-crossed: the crucifixion of Peter Meakin

The note pad had a surname scribbled across it, followed by a question mark. Of course, it could have meant anything: a reminder to make a lunch date, inquire about a mutual acquaintance, perhaps even send off a congratulatory bottle of French champagne, since the person mentioned had been honoured the previous week with a prestigious Walkley award for leadership in Australian journalism. Under the circumstances, though, none of those more benign options seemed very likely. The notation was sitting atop the desk of John Alexander, spotted in his Nine Network office by an eagle-eyed visitor in the first week of December, 2002. That wouldn't have been an easy time for him, with the *McLeod's Daughters* fiasco derailing his plans for drama; but he faced an even bigger hurdle trying to put his stamp on news and current affairs, encountering stiff resistance from the pugnacious veteran who headed that powerful arm of the network. Meakin was the name on the curious desktop citation and the question mark didn't bode well for him.

So long as the newscaff director remained at the network, he could only be viewed as an impediment to Alexander's grand designs. While Kerry's support might protect him from the purge list, that didn't mean Meakin couldn't be removed from the picture by more subtle means. If a Channel 9 executive as unflappable as John Stephens had been driven to resign over Alexander doing deals behind his back, it surely must have occurred to the Nine CEO that someone as volatile as Peter Meakin would hardly stand for it. At the very least, it's fair to presume that he really couldn't care if Meakin left as well. It's even more likely that Alexander actively set out to goad him into resigning as the newscaff boss began to discover one important decision after another being made in his area without him knowing the slightest thing about it.

It would be hard to find two people with less in common than Meakin and Alexander, the one prone to be as outspoken and direct as the other was tight-lipped and evasive. Both are of shortish build but to get an idea of how dissimilar they are, it helps to have seen the movie *Lord of the Rings* – the fearless bearded dwarf plunging with his mighty battle axe headlong into the fray compared to the lissom elf darting hither and thither plucking at his delicate bow like a harp string. No one was immune from Meakin's eviscerating jibes, not even Kerry Packer. On the day the mogul returned to reclaim Channel 9 from Alan Bond, all the other executives adopted the lowest possible profile to try to avoid his wrath but Meakin was more than happy to stick his neck out. 'Kerry's let everybody know he's back and good on him,' he remarked to the press. 'Now he can stop climbing the mast and doing King Kong impressions.'

One might have thought that the two men could at least find common ground in their journalism but the practical reality was just the opposite: nothing divided them more than the different perspectives from which they approached the art of mass communication. A quick review of Meakin's career shows him to be the quintessential television newsman. After a brief stint in newspapers, he got his start in the visual medium in a small country station in South Australia, going on to become a reporter in Perth and then an innovative news director at Channel 10 in Sydney. He made his switch to current affairs in the early 1970s, working as both a producer and highly provocative roving reporter for *A Current Affair*. His most memorable question is one he put to the Whitlam era's controversial Immigration Minister Al Grassby. It followed claims that the minister had misused his power to arrange temporary entry permits for several shady Italian gentlemen wanting to visit the Riverina area supposedly to attend a funeral. 'Mr Grassby,' Meakin cheerfully began, 'how long have you been a travel agent for the Mafia?' After that he was encouraged to focus on an exclusively behind-the-screen role.

By then our careers at Nine had begun to interweave. After an ill-fated attempt to launch a combined Sydney–Melbourne news service, I switched back to being a reporter under Meakin's watchful eye as my supervising producer. In 1978 it was a virtual toss-up as to which one of us might be chosen to take on the role of founding executive producer of *60 Minutes*, but I got the nod from Kerry, immediately appointing Peter my second-in-command. He proved to be a driving force behind the show's unprecedented ratings success and from there he would soon go on to co-ordinate all of the network's information output as head of newscaff.

That kind of solid CV can only be built upon years of accumulated experience: first-hand knowledge gained by putting together hundreds of newscaff programs and, within those programs, many thousands of different stories. Each effort leaves behind a precious grain of residual knowledge to draw upon in the unending quest for more effective coverage. Was the shot of the weeping woman held a second too long, should the camera have moved in for a tighter close-up; was the poignancy of the moment spoiled by a grab of commentary when silence would have delivered greater impact? Those are some of the fine points a production team might debate in preparing a report that attempts to convey a certain mood: for example, a community's grief over a tragic car accident. The art of presenting hard facts to a general audience can be even more exacting, particularly when dealing with complex political or economic developments. How can we make this story relevant to the everyday experiences of the typical viewer? If there are statistics that must be mentioned, what's the best way to enable people to visualise them?

Back in the 1990s Peter Meakin pushed for the introduction of a new lifestyle show, *Money*, that – in theory – seemed far too dry and cerebral for commercial TV. When sceptical program executives demanded to know who would care enough to watch, the newscaff chief had a ready answer for them. 'More people have hip pockets than backyards,' he pointed out, drawing a parallel with Don Burke's popular series. The key to such a concept was in making every segment, whether about comparing credit card fees or obtaining bank loans, as easily digestible as possible. His producers took that dictum almost literally with one of their earliest efforts: a report that tried to explain the intricate workings of the share market by showing the presenter, Paul Clitheroe, in a pizza parlour. 'Look, all a share is, is part of a business, just like this slice of pizza,' he enthused.

A newspaper might run a weekly advice column on finance and never know how many of its readers actually find it useful. The production team on *Money* could count on an accurate measurement of the number of viewers watching each edition, their ages and incomes, the segments they found interesting enough to tune into or boring enough to switch off. With that kind of knowledge it was possible to make continual adjustments to content and treatment, improving performance week by week. The fact-filled program was to prove a phenomenal hit.

It should be clear enough, then, that the visual medium is a world unto itself, even to the point of having its own language, the means by which TV professionals tell each other about the countless little tricks they've discovered over the years for presenting a particular type of story to best advantage. If John Alexander had shown any interest in learning that language, he would have found no wiser teacher than Peter Meakin, towards the end of 2002 just turning 60, with more than four decades in the news business, if one includes his brief apprenticeship in print journalism. At that age Meakin was not likely to be harbouring any deep-seated political ambitions, such as wanting to take charge of the network or move into the hierarchy at Park Street. Yet Alexander appeared to see him precisely in those terms, as a political adversary – with David Leckie gone, the only one left of Nine's old guard with clout enough to challenge his authority. In that sense, Meakin's vast experience in information-based programming actually counted against him, viewed as a threat rather than an irreplaceable asset.

Not all of Alexander's escapades were conducted on a lone-wolf basis, like his clandestine wooing of Susan Bower for the job of head of drama. He frequently consulted with Kerry or James or an influential PBL board member like Sam Chisholm in deciding upon a desirable course of action in terms of programming or more efficient administration. However, even when he set out to achieve a goal agreed upon by others at Park Street, the means he resorted to were peculiarly his own, tailor-made to a personality uncomfortable with direct confrontation. He had launched his campaign to unseat Mike Munro at *ACA* as early as July, 2002, possibly after discussions with Kerry but in any case well before Meakin ever got wind of it. By August, it appears he had a second newscaff presenter in his sights. Nine's finance editor, Michael Pascoe, was well known to viewers of *Business Sunday* for his droll comments on the foibles of various leaders of the business community. Unfortunately, egg on the face is not a good look for a CBD mover and shaker in his pin-striped Zegna suit. Some of the victims of Pascoe's distinctive brand of ego-puncturing satire began to complain directly to their contacts in the Park Street hierarchy.

Suggestions of censorship are notoriously hard to pin down. No one at Nine was ever ordered in so many words: *Tell Pascoe to pull in his claws.* However, a familiar phrase began to be heard within PBL's inner circle with ominous repetition. 'He's not taken seriously around the town.' That evaluation might have been laughable if it hadn't had such dire implications. If Pascoe had any credibility problem at all, it was in being taken far too seriously by the corporate heavyweights he poked fun at from time to time. The heads of Woolworths, Westfield and Macquarie Bank all felt his barbs but in Pascoe's own estim-ation, he probably stretched his luck a bridge too far by taking on Rupert Murdoch's News Ltd, at that particular point in time enjoying a particularly cosy relationship with the Packers.

Wherever the critical spark might have come from, the fuse was well and truly lit by late August 2002. *Crikey*, a gossipy e-mail newsletter avidly read by journalists, carried the first whisper.

'Pascoe is having his turf stomped all over,' wrote an arch-rival, Mark Westfield, economics commentator for the ABC's *7.30 Report*, as well as columnist for the *Australian*. 'He can't get a scoop anymore and it's starting to show in the lack of coverage he's getting in the Monday newspapers.' That acerbic observation was clearly a payback for Pascoe's trenchant criticism of some aspects of business coverage on the ABC. Westfield, however, soon moved on to the nitty-gritty. 'The other interesting factor in Pascoe's anger of late is the fact his position is uncertain. His job is being offered around. I was offered the job a few months ago. Nine no longer wants him, so he's lashing out at his rivals. Grow up, Michael. You're on the skids.'

Westfied gave no indication of who at PBL or Nine might have approached him with the purported job offer. Peter Meakin certainly knew nothing about it and dismissed the claim as mere mischief-making between journalistic competitors. Interestingly enough, Pascoe decided to put the allegation directly to Alexander himself via e-mail, though with a bit of his typical tongue-in-cheek humour in asking whether he knew of any basis for Westfield's claim.

From: Pascoe, Michael
Sent: Friday, 30 August, 2002, 6.06 pm
To: Alexander, John
Subject: feuding banjos.

John,
While trying to build credentials for a job on Media Watch I've been taking a few swings at easy targets, one of which, Mark Westfield, has tried to hit back via Crikey. Before dealing with it, I need to know what reed he might be leaning on. Even a defamation lightning rod like Westfield would tend to need something to work with, so, is anyone at the PBL end a fan of his?

From: Alexander, John
Sent: Saturday, 31 August, 2002, 4.28 pm
To: Pascoe, Michael
Subject: Re: feuding banjos.

Michael,
I think if Mark Westfield was being offered a job at PBL, I would know about it . . . and I know nothing about it. I doubt if we could afford the legal bills even if there was a vacancy – and there isn't. His name has never been mentioned to me in any capacity in four years at PBL by my betters . . . neither positively or negatively – the latter is usually reserved for Fairfax journalists. Hope this clarifies things.

From: Pascoe, Michael
Sent: Saturday, 31 August, 2002, 5.11 pm
To: Alexander, John
Subject: Re: feuding banjos.

John,
Thanks for that – I shall go forth and kick head.

Which he proceeded to do in a lengthy rebuttal, ending on a sardonic note that would soon come back to haunt him. 'But Westfield saved his best concoction to last,' Pascoe wrote in his *Crikey* article. 'Heaven knows, strange things happen in television, but his claim to Channel 9 being so keen to have him caused plenty of laughter around here.'

Sadly for Pascoe, though, whatever laughter there was would soon ring hollow. His days were definitely numbered – the only question being how much longer it would take for Alexander to secretly seek out a suitable replacement. That wasn't easy to do in a country where credible financial reporters were thin on the ground and tended to move in the same social circles. In early November, 2002, Alexander approached Channel 7's David Koch, asking him to replace Pascoe in a determined pitch that was to extend over two meetings. This was before Kochie, as loyal fans know him, went on to win astounding popularity as the co-host of Seven's *Sunrise*, but even then he wasn't interested. He simply couldn't stomach the way Alexander proceeded to heap scorn on Pascoe's performance and reputation. He quickly broke off negotiations with one thought foremost in his mind. *If it could happen to him, it could happen to me.*

Peter Meakin knew, of course, that Pascoe had his critics at Park Street. Kerry Packer himself had once complained to him about the business commentator. Yet the newscaff chief was well used to defending his reporters and presenters against Packer's habitual grumbling and confident enough about Pascoe's future at Nine to promise him a new two-year contract after the Christmas break. As it turned out, the business reporter's impending fate wasn't the only surprise in store for him.

In early November, 2002, again without speaking to Meakin, Alexander commenced negotiations to bring Jana Wendt back to Channel 9 after an absence of seven years. There was no doubt that he was encouraged to do so by Sam Chisholm, who considered Wendt to be one of the truly great talents to come out of the network's Golden Age, 'as good as anybody in the world'. Jana, of course, had become a household name through her work as the first female reporter on *60 Minutes* and later as host of *A Current Affair*, leaving viewers agog with her razor-sharp interviewing. She might not have had the wide popular appeal of a Graham Kennedy, Mike Walsh or Ray Martin, but in the history of Australian television no one came closer to the archetypal image of a Hollywood movie star, set apart by her electric presence – a mystique that put Jana in a class all her own. Her importance to Nine in the 1980s and 1990s was not just in her drawing power. With her intelligence, poise and sophisticated femininity she became a role model for an entire generation of aspiring Australian career women.

Still, by the mid-1990s Jana's career had begun to falter – a reflection of the inherent small-mindedness of the Australian television industry, reluctant to allow its veteran presenters to explore new horizons so that they begin to feel caged in, imprisoned in some repetitious, stereotypical role. In 1995, frustrated by what she saw as a lack of innovative thinking at Nine, the star switched channels, moving to the Seven Network to host a new public affairs program called *Witness*. That misadventure would soon end in a bitter lawsuit, with Wendt claiming she had been misled by promises the new show would tackle more serious topics than its producers were actually prepared to do. From there she packaged interview programs for the ABC before moving to SBS to anchor *Dateline*, with its strong emphasis on international coverage. That certainly was a most serious program, with the size of audience to show for it. If Jana often got a 33 per cent rating at *ACA*, she was lucky to get 3 per cent at SBS.

Within commercial TV circles, Jana was depicted as 'difficult' because she insisted on having a say in the kinds of stories she was asked to present. In one famous incident she had stormed out of the *ACA* cottage in protest over a tasteless tale about topless sales girls that had somehow been slipped into the line-up at the last minute. As far as she was concerned – and any number of her counterparts in US television agreed with her – it was very much in a network's interest to protect a star's image and she had a perfect right to have editorial input into the programs she anchored. Sam Chisholm was by then long gone from Nine but he gave Jana the strongest possible backing during an interview for *Compulsive Viewing*.

'It's a searing indictment of television management that she dropped off the commercial screen,' Chisholm told me with great feeling. 'People with Jana's skills and talent are rare. They are not just run-of-the-mill talent, so they don't have run-of-the-mill attitudes. It is very easy for management to drive them away by putting them in the too-hard basket, to say "Oh, this is too hard,

I'll take mediocrity." Mediocrity is always easy to manage, but our business is not about mediocrity.'

That, indeed, was the kind of thinking that created Nine's galaxy of stars during the glory years but by 2002 the main issue was whether it was worth the risk to bring Jana back after being away from Nine for so long. As far as Meakin was concerned, she had simply dropped off the radar of commercial TV. While he respected her abilities, there were other talented female presenters making their way up the ladder at Nine and they would have every reason to resent Wendt stepping into some high-profile presenter's role that could have been theirs. By the time the newscaff boss heard of Alexander's secret negotiations with Wendt, though, her return was virtually a fait accompli. Kerry, James and Sam Chisholm all pronounced themselves delighted to have her back, arguing the move was 'good for our perception'. Meakin had little choice but to fight a rearguard action over the details of her contract, demanding a strict limit on her annual salary so as not to create havoc in the prevailing pay scale relativities. More importantly, knowing Jana's sensitivity about program content, he wanted clear instructions that she was to work in whatever current affairs role management chose for her, whether *60 Minutes*, *Today*, *Sunday* or special reports as they arose. In this he had the full support of David Gyngell, but their protests were to no avail.

For Meakin, it had been a particularly humiliating episode. 'There were reports that Jana was being talked to by people at Channel 9, and I was denying them in good faith because I didn't know anything about it. "No, we're not talking to Jana," I kept saying, and then I suddenly find there's a deal done.' In his mind the issue went much further than the signing of a new presenter.

'I had no real problem with Jana,' Meakin says, looking back on that episode. 'I just thought: "This has all been taken out of my hands."' Perhaps the passage of years has mellowed his memory, because he certainly expressed the deep indignation he felt at the time directly to Kerry Packer.

'This is fucking ridiculous, what do we want her back for?' Meakin exploded, according to a witness who attended a meeting hastily convened at the Willoughby offices to discuss the merits of Wendt's return.

'C'mon, son, it'll work out . . .' Packer tried to calm him, but didn't get a chance to finish his sentence.

'No, Kerry,' he snapped, 'I'm not happy here.' He at least agreed to Packer's urging not to do anything rash. 'I'll let you know, Kerry,' he assured the boss of bosses, 'I won't just walk out on you. If I decide to leave, I'll give you six months' notice.'

The veteran newsman didn't mince his words with John Alexander, either. 'I don't like being put in a position where people are being appointed in my section without me knowing about it,' he told him bluntly. To which Alexander gave the kind of unctuous reply Meakin would never forget.

'Mea culpa,' he apologised, 'mea maxima culpa. It won't happen again.'

'Okay, fine,' Meakin shrugged, and promptly dropped the issue, assuming that the contretemps had cleared the air between them and he could trust Alexander to keep his word. The truth was, however, that in the same time frame when Alexander was vowing *it won't happen again* he was actually in the process of secret talks with David Koch. After Koch finally rejected his advances, he set out without a qualm to sign up Ross Greenwood, an Australian-born financial writer then working in London. The appointment was destined to raise eyebrows considering Greenwood's relative lack of on-camera experience but that, in itself, only served to prove how determined Alexander had been to be rid of Pascoe. Even with Greenwood lined up to make his debut in the 2003 program schedule, however, the network head still said nothing to Meakin, leaving him completely in the dark until well into the new year.

Mea culpa, mea maxima culpa. On Friday, 7 February, 2003, John Alexander called his director of news and current affairs into his office at Willoughby to show him those words meant absolutely nothing. 'We want Pascoe out,' he commanded. 'Why?' Meakin asked, and was struck by the way his CEO's explanation matched Kerry's earlier complaint word for word. 'He's not taken seriously around the town,' Alexander replied.

By any standard this was a dark moment in the proud history of Channel 9 news and current affairs. Senior management certainly had a say in which presenter fronted a particular newscaff program but generally stayed well clear of the day-to-day business of TV journalism. Not since the so-called Soap Powder Inquiry of the mid-1970s – a scandal involving an attempt to appease important advertisers – had Park Street directly intervened to order the sacking of an on-camera reporter in such an arbitrary manner.

Meakin was disgusted enough with the instruction he had just been given. 'I think you're going to find that this sacking will have wider implications,' he warned the CEO. He instinctively sensed, however, that Alexander had an even more unpleasant surprise waiting for him.

'Have you already hired someone as a replacement?' he demanded to know. He anticipated the answer but it still rocked him like a kick in the stomach.

'Yes, we have,' Alexander replied. Meakin immediately whirled around and stormed out of the room, too enraged even to remember whether or not the name Ross Greenwood came up at that point. He called Pascoe in to break the news. The business reporter understood the situation totally and has nothing but praise for the way the newscaff chief stood up for him.

By Monday, Peter Meakin had made up his mind to quit the network he had served for close to three decades. Still, he felt he owed one last obligation to the man who had done so much to make Nine a powerhouse of television journalism and in that process, given him the most exciting and fulfilling career he ever could have hoped for. He put in a call to Kerry Packer.

'I've decided to leave,' he informed him.

'Why?'

'Because of John Alexander. I can't work with the duplicitous bastard; he's a 24-carat cunt.'

'Well, son, can we talk about it?' Kerry asked.

'I can't see much point in the conversation, Kerry,' Meakin responded, 'because you've made your choice. I accept that and I don't want to play games like it's him or me.'

Packer took a moment to gather his thoughts.

'Well, can we stay friends?' he asked.

'Yes, that suits me fine,' the newscaff boss signed off for the last time.

But he hadn't quite finished with John Alexander yet. Walking along the third-floor corridor of power around four o'clock that afternoon, he happened to notice David Gyngell's door open, and who should be sitting there with him but the person he had recently been describing to Kerry in such colourful language. He barged in uninvited to let his nemesis know to his face what he thought of him and his language certainly didn't get any more temperate. His epithets were just that – words of abuse meant to sting rather than convey any sensible meaning – and all the more biting as he spoke in the low guttural growl of cold fury.

'You're a spineless cunt . . . a disgrace to this network . . .' Alexander didn't say a word, didn't even raise a hand to symbolically fend off the onslaught. David Gyngell was clearly embarrassed on his behalf and did what he could to get Meakin to end his tirade.

'Listen, mate,' Gyngell broke in, 'I don't want to hear all this shit – you've made your decision, we know you've already spoken to Kerry . . .' That, however, only encouraged Meakin to switch to a new line of attack, speaking out in defence of the deputy CEO as someone who knew and loved the television industry, yet had to suffer the indignity of cleaning up Alexander's toxic waste. 'This young bloke here,' Meakin pointed, 'why the fuck are you interfering with him? He at least knows what he's doing and he's trying to learn and he respects the place and the people who work here. You don't have a fucking clue, yet you stand here meddling. You're just a fucking little cunt, and I'm out of here.'

And with that he was gone. The spray he gave Alexander probably lasted no more than two minutes. He went to the newsroom to break the news of his departure, an announcement met with stunned silence. Within a quarter of an hour he was gone from the building, leaving his loyal assistant, Helen Biven, to pack up his personal effects. The network promptly put him on three months' gardening leave to serve out the rest of the contract. Strangely, during that time, his name remained on the coveted parking space just outside the main entrance. That, however, merely served to build up false hopes among the colleagues who desperately wished there was still a chance of his returning.

What they couldn't know was that Peter Meakin was about to follow John Stephens to the Seven Network, with David Leckie soon to join them.

CHAPTER 6

The Block: a rainbow amid the storm clouds

Without a doubt it was one of the most brilliant concepts ever to land on the desk of an Australian TV executive. Two young hotshot producers named Julian Cress and David Barbour came up with the idea over lunch on a Friday, spent the weekend working out the right kind of proposal needed to sell it, presented it to Channel 9 on the Tuesday and virtually had themselves a deal by Wednesday. If their idea for a reality series broke new ground, their 'pitch' was even more audacious – printed on A3 paper, twice the size of a normal page so that it would be impossible for a sceptical programmer simply to file away and forget about. But who would be unimaginative enough not to be intrigued by this?

What do you get when you mix . . .

BIG BROTHER with RENOVATION RESCUE with SYLVANIA WATERS with CHANGING ROOMS with MELROSE PLACE with SURVIVOR with LOCATION, LOCATION?

The six-page document went on to explain the basic format:

Imagine four attractive and determined young couples aged between 20–35. They move in next door to each other to chase the Australian dream. And only one can get it. They'll be up to their guts in makeover mayhem. They literally must live and breathe the renovation to achieve the apartment of their dreams, each and every home improvement idea jealously guarded from the other players. Between all the trials and tribulations of their normal daily lives – work, love, friends and foes – they must also out-paint, out-design, outwit and out-maneouver their new neighbours. With the cameras watching 24/7, we'll see every tear, tantrum, lovers' tiff, conspiratorial scheme and power play. Because all is fair in love and real estate.

Cress and Barbour then proceeded to set out the game rules for the series contestants, ranging from their renovation budgets ($40,000 each) to the prize money, geared to a percentage of the profit on the sale price. All that took a lot of explaining, though, which prompted a tongue-in-cheek apology. 'Hey, it's a big show.'

Indeed, it would be hard to get a bigger Australian show than *The Block,* with the 'set' alone – a run-down apartment building in the trendy beachside suburb of Bondi – destined to cost just under $2 million, in addition to production expenses to cover thirteen weeks of a multi-crew shoot. The beauty, of course, was that if it all worked out, the set could be resold at a profit.

Cress and Barbour were already well-established producers at Nine, Cress working for *60 Minutes* and Barbour involved in a number of lifestyle formats dealing with home improvement or renovation, such as *Our House* and *Changing Rooms*. They hit upon their brainwave in early September, 2002, deciding to try it out first on Peter Meakin.

'Oh Christ, you think because it's on bigger paper, I'm going to want to make it?' he grumbled when he saw the size of the pitch they handed him.

'Absolutely,' they urged him on. And they were right, because by the time he got halfway down the first page, he knew it was worth passing up the line. That was at ten o'clock. Meakin carried the proposal into the weekly programmer's meeting scheduled for 10.30. From there it went to David Gyngell, who realised immediately that this was the project he had been looking for since he joined PBL, the chance to prove he had a nose for a hit and the courage to stake his career on it. In theory, as deputy CEO, he should have put the proposition to Ian Johnson, who in early September was still officially head of the network, or directly to John Alexander as chief of PBL Media. The simple truth, however, was that Johnson, as an interim manager, was not likely to want to involve himself in such a major decision, while Alexander had no experience in assessing program proposals and his brief from the Packers had been to reduce costs, not add millions to them for a show that might turn out to be a total disaster. To David Gyngell, the biggest risk by far was to see such a red-hot concept put on ice for weeks or even months of high-level dithering.

'I think this is a good idea,' Peter Meakin affirmed.

'Yes, I think it's pretty good,' John Stephens agreed. 'But we've got to go spending $2 million buying a building. We're never going to be able to do that.'

David Gyngell asserted his right to the deciding vote.

'Well, it sounds like you're spending $2 million but you do sell it in the end, so you're not losing money – it's just capital outlay,' he explained. 'I want to do it, and I want to do it in Bondi Beach because it's a very hot area. I understand the real estate there because that's where I've spent all my life. Let's look for a block in Bondi.'

The question of location would later become a source of considerable debate, with some programming advisers warning that the Melbourne audience would be put off if the site was too closely identified with Sydney. They suggested the series be shot in a nondescript setting that could be in either capital and thus not offend any viewers. Cress and Barbour, on the other hand, had always envisaged Bondi as a must-see element in the show – the very heart of Sydney's crazy property boom and a talking point for aspirational couples no matter where they might live. 'Our theory was that as property prices were going through the roof in Sydney, the rest of Australia could tune in and say, "See, I told you they were bloody crazy there. Look what you get for $600,000 – nothing but a two-bedroom apartment!"' David Barbour explains. They were naturally delighted to have Gyngell on their side.

Without even seeking Kerry Packer's approval, at that point, the 35-year-old deputy CEO let the two producers know that he was prepared to commit the network to backing their idea and needed to get a production budget from them immediately. The implications of that bold decision were enormous. First, it was a clear demonstration that, despite the upheaval following the dismissal of David Leckie, Nine remained a formidable player within the commercial TV industry, capable of acting quickly and decisively to take up a daring new format untested in any other TV market in the world. Not only was the set-up cost for *The Block* extraordinarily high, but there was no chance to pre-test the concept with a pilot that could give an inkling of audience reaction. The whole series would have to be shot before management saw the first ratings point.

There was a lot more riding on *The Block* than ratings, however. David Gyngell was beginning to demonstrate just the right qualities of leadership so desperately needed at this critical turning point in Nine's history. If Park Street was determined to transform its television arm into a leaner, meaner broadcaster, the worst possible way to go about it was to put the network under a manager with a cost-slashing mentality but no practical knowledge of the medium. Amid shrinking revenues and increased competition, twenty-first-century television cried out for a CEO with creative flair – someone who knew enough about program-making to show how to do things cheaper but better, a hands-on motivator capable of inspiring those around him to achieve the biggest bang for the buck.

Nine's previous two CEOs, Sam Chisholm and David Leckie, were both strong leaders with a knack for hiring the right people and giving them the resources to do their jobs; but neither fancied themselves as having any special feeling for the creative side of the business. David Gyngell, by contrast, was deeply absorbed in what might be called the art of showmanship, of finding new ways to attract and hold viewers in a period where the free-to-air audience was being steadily eroded by the Internet, pay TV and other distractions. It was important, of course, to have a keen eye for any program concept capable of standing out in that crowded environment. Hit shows, however, were only one part of the equation. A network's entire prime time schedule needed to be structured in such a way as to have across-the-board appeal to advertisers concerned with who watched, as well as how many. Programming strategy – putting the right content to air with the right promotion to attract the right audience – was undoubtedly the single most critical element of success and Gyngell set out to learn as much about it as he possibly could.

Ironically, Channel 9 had not seen a managing director with that kind of expertise since the reign of Bruce Gyngell, David's father. He, too, faced an uphill struggle to outperform the competition with limited finances and found the solution to be a resource costing not a penny more – just a little extra use of the imagination. One example of the senior Gyngell's talent as a consummate showman seems almost too obvious for a modern TV viewer to grasp. In those early days of Australian television the stations normally relied on newspaper ads or billboards to publicise their programs. The mindset of the era was such that TV executives didn't think of using their own air time to plug their own shows. At most, there might be a still photograph of a cowboy with an announcement about what was to be on *Gunsmoke* for that week. Bruce Gyngell started copying selected clips from the actual programs and splicing them together into action-filled 'promos' – much like movie trailers – to pull the audiences in. Don't miss this exciting episode, viewers were urged. And they didn't. Within three months, ratings had jumped 10 per cent compared to the results of the newspaper ads. Bruce, though, was more than a P.T. Barnum figure pulling people in with his promotional gimmicks and clever scheduling. His success flowed from his profound insights into the basic nature of the free-to-air audience. Just before the legendary figure died from a brain tumour at the age of 71, he agreed to reveal some of his programming philosophy in an interview for *Compulsive Viewing*.

> Broadcasting is not a mass medium in my view. It's about finding ways to appeal to a myriad of minorities that come together in a mass – minorities which are constantly appearing and disappearing and reclustering, as it were. As a broadcaster you are licensed to serve the environment of a particular area and you have a responsibility to all those people in it. If you are going to be a successful broadcaster, then everybody in your potential area must be looking at you some time or another.

Those words are even more relevant today as the 'old media' networks try to reposition themselves to cope with a rapidly fragmenting viewership. The free-to-air audience may be in a constant state of flux, with web surfers and cable TV samplers drifting in and out of the picture, but it is still possible to find ways to bring viewers together en masse. All it needs is the stuff that made Bruce Gyngell the exceptional TV executive that he was – a little extra imagination. David Gyngell had grown up listening to his father's thoughtful analysis; but ultimately, he also knew from his dad that all such reasoning was worthless without the inbuilt antennae to lead you in the right direction.

'If you want to find shows that attract a fifteen-year-old and a 45-year-old and a 75-year-old,' he would later note, citing the borderline difference between a mega-hit and a flop, 'you have to have the right instincts. They're 49 per cent to 51 per cent calls. A 51 per cent is a winner and a 49 per cent is a failure, so it's very, very close. You either have a gut for it or you don't.'

The Block, then, would prove to be his moment of truth, the first time the son of Bruce Gyngell had his own gut instincts put to the test. And what a test it would be. This wasn't some inexpensive quiz show format that could be whisked off air after a single dismal showing. If it failed it would not only be the most spectacular flop in the network's history but also the longest-running because there was no way the thirteen-week series could be aborted after all the commitments made to sponsors about displaying products ranging from power tools to paints, tiles, kitchenware, furniture and even the cars used to get the couples around town. As far as the deputy CEO was concerned, though, failure simply wasn't an option as he turned up at the monthly TV management meeting at Park Street to try to convince Kerry Packer he was on to a winner.

'What are you, fucking Donald Trump now?' Kerry taunted him. 'You're still learning about television, yet you want to be some kind of property developer, going out and buying a building.'

'Kerry, I just believe in this project,' Gyngell replied, with calm insistence. 'I believe in the guys who are making it. I believe it's a smart idea.'

Packer was well aware of the younger Gyngell's keenness to become more involved in content and presentation. 'Would you stop meddling in the fucking programming every day?' he would often chide him. 'You know, you're not your old man yet.' But there was no doubt the proprietor was inwardly pleased that someone as dear to him as a second son showed such passion for the network he adored above all else. James certainly had a solid grounding in the business of television but that's the way he treated it, as a business like any other, to be judged coolly and dispassionately, on its profitability alone. David, on the other hand, saw Nine more as a living organism, in need of a bit of tender loving care and encouragement if it was to produce its best. Like Kerry, he had a fire in the belly to keep Nine ahead of its competition, whatever it took. If Bruce's boy thought *The Block* could help do that, Packer was prepared to let him have a go.

'Well, I don't know if it's going to work or not,' Kerry finally told him with a shrug that signalled, *I'll give you this one, do what you want.* It was hardly a ringing endorsement, but no one else at the meeting was game enough to question the sizeable chunk of cash involved. David Gyngell left Park Street that day in charge of a show that could bring him a giant step closer to running Channel 9, as his father had done. Either that or send him back to selling surfboards. As soon as he returned to Willoughby, he sought out Julian Cress and David Barbour. They were in a meeting, attempting to persuade Jamie Durie, the popular landscape gardening guru, to take on the role of presenter for *The Block.*

'Guys, my kahunas are on the line here, so are yours, so you better get on with it,' Gyngell happily informed them.

Cress and Barbour. They sound like a 1930s vaudeville act at Her Majesty's Theatre and they certainly exhibited the same sheer pluck and inexhaustible optimism. Neither will easily forget the fateful Friday they showed David Gyngell a brochure of the apartment building they had picked as the setting for their series.

'Is this the one you want, boys?' he asked them.

'It's the best we've seen,' they replied.

With that he picked up the phone, called the Channel 9 finance department, and said, 'Send someone down with a cheque book.' He signed with a flourish and handed it over – the proverbial blank cheque. 'Go get it!' he declared, waving them away to attend the auction the next day.

From there on, the two producers found themselves swept up in a perpetual motion machine, spending endless hours in auditions, budget meetings, production meetings and pep talks with potential sponsors.

'It was a very exciting time,' Julian recalls. 'It was our baby. We believed in it. And we just went out and we went really hard.'

As the moment approached to start taping, it was natural enough to be stricken with butterflies, though theirs were more the size of raptors. Each of the four couples had been carefully selected to add their own special spice to the ferment, but no one could really be sure of how well they would interact until the first scenes were played back on video. Julian and David put up a sign in their office with two words to sum up everything the show was about. *Human Drama*. Romeos and Juliets scampering around the stage in paint-stained blue jeans. All the renovation frenzy, fascinating as it might be, was merely a backdrop to the bitchery and backbiting, the plotting and conniving, the lechery and treachery of the eight occupants of *The Block*. Lest the competitors begin to get along too well with each other – the dreaded Stockholm Syndrome – Cress and Barbour were always ready to stir the pot by planting a hint here and there about one neighbour's derisive put-down of another. The two producers had done their homework well, however. Once the residents were in situ, their inherent rivalry, jealousy and greed soon became self-sustaining, like a nuclear reaction. The masterstroke was to inject Warren and Gavin into the mix – gay partners who tipped the 'battling couples' formula into a whole new dimension, unpredictably awry. Waz and Gav's penchant for parading around in their underpants was the stuff that talk-back radio is made of.

Surely, though, Cress and Barbour must have put a foot wrong somewhere. As it happened, their biggest mistake was in the title they originally chose for the series. They wanted it to be called 'Blockbuster' but the Channel 9 lawyers immediately recognised a potential trademark conflict with the giant video and DVD rental chain. In this case, the enforced change of name was fortuitous. *The Block* is short, sharp and bristling with delicious intrigue. Blockbuster could only have been an encouragement to cynical TV critics to refer to the show as a bomb.

The producers also miscalculated on another aspect of the series, but their instant solution has much to tell us about the magic of the television medium. As Cress and Barbour began assembling the first half-hour episode they realised they had done their jobs too well. The 'human drama' they had set out to capture was simply too abundant and too riveting to fit into such limited time. So what were they going to do about it? They were due to give the first preview screening to the Channel 9 bigwigs that morning – David Gyngell, John Stephens, his chief programming assistant, Michael Healy and, most daunting of all, John Alexander. Cress and Barbour decided upon a course of action that would prove either disastrously foolhardy or a stroke of genius: bluffing their way through the showing, not mentioning a word about length.

'We didn't tell them anything when we stuck the tape in,' David Barbour chuckles even today when he looks back on that stressful moment. 'We made the decision just to show it to them and see how they responded. So we got to the end of it and they all said "Oh, fuck, that's terrific." And we went, "Good! It's an hour!"'

The Channel 9 executives could hardly believe how quickly the preview flew by, but that didn't mean they were prepared to let the dynamic duo get away with filching an extra half-hour of precious prime time. 'Is this an hour – can we possibly run it for that long?' the Nine programmers began grumbling. Cress and Barbour countered with a question that stopped them in their tracks. 'What would you cut out?'

The executives looked at one another and agreed. 'Nothing, really.'

The Block, then, was destined to take up a full hour of one of the prestige time slots of Australian television – from 6.30 to 7.30 Sunday night, leading into *60 Minutes*. The first episode went to air on 1 June, 2003. Cress held a party for all the production staff and their families to watch, and naturally there was intense speculation about what the 'numbers' would be. At that stage Channel 9 News at 6 pm was rating well over a million viewers and the producers figured the worst thing that could happen was if they dropped out after the news. They were confident enough, however, to have negotiated a bonus of an extra $1000 each for every week that *The Block* reached 1.6 million viewers or more an episode. They even had the cheek to seek a larger bonus if the show attracted more than 2 million. A station executive virtually laughed them out of the room for raising a possibility too ridiculous for serious discussion.

The next morning they got to their production office at Bondi at 7 am to sweat it out until 8.30 or so when the results of the Nielsen audience survey usually started coming in. The God of Ratings, however, loves to play cruel tricks at crucial moments like this. *The Block* computer went down, so the producers had to get the figures by phone from a publicist at Channel 9.

'The numbers were so big we kept asking if they were right, and could she check them again,' Barbour recalls. When they tallied up all the figures from the five metropolitan markets, they came to over 2 million, with the big surprise being that there were even more viewers in Melbourne than Sydney. The show would go on to become the highest-rating series ever in the history of Australian television, with an average weekly audience of 2,346,636. Its grand climax, centred around the auctioning of the four apartments, not only collected an astounding 53.2 per cent share of the total national viewing audience but created traffic jams in Bondi from the crowds turning up at the scene. Waz and Gav didn't end up winning the top prize but they became household names, helped along by outraged radio talk-show hosts like John Laws and Steve Price of Sydney's 2UE. Both protested vehemently about having to watch two homosexuals prancing around in their underwear in a time slot once reserved for the innocent delights of *The Wonderful World of Disney*.

'I grew up watching *The Wonderful World of Disney* and look at me now,' Waz retorted, to the delight of his 2 million plus fans.

Kerry Packer was overseas during the entire three months the show was on air, but as always rang up David Gyngell each morning to discuss the network's ratings. He was invariably amazed to hear how well *The Block* was doing.

'Shit, tearing up a bunch of concrete rates that well?' was all he could say. 'There must be nothing else on.'

*

Ironically, for all its dazzling success, *The Block* would stand as a sobering testament to everything that was going wrong at Channel 9, its rapid descent from supreme self-confidence into a sorry state of disorder and disillusionment. For a start, two senior executives who helped get the show off the ground, Peter Meakin and John Stephens, wouldn't be around to share in the celebrations. Instead, those two highly experienced veterans were now at Channel 7, along with David Leckie, rallying their forces for the first sustained challenge in nearly three decades to Nine's ascendancy.

Yet, there can be no more painful example of the network's creative decay than the fate in store for Cress and Barbour themselves, wildly successful in-house producers who would have been treated as superheroes only a few years earlier. But that's a story for another chapter.

CHAPTER 7

Sunrise: Seven sees the light

Gathering dust in the files of the Channel 7 programming department was a most embarrassing piece of audience research – or so it seemed at the time. A survey group of typical viewers was presented with a large selection of photographs and asked to pick out the ones they thought best suited the image of each of the three commercial networks. The composite that most of them chose for Channel 10 was predictable enough considering its well-known focus on the youth market. There were lots of bikini babes, rave parties, Coca-Cola bottles and zippy little Hondas. The photos that featured in the depiction of the Nine Network were the embodiment of wealth and power – a BMW, a Rolex watch, a mansion overlooking the harbour. The overall theme was strongly masculine: successful, well-dressed men with glamorous women to show off by their sides. After that, the third photo display could only be regarded as mortifying. The Seven Network's image consisted of a plate of roast chicken with three vegies, a Holden Commodore and a backyard washing line.

Back in 1999, when that survey was taken, all anybody wanted to do with it was lock it away and forget about it, praying it would never leak out. It seemed to confirm Channel 7's destiny to be forever second, good for a soapie wedding, sitcom or quiz show from time to time, but too suburbanly daggy for comfort – the Edna Everage of Aussie TV. Over the next couple of years, Seven programmers did their best to position the network as far away from that dowdy appearance as possible, spending a fortune on new promotional campaigns infused with sophistication and dazzling colour. When David Leckie took command in April, 2003, his first instinct was to go even further, trying to beat Nine at its own game with an *anything you can do we can do better* approach. In the power image stakes, however, the Edna Everage channel could only ever end up looking like a satirical imitation and that strategy was doomed to failure. Not only did Seven's ratings decline slightly in the 2004 season, despite featuring the Athens Olympics, but Channel 10, like some cheeky dingo, crept up to snatch away second place in the 25 to 54 age group. It was at that low point in Leckie's reign, however, that he suddenly saw the light – the ember of hope still glowing away within that discouraging research report.

'We thought Seven should become like Nine, but we're not Nine,' Leckie would later reflect. 'We're heartland Australia. The key to our success is being comfortable with what we are.'

Heartland Australia. It was all there in the Channel 7 montage: the simple but satisfying home-cooked meal of roast chook, the reliable Holden parked in the driveway, the laundry hanging out to dry in the bright Australian sunshine in a backyard where kids could grow up healthy, happy and secure. What was so wrong with being suburban? Who cared about looking a bit daggy in the land of the laid-back Aussie? As the first cracks began to appear in Nine's glossy, all-conquering image, the perennial also-rans at Seven started to feel empowered with a homespun persona of their own. The seeds of that transformation had actually been planted even before the arrival of Leckie, in an obscure little patch of morning programming that would come to symbolise the very essence of television's heartland. With the rise and rise of a show called *Sunrise*, the mighty Nine Network would begin to feel the first tremors of imminent danger, not only weakened from within but threatened from without.

Sunrise had been around in one form or another since the mid-1990s but its direct confrontation with Nine's long-running and highly successful *Today* in the 6 am to 9 am slot began in earnest in October, 2002. It was then that a 27-year-old dynamo named Adam Boland put his distinctive stamp on what had previously been an almost totally news-oriented format. Boland comes across as Seven's version of Julian Cress and David Barbour rolled into one, a creative hotshot with more steam coming out his ears than Old Faithful. As a producer he had something going for him only a second-place network like Seven could provide – virtually no resources whatsoever. Almost every change he was to introduce into the program's weary old news-and-views format had to be manufactured out of sheer imagination. In that he was helped immensely by his early beginnings in radio, starting as a journalist at 4BC in Brisbane and moving on to 3AW in Melbourne. Television is often thought of as an 'intimate' medium, with the audience able to see a presenter's face; but the truth is, radio, at its best, relates to its listeners in a way TV is rarely capable of matching.

'Radio taught me a sense of immediacy,' Boland says, 'but most of all, it taught me how to interact with the audience, because whether it's AM or FM, they are all driven now by listening to their audience. I never understood why TV couldn't get that. Well, we do get that now, and that's what *Sunrise* does. It has very much the same focus as radio, our agenda firmly driven by what we think our viewers will like, not what the Canberra gallery perceives as exciting.'

With that unique perspective Boland decided on a format that would set its presenters free to discuss the talking points of the day with absolute spontaneity, very much like the all-in family banter around a breakfast table. The latest news would be read on the half-hour and might become a peg for discussion, but not necessarily – not if there were issues to debate of more relevance to an audience largely made up of switched-on, 40-something women, many of them juggling kids and jobs. In that kind of context, a news item on Brazilian inflation was more than likely to spark some good-natured jibing about the pros and cons of a Brazilian wax. Boland encouraged his hosts to express whatever opinions popped into their heads and to inject as much of their personal life into the conversation as possible. One of the first and most important of his innovations was to encourage viewers to send in e-mails as well as letters to give his presenters some up-to-the-minute audience reaction to bounce off of. 'Don't think twice before you talk,' was the simple sermon he preached to his on-camera team. Once they stopped to consider their remarks, they would begin to worry about whether some people might be offended – and that could only lead to self-censorship.

Boland's singular vision for *Sunrise* was a sure-fire recipe for either disaster or runaway success. On some mornings it could well contain a mixture of each if one of the presenters inadvertently overstepped the bounds of good taste. Such uncertainty, however, only served to add an extra edge of interest to the show. Compared to its opposition, the new *Sunrise* dawned as a breath of fresh air. That was in no way a criticism of *Today*'s presenters, Steve Liebmann and Tracy Grimshaw. The fact was they were locked into a format that had become highly ritualised over twenty years, with the day's news largely dictating the interviews and commentary to follow. The program prided itself on being able to attract leading politicians or expert analysts to put their spin on the morning's headlines – a source of prestige, no doubt, but also a potential turn-off for viewers who had more practical, everyday matters on their minds. *Today*, in fact, seemed to be growing more and more insulated from the topics viewers really cared about, although up until then it had largely been protected from any backlash by the lack of serious opposition. With a respected journalist like Liebmann at the helm, the program positively reeked of authority. That air of authority, however, became its biggest liability once audiences had a chance to switch to a rival show that was far more relaxed and fun. And switch they did at astonishing speed.

Boland took command of the show when it was averaging 91,000 viewers compared to *Today*'s 418,000. Within three months the *Sunrise* audience had jumped more than 30 per cent, with *Today* dipping slightly to 412,000. In January to March, 2003, the Seven program was up to 123,000, with *Today* dropping to 400,000. By December of that year, the tide had turned dramatically, with *Sunrise* at 227,000 and Nine's morning show down to an average of 246,000.

Such a turn around would cause alarm in any circumstances, but *Sunrise* was gaining strength in a period of great upheaval when Nine was missing the steadying influence of its three most experienced managers – David Leckie, Peter Meakin and John Stephens. Seven, of course, had drawn blood before with a win here and there in the entertainment schedule, a compelling drama or popular game show. What made this onslaught all the more disconcerting was that it was coming from an entirely unexpected direction – a head-on challenge to Nine's supremacy in current affairs. Other worrisome changes were occurring within the news arena as well and it would not be long before Park Street hit the panic button, resulting in even more disorder and confusion.

Meanwhile, two bemused Channel 7 presenters found themselves plucked from relative obscurity to become the very face of the Heartland network. *Sunrise* hosts Melissa Doyle and David Koch would soon go on to achieve the highest degree of fame possible in the pantheon of Australian stardom – recognised by a single moniker: Mel in her case, Kochie, in his. Yet, even to refer to them as 'stars' was to misunderstand their unique relationship with their adoring audiences. If you happened to spot some other famous TV celebrity, Jana perhaps, shopping in a department store for a new bra, would you have the nerve to walk up and suggest a brand to suit her? That kind of thing happened to Mel all the time, accepted as being just one of the girls except she spent her mornings in front of a TV camera. It was very much the same with Kochie, middle-aged and balding but obviously seen by many of his fans as eminently approachable and as cuddly as a teddy bear.

'For an old bloke like me to have teenage girls come up in the street and want to give you a hug is weird,' Koch admits, 'but it's one of the really nice things about the show, the number of teenagers – kids the same age as my daughters – who relate to it. It's easy to forget sometimes how many Australian households have single parents. A lot of those households seem to have adopted us as their family and I'm their daggy dad.'

Daggy is an adjective that's used with much pride at *Sunrise*, distinguishing it from the way Channel 9 productions are invariably described, with words like slick, polished and professional.

'Daggy is not afraid to be natural,' Koch suggests, 'not afraid to have an ordinary sense of humour, nothing put on. It's the opposite of manufactured. Television in the past has tended to try to manufacture personas but you just can't get away with that on a breakfast show. With three hours of live TV, you can't pretend to be something you're not. You've got to be yourself or viewers will quickly see through you.'

Doyle, for her part, points out that as a mother of two, well into her thirties, she hardly qualifies as one of the 'cardboard cut-out' presenters who used to dominate the TV screens. 'I think our typical viewer is us,' she begins to explain when I ask her who she sees as the *Sunrise* audience. Then she changes her mind to come up with a far more perceptive answer. 'No, rather than being us, I think we're them, if that makes any sense to you. I go home and walk out of here to a house that needs cleaning, and washing that needs to be done. I pick up my son every day from school – and to be there at the school gate at three o'clock is very important to me. I shop at the local supermarket up the road and have a chat with everyone there. And we're all like that here, we all go home to relatively normal lives.'

If what they go home to is normal, what they come to every morning is anything but. Mel and I are having our chat just after 5 am. She wakes up each day at 3.25 am to arrive at the studios by 4 am, her hair freshly shampooed and wet for the hairdresser to blow-dry and style. She spends an hour reading the newspapers and getting briefed on the production rundown, then almost another full hour in styling and makeup before fronting the cameras for the three-hour show. That's a five-hour stint before a lot of workers have even arrived at the shop or office and there are still promos to shoot for the next day's program and possibly press interviews as well. Can anyone really hope to go on to lead a normal existence with such an exhausting daily routine? But that's why the spontaneous switch in Doyle's answer to my first question is so revealing. *I think we're them.* For all that she has to cope with, she still genuinely thinks of herself as being no different to the people who watch her.

It's a rare presenter, indeed, who really believes that. Television history is filled with Jekyll-and-Hyde personalities who made their fortunes pretending to be just like the wholesome boy or girl next door while secretly looking down upon their fans as loathsome trailer trash. They could easily get away with such deception in the past because their producers effectively shielded them behind a thick glass wall, orchestrating their every word and even gesture to such an extent that the term 'live' television becomes virtually meaningless.

Sunrise certainly gives its on-camera people strong professional backup, with its researchers and producers working virtually around the clock to piece together the next day's rundown, a document akin to a giant jigsaw puzzle encompassing twenty or more different segments and hundreds of camera directions. One key producer, David Walters, presides over the three hours of morning TV like a football coach, constantly calling plays to his team from the studio control room. He might suggest a question here, a quip there. On the morning I attend, the big news is the North Korean nuclear test staged by a defiant President Kim Jong II. In a more traditional current affairs program learned commentators would no doubt pontificate on how this might threaten the cause of non-proliferation, leading to an all-out arms race. Walters, however, gets on his intercom to Kochie to suggest summing up the issue in a lot simpler language: North Korea's nervous neighbours were trying to 'keep up with the Jongses'.

Walters, like Boland, has a strong radio background, and is careful not to let his prompting intrude on the program's inherent spontaneity. What makes *Sunrise* so different from its opposition is that its presenters ultimately stand or fall on their own instinctive reactions. Koch and Doyle were singled out as ideal hosts for the very reason that they seemed to be in tune with the Australian mainstream – and that was almost a guarantee that they would frequently come up with views that were anything but politically correct. Koch has been called to answer before a state anti-discrimination board for an off-the-cuff remark about transsexuals. No doubt he also left many of his viewers gobs-macked when he let them in on how embarrassing it can be to get an erection in front of your mother-in-law.

Though the show comes across as brand new, it's very much retro-TV, reminiscent of what it must have been like before there was ever an auto-cue. That, indeed, accounts for a large part of its charm. Not since the early days of Graham Kennedy have Australian audiences had a chance to see live television that can suddenly go so terribly wrong.

'I thought the hosts needed to be more than just people who read an auto-cue,' Boland agrees, looking back on his original inspiration for the *Sunrise* concept. 'That's why I went for Kochie, even though he was a finance reporter. When he did his business segment, he'd always add a cheeky little comment at the end. You could see he was this guy full of energy, bursting to explode – so why not just let him go?'

Boland used the simplest possible argument to persuade Channel 7 to let him experiment with the show, then barely a blip on the ratings scale. 'What have we got to lose?' It was an argument that time and time again has proved the crucial turning point for a second-ranking competitor, the rallying cry needed to infuse it with the confidence and the courage to take on a long-reigning champion.

Still, it would be wrong to assume that from then on the young executive producer had everything going his way. Just as the Nine Network suffered from its rivalries and intrigues, the Seven Network, too, was riddled with faction fighting – petty squab-bling between departments over resources and prestige but in particular, between a conservative old guard quite content to have things rolling along as they were and those eager for change.

Boland, with his faith in the immediacy of radio, began pushing the limit when he introduced a breathless new opening to the program. *Now, from Brekkie Central right across Australia, this is Sunrise with Kochie and Mel.* The reaction from a senior programming executive was one of sheer horror; and it wasn't just *Brekkie Central* he hated.

'What's this "Kochie" and "Mel" business?' he demanded. 'Their names are David Koch and Melissa Doyle.'

'Well, we're just trying to make it a little more personal and friendly,' Boland fought back, 'like you might hear on a radio show.'

'You risk undermining the credibility of the network!' the executive rebuked him, ordering him to stop all this name-shortening nonsense at once.

From then on, he was kept busy fielding calls from the network's opinion police, worried officials keeping a tight check on all views expressed on the program, especially Koch's. 'You can't let him say things like that,' Boland was continually admonished. He went through the motions of toning down the concept as he was directed, but made sure that every guest who came on the program was encouraged to keep referring to the hosts as Kochie and Mel, so that the air of informality was soon firmly established whether Seven's programming department liked it or not. He was only to hear later how close he came to losing his job over such gross insubordination.

'There was this crucial executive meeting I wasn't invited to attend,' Boland recounts. 'I'm told that several executives spoke out, demanding that the news department pull us into line. "You've got to do something about this *Sunrise* show, it's going to cause the network a lot of damage, they're out of control, they're doing silly things."' Fortunately for Boland, he turned out to have at least one devoted fan at that torrid session. His name was Ryan Stokes, son of Kerry Stokes, Seven's largest shareholder.

'You know what?' he told the group. 'I've seen a lot of breakfast shows around the world and this one is really special.'

His support was enough to temporarily subdue the show's detractors, giving it the extra few months it needed before the ratings started to speak for themselves. 'It was probably our get-out-of-jail-free card,' Boland says, thinking back to those scarier times, 'because at that point the audience hadn't really grown all that much. Then, all of a sudden, we were taking off under our own steam and they left us pretty much alone after that.'

Just before Christmas in 2003, a little over a year after Boland took over, *Sunrise* beat *Today* for the first time, averaging 261,000 viewers for the week compared to 257,000 for its rival. In keeping with the mysterious nature of the Ratings God, that supposedly didn't count because it was out of the official survey season. The *Sunrise* crew soon made up for it with another win at the very start of the new ratings season, 8 February, 2004, climbing to 265,000 viewers compared to 256,000. Not long after that, Seven began to win the mornings consistently and by ever bigger margins, taking over the role of undisputed leader.

Today, then, would be the first of Channel 9's redoubtable array of newscaff offerings to be toppled by a program of the same genre. That's an important distinction because it had always been possible for an information-based program, even one as strong as *60 Minutes*, to be beaten by an entirely different type of show. As executive producer of *60 Minutes* through the 1980s, I remember the shock of losing to Channel 7 one Sunday night after years of beating all comers. At least I was able to comfort myself that it was only some bizarre imported sitcom about a cute, furry extraterrestrial named *Alf*, as far away from reality as it was possible to get. *Today*'s loss to *Sunrise* may have been out of prime time, but its psychological impact was considerable – all the more unnerving in light of the gains that Seven's *Today Tonight* was making against *A Current Affair* at 6.30. The danger signs were inescapable: an arch-rival in the process of gaining creative force just as the Packer network began to falter.

By the start of the 2005 ratings season, *Sunrise* was averaging 290,000 to *Today*'s 215,000. In that same year *Today Tonight* would out-rate *ACA* nationally for the first time. Within the newscaff competition between the two networks, however, the most important battle of all was the nightly news – and there, too, Seven would begin making its way steadily towards the high ground.

CHAPTER 8

Good news, bad news

The nightly news has always been a key indicator of the health of the entire Nine network. Strong ratings at 6 to 6.30 pm tend to encourage a natural flow-on of viewers through the evening but there is much more to the equation than that. Nine's reputation for being first and best in its coverage of major events was Kerry Packer's greatest source of pride. To maintain that fine tradition he made sure the three PBL-owned channels in Sydney, Melbourne and Brisbane got the editorial and technical resources they needed to keep well ahead of their opposition. Each of the three stations could boast the highest-paid anchors, reporters and producers in the business. While they operated independently, Sydney served as the co-ordinating centre and pretty well had its pick of the nation's most talented television journalists. Morale at the Willoughby newsroom couldn't have been higher at the start of the new century, spurred on by wide recognition of Nine's superb coverage of the 9/11 terror attack in the United States in 2001 and the Bali bombings of 2002. Such acclaim went a long way to boosting the spirits of the entire Nine Network staff right down to the receptionists and security guards. As the slogan went, *more people get their news from Channel 9 than any other source.* A notable exception, unfortunately, would turn out to be the Channel 9 newsroom itself, about to be hit by one top-level shake-up after another with its journalists always last to know what was happening.

At the end of the 2002 ratings season Brian Henderson told Sydney viewers 'the way it is' for the last time, retiring after 38 years. A news anchor is undoubtedly the most crucial link in the bond between a TV station and the community it serves; and there can be no more worrying period than the changeover when a much-loved figure like 'Hendo' inevitably signs off. The issue of his replacement had pretty much been settled long before. Jim Waley, TCN 9's backup newsreader, had all the right credentials for the job as an experienced and respected newsman. Some exec-utives privately held concerns that he might come across as too much of a heavyweight: a solid yeoman type, but lacking in charisma. Kerry Packer, however, made it clear that he favoured Waley, silencing all but the bravest opposition. John Alexander was reported to personally favour the ABC's Juanita Phillips – formerly a high-profile CNN anchor – as his candidate for the job but didn't attempt to push the point. Only David Gyngell had been prepared to raise a dissenting voice from the earliest stage of the debate, arguing that Waley was making an important contri-bution to the network where he was, serving as host of the highly praised *Sunday* program, as well as anchoring the Sunday night news – usually the most watched bulletin of the week. Gyngell's preferred candidate to succeed Henderson was Ian Ross, a popular member of the reserve newsreading team who stood out with his more relaxed style of presentation. Ross might not have the gravitas of Waley but Gyngell sensed that he had wider appeal for a general audience, with the added advantage of even looking a bit like Hendo. Obviously, the Seven Network shared much the same view because it snatched Ian Ross out of semi-retirement to present its own six o'clock news service.

For the Sydney newsroom of Channel 9, then, the launch of the 2003 ratings season was fraught with unknowns. The departure of a long-serving newsreader always raised the possibility of a large-scale defection of viewers, whoever his replacement might be. GTV 9 had faced the same problem four years earlier when Melbourne's favourite son, Brian Naylor, retired. Despite some pressure to look outside Nine for a fresh new face, GTV's veteran news director John Sorell insisted on sticking with Peter Hitchener, Naylor's long-time offsider, and was rewarded with even higher ratings. 'We promoted from within the family and I think Melbourne people appreciated that,' he said at the time. Still, there was no way of guessing the reaction to Jim Waley's accession to the throne, especially since he would be pitted head-to-head against a former colleague who, over many years, had established his own devoted following within the Channel 9 audience.

A wild card had also been thrown into the Waley–Ross contest with Seven introducing a 'hot' new game show in the time slot leading up to the news. *Deal or No Deal* would quickly overtake its competition on Nine and start delivering a significant shift of audience numbers to the doorstep of Channel 7 news at 6 pm. Within the industry it was widely accepted that news ratings were directly affected by a rise or fall in the ratings of the lead-in program. The only question was just what degree of influence that might have compared to the pulling power of the anchor. Losing viewers at 5.30 to 6 pm certainly did Nine no favours.

Amid all the razzamatazz of commercial TV, newsrooms stand out for their stolid, deadpan professionalism – much like Houston control, doing exciting things, perhaps, but as coolly and calmly as possible. They operate on the principle that stability and reliability are the two absolute essentials for a successful nightly news service. With viewers having to cope with disturbing accounts of accidents, murders, wars and scandals being pumped into their living rooms every night, the last thing they need is a disruption to the kind of bulletin they've grown used to over the years. Just like their audiences, the journalists who churn out the nightly news are also sensitive to instability around them – understandable considering the immense deadline pressures they have to cope with. They are trained to repress their emotions as far as is humanly possible; but that's exactly why they can become so easily unnerved – anxious, fearful, even paranoid – when there's any sign of disorder within their working environment. The sacking of David Leckie and ascendancy of John Alexander had already triggered more than enough rumour-mongering and speculation. The sudden resignation of Peter Meakin at the very start of this critical transition year left the TCN newsroom totally shell-shocked.

'The mood was one of sheer gloom when Peter left,' recalls Paul Fenn, who was news director of TCN at the time. 'He gave the newsroom a lot of independence, room to move without consulting him on everything we did. At the same time – and I'm speaking personally now – just knowing he was there to lean on and give advice was a wonderful comfort. He had such a great knowledge of television and everyone admired him for that.'

The circumstances surrounding Meakin's departure were certainly not lost on Fenn or his staff – the fact that he stormed off in protest over Alexander's direct order to dismiss a reporter who was merely doing his job. Without Meakin to guard against further Park Street encroachment, how much more interference would there be in the news department's hard-won editorial independence? It takes only a brief reminder of the bad old days to understand how hard-won it had been.

During the mid-1970s, Channel 9 in Sydney bore the brunt of an embarrassing scandal exposing the way commercial TV managements misused their news departments to curry favour with important advertisers. Until then, stations not only routinely banned coverage that might offend a sponsor but made sure there was always a pleasing little item to promote a department store fashion parade or opening of a shopping mall. The issue came to a head in August, 1974, over what should have been a big news story involving the inflated cost of laundry detergents, a major item on most grocery lists. A federal parliamentary inquiry accused leading soap manufacturers of cynically exploiting Australian housewives by bumping up their prices to pay for saturation TV ads that were both misleading and nonsensical – claims, for example, that 'Rinso gets things whiter' when it was made from the same basic formula as a competing product like 'lemon charged' Fab. Citing one reason or another, however, none of Sydney's commercial TV stations saw fit to give air time to the parliamentary finding. A Channel 9 journalist, furious that the story he filed had been dropped after intervention by the sales director (who then happened to be Sam Chisholm), showed up on the ABC a few nights later to blow the whistle on the whole sordid affair. He was promptly sacked by an enraged Kerry Packer who had just taken charge of the network after his father's death.

In a subsequent investigation, the Australian Broadcasting Tribunal warned that TV stations could be stripped of their government-issued licences if found guilty of meddling in the editorial freedom of their news departments to further their own commercial interests. Every management, of course, has the right to move journalists to different programs or reduce staff levels but PBL's singling out of Michael Pascoe for dismissal was the first such incident to raise suspicion of corporate impropriety since those dark days before the Soap Powder controversy. Meakin's departure thus stirred up some old ghosts to haunt a demoralised newsroom, though there was more immediate concern over the future of the network's newscaff division in its battle to remain number one.

'Everyone in the newsroom knew we had lost the very core of the operations – Peter Meakin, David Leckie, John Stephens,' Fenn explains. 'They hadn't just gone, they went over to join the Seven Network and that made it all the more worrying for us. We used to say to ourselves, "There's the door to the newsroom over there and we don't know what's going on outside it, so let's just try to get on as best we can."'

Fenn was a classic example of the unflappable, no-nonsense TV news boss. At the point Meakin left he had been in charge of the Sydney news for eleven successful years and spent almost the same time as assistant news director. He would soon find out what it was like to deal with John Alexander directly. Fenn thought it his duty to warn the PBL Media chief to expect an inevitable decline in the news ratings as 2003 progressed.

'Why?' Alexander snapped.

'Number one, we've lost the best newsreader Sydney has ever seen,' the veteran news director tried to explain, 'and as good as Jim is, he's not in that category. But we've also got trouble with our lead-in and it's just going to be a very difficult period for us.' Fenn won't easily forget the vehemence of Alexander's response. 'Don't dare blame the lead-in. The news should always win, no matter what the lead-in.'

The TV newsman could only shake his head in dismay. 'Every program on television is affected by what goes ahead of it,' he thought, but kept it to himself. As he predicted, the Seven news with Ian Ross continued to nibble away at Nine's ratings through 2003 and into 2004, with the gap between the two narrowing to as close as 10 per cent Monday to Friday compared to the runaway margins of the past. The mounting pressure on Jim Waley was compounded by a melanoma scare that sent him to hospital for surgery and time off for recuperation just at the stage when he most needed to impose his own distinctive imprint on the bulletin.

In an even bigger blow to morale, however, the already jittery newscaff staff would be plunged into a chaotic three years of chop and change at the most senior levels. First, David Gyngell temporarily stepped into Meakin's shoes as head of news and current affairs even though he had no journalistic training. Park Street soon intervened to locate a candidate overseas, an Australian-born journalist named Jim Rudder who was known to Sam Chisholm through his work at Sky, the UK pay TV station.

Rudder had spent years away from Australia and was sceptically regarded by his new colleagues at Nine as having little feel for the local free-to-air market. As a consequence he was given short shrift by those he was supposed to be leading. Barely thirteen months into the job he would tender his resignation for 'personal reasons'. That was long enough, though, to cause considerable resentment among those who saw him as Alexander's surrogate executioner, dismissing or reassigning a number of TV journalists considered too much a part of the old Nine culture. By far his most controversial move, with dire repercussions, was to appoint a new executive producer at *Sunday*, a reporter named John Lyons who had made his name in print journalism, but still had much to learn about the special scripting and editing skills required for television. As a newspaperman Lyons was known to be in Alexander's favoured inner circle. Stephen Rice, the long-time boss of *Sunday*, was simply told by Rudder that 'it was time for a change'.

Paul Fenn would soon be dismissed as well, axed by Rudder though there could be no doubt who was behind the scenes sharpening the blade for him. The news director had been warned by Meakin two years earlier that Alexander hadn't been keen to renew his contract, regarding Fenn as a dinosaur who stood in the way of his plan to move Channel 9 upmarket. On the day he was sacked, in April, 2004, Nine news ranked as number one of all programs. That, however, was but a small taste of the bitter irony surrounding his demise. 'Fennie', as he was affectionately known to his news staff, had been in hospital for some days, in intensive care with internal troubles that would eventually lead to surgery to remove his gall bladder. He went through an agonising time, losing 18 kilos, but nothing worse than reading a report in *Crikey*, the e-mail newsletter, that he was about to be fired. On the day after the news director returned to work, Rudder called him into his office.

'There's no easy way to do this,' the newscaff boss began.

'Well, you're going to fire me,' Fennie interrupted. 'I read it in *Crikey*.'

'Oh well, you just made it easier,' Rudder said with relief.

'Not really,' Fenn replied, 'because after 25 successful years in this place, I don't want to be sacked by someone I have no respect for.' With that stinging rebuke he demanded to see David Gyngell, so he could at least hear the news confirmed by an executive who wielded real power. Gyngell had been one of those trying to convince Park Street that the main problem with the news was its poor lead-in. 'I don't know why we're doing this. This isn't going to win us one ratings point,' he told Fenn apologetically.

On his way out of Gyngell's door, the sacked news executive serendipitously bumped into John Alexander of all people. He immediately thought back to something very odd that had happened while he was still in the intensive care ward. One of the nursing sisters informed him that a woman from Channel 9 named Tina Rados had phoned to inquire about him – not his condition but whether he was still in hospital. Tina happens to be the name of John Alexander's PA. Suddenly, it all became clear. Alexander had obviously been pressing Rudder to find out why Fenn hadn't been fired yet, growing impatient when advised the news director was still in hospital due to unexpected complications. Tina must have been instructed to ring the ward on Alexander's behalf and check up to see if Rudder was telling the truth.

'Oh, Paul, how are you going?' the CEO inquired solicitously, though he was clearly embarrassed by the unexpected encounter.

'You should have got your secretary to ask me that when she rang,' Fenn blithely replied.

The appointment of Fenn's replacement had clearly been lined up well in advance of his dismissal but the announcement of who it was hit the newsroom like a veritable bolt from the blue. Max Uechtritz had built his career in the ABC, rising from award-winning reporter to head of the public broadcaster's national news. He was certainly well qualified to deliver the kind of upmarket bulletin Alexander envisaged, but the cosseted, ratings-free culture he came from was so alien to commercial TV he might as well have descended from a distant planet. Word soon got around at Nine that their new news boss had admitted never bothering to learn how to read a ratings sheet. He might have been joking, of course, but there could be no question about his thorough indoctrination in the highly stratified, bureaucratic ways of ABC administration. With the approach of the festive season, he decreed that Nine news would have two Christmas parties: a chartered harbour cruise for the reporters and senior managers and a suitably downmarket affair in the canteen for the crews and technicians. Jim Waley, for one, couldn't believe it. 'How on earth can you have an A and B Christmas party? You're splitting the newsroom,' the anchor protested. 'That's terrible for the morale, which is already bad enough.' When Uechtritz persisted, Waley decided to boycott both functions.

If Uechtritz's style was more cerebral and less hands-on than commercial newsrooms are used to, there was certainly no doubting his professional abilities. He was keen – as Alexander was – to see the news break more hard stories in local politics and finance, though some of the older hands questioned the relevance of such 'scoops' to a mainstream audience. The ratings continued to slide on his watch and he would be gone as quickly as Jim Rudder. His replacement was to be a senior journalist poached from Channel 7 and not long after that, someone else would be found to replace the replacement – counting Paul Fenn, four Sydney news directors in two years, not to mention the constant shifting of senior producers to suit the whims of each incumbent. That was a mighty lot of disruption for any newsroom to cope with, let alone one that was still somehow managing to keep ahead in the ratings, if only just.

Inevitably, though, Jim Waley himself would end up paying the heaviest price, not only targeted for execution but typically, left to dangle ignominiously for months amid hostile press speculation and even ridicule. The first warning signs appeared in mid-2004 when the anchor was sent on assignment to Baghdad to mark a hopeful turning point in the Iraq War: the transference of power to a new transitional government. Waley was a seasoned reporter and if this trip was conceived largely for promotional purposes, it still made a lot more sense than some of the publicity stunts commercial channels had tried to get away with in the past. In the days when most newsreaders had no journalistic experience whatsoever, they were still featured in promos and full-page newspaper ads climbing out of a helicopter as if they were racing to cover a hot news story. The press, of course, loved to lampoon such silly pretence and with good reason.

Waley, for his part, had proven credentials as a war correspondent, winning considerable praise for his coverage of the Bosnian conflict for *Sunday*. Still, Iraq posed a far greater danger to him than anywhere else he had ever been – not so much physically as in its potential to cause irreparable harm to his public image. American networks sent their anchors to important trouble spots as a matter of routine but only Sydney's Channel 9 had the audacity – and the money – to send Waley to Baghdad. The Australian press loved nothing better than to cut down one of the television world's tall poppies. They were quick, then, to make the most out of the storm in a teacup triggered by the news-reader's first live cross to Sydney. Waley, it was noted with a sneer, addressed the camera wearing a flak jacket while a Channel 7 reporter stood barely 10 metres from him giving his own piece to camera in plain civilian clothing. Seven's publicity department wasted no time in stirring the pot, pointing out that the site was within a secure perimeter known as the Green Zone in which most other reporters felt they could roam freely without need of protective gear. 'Is Waley's flak jacket from Nine's wardrobe department?' a newspaper columnist pondered. 'Will he be forced to do his own hair and makeup before each bulletin?' The clear imputation was that Waley was merely putting on an act for the camera – a faked scene reminiscent of those spurious old public-ity photos of newsreaders in helicopters. It was both a cruel and most unfair comparison since the Green Zone did come under occasional mortar fire and Waley was merely following instruc-tions given to him by the Nine Network's security advisers.

Nine, by that time, had spent millions of dollars in the campaign to introduce its recently installed anchor to the Sydney market. There were any number of ways to counter this unfavourable spurt of publicity over the flak jacket. As a simple example one could easily imagine the network publishing a full-page newspaper ad listing Waley's impressive achievements as a reporter covering dangerous assignments with a headline reading *No News Anchor to Match Him*, which would have been perfectly true compared to Ian Ross or any other rival. That small effort would at least have been better than the dead silence emanating from both Willoughby and Park Street. Even before the Baghdad brouhaha, leaks had begun to appear in the gossip columns suggesting Nine was considering whether to 'cut and run', abandoning Waley for a younger journalist, Mark Ferguson. A publicity spokesman for the channel described such speculation as 'absolute nonsense' but that hardly stood as a denial from the very top of Nine's chain of command, which in May of 2004 would still have been John Alexander as chief executive officer of the network, as well as head of PBL Media.

Waley maintained an outward calm throughout this period of hurtful publicity but he admitted to friends that he was devastated by Nine's failure to give him wholehearted support. It was impossible to know for sure how much of the damaging press comment was planted by Seven as it closed in on Nine's ratings lead and how much could have actually come from among those wanting to see Mark Ferguson eased into the anchor slot. 'It was a time when Mark's rise was being endorsed by various people and I could see there was definitely a campaign against me,' Waley agrees, looking back on that distressing period in his long career. David Gyngell at least went through the motions of rising to Waley's defence. In July, 2004, he stepped in to deny rumours that Waley was upset enough over the flak jacket controversy to offer his resignation immediately upon his return from Iraq. 'Jim ain't going anywhere,' Gyngell jibed in a statement to the press. 'He has a five-year contract and will not be leaving. If you were paid as much as Jim Waley, you wouldn't be resigning either.' It was the first high-level comment in weeks of speculation, but it could hardly be described as a ringing endorsement either. What Gyngell didn't say is: he's our anchor and we're behind him 100 per cent. He couldn't because he knew by then that he was likely to be caught out in a blatant lie. The new CEO sincerely wanted Waley to stay with Channel 9, but the feeling at Park Street – Kerry Packer included – was that Seven news was drawing too close for comfort and a fresh face was urgently needed to anchor the Sydney news.

For all its troubles, Nine news would rise to the occasion once again when a mighty tsunami struck over the Christmas period in 2004, inflicting death and destruction through much of Southeast Asia. Nine's blanket coverage not only surpassed its reportage of 9/11 and the Bali bombings but was of far greater international significance, eagerly snatched up by the world's major networks, including CNN, BBC, CBS and American ABC. Mark Ferguson, the handsome young fill-in anchor for Waley over the summer break, performed brilliantly – handling the many throws to the network's far-flung correspondents with cool precision. For Ferguson it was one of those fabled opportunities of a lifetime. Jim Waley, meanwhile, was enjoying a well-deserved holiday in Egypt. He was travelling through remote areas where communications were difficult but even then was beginning to wonder why no one at the office had even bothered to try to contact him to see how soon he could get back to Sydney.

The answer was awaiting him when David Gyngell called him into a meeting in early January, 2005. In the previous ratings season Nine had still managed to win most nights but Seven was continually gaining ground, on a national five-city basis behind by less than 200,000 viewers across the week compared to twice that in the 2002 weekly averages. Gyngell was still firmly convinced that most of the problem could be attributed to Seven's stronger lead-in at 5.30 to 6 pm, but he came to agree that it was time to shift Waley out of the anchor's chair.

'Look, it may take three or four years for Nine to regain the ascendancy at 6 pm, but if we're going to make a move we have to make it now,' he began. 'We want to start targeting a younger audience and it's the feeling at Park Street that Mark is the best person to do the job.' Whether the decision was right or wrong, it was as illogical as any decision could be. The nightly news has always been skewed towards an older audience. It would be hard to find supporting evidence anywhere in the world that a younger newsreader attracted a younger audience. Waley would have much rather been told the obvious truth: that Park Street had simply lost its nerve and was seeking a quick fix rather than hanging in for the long haul as news traditionally demanded. Brian Henderson himself had spent years in the ratings wilderness, often struggling along in second or even third place, before he succeeded in winning the hearts and minds of the Sydney audience.

Waley's ordeal was not over even then, however. It would degenerate into a tense stand-off as Nine's lawyers insisted that he could be reassigned to his old position as host of *Sunday* without any penalty for breaking his anchor contract. The fact that Jana Wendt had by then been hosting *Sunday* for two full years appeared to matter little. What everyone seemed to forget was that Waley had been told by Kerry Packer himself to give up his appearances on *Sunday*. 'The news is too important to us, son,' Kerry urged him. 'We want you to be able to concentrate full time on it.' So it was that the first contract initially proposed – providing that Waley would serve both as news anchor and host of *Sunday* – was set aside in favour of a contract strictly confined to the news. The Channel 9 lawyers brought the superseded contract to the meeting, insisting that it proved he had no right to a payout. Waley's lawyer pointed out the simple fact that it had never been signed. The only signed and valid agreement guaranteed him five years reading the news, which meant three years still to run. Even then, Waley was reluctantly forced to threaten a messy court action before Nine finally caved in. It was a preview of the heavy-handed tactics to come in the network's future dealings with its key personnel.

On the day he left Channel 9, after a career that began there in 1968, Jim Waley asked if he could at least send an e-mail to his many long-time associates explaining: 'Sorry I can't say goodbye in person but it's been wonderful working for you and good luck for the future.' Nine's lawyers refused to allow it.

In the 2005 ratings season, with Mark Ferguson replacing Jim Waley in the anchor chair, the Nine Network would continue its downward slide, dropping to second place behind Seven in the national rankings for the first time in decades. As television history goes, it was a significant psychological turning point, not so much a measure of Channel 7's success as a symbol of just how much ground the Packer network had lost since those days when it could rightfully boast: *more people get their news from Channel 9 than any other source.*

CHAPTER 9

Passions rising:
the Gyngell bombshell

'We need to keep James and Alexander out of the place – they're going to fuck the joint.'

It was the language of an ageing, ailing monarch, too weak to stand against the tides of change, but still conniving to thwart the ambitions of his son, the prince. Kerry Packer certainly saw merit in the argument that the Nine Network had grown too fat and lazy. Perhaps he even paid lip service to the principle that profits should be given priority over ratings. Yet, whatever Kerry's head might tell him was the rational thing to do, every fibre of his emotional being told him just the opposite. He was like an addict, hooked on winning, and there was no way he was ever going to be weaned off his top-of-the-ratings highs.

'I don't give a fuck how much we make,' he confided to a

trusted confidant not long before the end. 'I'm old and I'm dying. I don't want to lose.'

Packer's ambivalence on the issue of cost-cutting at Channel 9 goes a long way to explain the increasingly mixed signals emanating from PBL headquarters leading up to his death. One moment he might fly into a rage over a programmer's decision to 'waste' the first run of a low-rating black comedy like *The Sopranos* by playing it during the summer months. Then, acting on a mere whim, he could commit the network to spending millions on a risky purchase no one else would touch. 'Kerry, you should have this,' Donald Trump, the New York property developer, urged him. And with that, he agreed to pay a whopping $180,000 an episode – five times more than the normal rate – for a full three-year run of *The Apprentice*, a show that proved to have little appeal for Australian viewers. Time and again he would give his begrudging approval to some efficiency measure put to him by James and Alexander, only to change his mind and reverse the decision at the last moment. His waxing and waning could have but one result – a paralysing rift within the inner core of the Packer empire, pitting father against son.

Packer senior had started off with high hopes that John Alexander could do for television what he did for print, reducing expenditure without damaging the basic product. Amid the fallout from Alexander's disruptive tactics, however, he soon came to regret letting the PBL Media chief anywhere near Nine. His son had no such qualms. He was committed to extracting maximum returns from the network and accepted the risk of inflicting some collateral damage here and there to achieve the necessary results. Still, blood was thicker than PBL scrip and James Packer was not prepared to stage a showdown with his dad over the issue. Kerry, too, seemed eager to avoid open hostilities, though that obviously didn't stop him sharing his true feelings with others, as evidenced by the quote that began this chapter. So it was that their conflict over Nine would be fought out in the form of a shadow play, with angry gestures here or there but not much in the way of direct confrontation.

To understand the strange stand-off between the two Packers it helps to know a little of the highly competitive nature of their relationship. Kerry, like his father before him, was a strict disciplinarian, though determined to show his son a lot more love and respect than he ever received from Sir Frank. In raising Jamie – as he was then known – he assumed the role of a stern but fair sergeant major, daring the boy on by example, using sport, in the main, to constantly test his courage and resiliency. By the time Jamie reached adolescence, he showed himself capable of meeting every challenge his father could throw at him. Their rivalry couldn't have been demonstrated in a more tangible way than in a device Packer senior imported from the United States as a coaching aid to improve Jamie's cricketing skills. The elder Packer thought of a cricket batsman facing up to a champion fast bowler as one of the ultimate measures of bravery. With that in mind, he and his son padded up in the backyard of their Bellevue Hill home every weekend to face the awesome deliveries of an American-made baseball throwing machine. Converted to cricket, it could hurl a ball at 192 kilometres an hour, faster than anything experienced in a test match. Jamie's cricket coach did his best to convince Kerry that even the most promising fourteen-year-old would be doing well to handle a ball hurled at half that speed. 'What are you trying to do, turn him into a wuss?' the father complained. 'C'mon, he's a man! Turn it up a bit.' Clive Lloyd, then the captain of the West Indies cricket team, attended the backyard sessions one day and refused to take on the machine at the same 160 kilometre per hour speeds set to test the nerve of the Packers, father and son.

As Jamie became James, going through his late teens and into manhood, their obsessive competitiveness became a kind of bonding ritual, acted out in many different ways – sometimes including their good-natured vying for the favours of the same young woman. It was nothing new, then, for father and son to challenge each other in any endeavour, business hardly proving an exception. If the contest looked like getting out of hand, as might happen from time to time, they could always turn to surrogates to champion their differing points of view. In a strange way, then, it suited both of them to have John Alexander as an insulator, putting enough space between them to take the heat out of the situation.

There was someone else, however, who was destined to pay a heavy personal price in this drawn-out clash of wills. The psychological tug-of-war between the Packers left David Gyngell in an invidious position, caught between the two men he admired most in all the world – Kerry as a second father, James like a brother and his closest mate. From the time he effectively took charge of the network, though still a deputy, he had two conflicting messages ringing in his ears. James and Alexander kept urging him to stand firm against Kerry's profligate influence. *You've got to keep telling him: don't do this, push back on him, you're not pushing back hard enough* – that was the gist of advice that made about as much sense as telling someone how to grapple with a sumo wrestler. Meanwhile, he had Packer senior on the phone to him every day, up to perhaps four hours on a Sunday, engrossed in rambling conversations covering the entire spectrum of programming from potential hits on offer from overseas to ways to improve the performance of a struggling quiz show. Kerry's message, too, was deceptively simple. *C'mon son, I need you to help me on this. Otherwise, if they want to save a lot of money, let's just put a test pattern to air.*

David Gyngell tried as best he could to stay true to his own inner voice. He sensed there was a way through this father–son impasse that might not be to either Packer's liking but could still be shown to be in the best interests of both. As much as he was with Kerry in wanting to maintain Nine's ratings supremacy, Gyngell accepted that didn't necessarily mean having to be number one in every time slot, every night, every week of the survey. Packer's win-at-any-cost mentality might have been a doctrine suited to the Golden Age but was as outdated as trench warfare in an era of shrinking audiences and soaring expenditure. The clever strategist had to be prepared to surrender ground here or there so long as he ended up winning the war. At the same time, Gyngell had no quarrel with the emphasis James and J.A. placed on the need to get better returns from the network. Where he differed was in their almost total preoccupation with costs. Profit could be obtained by increasing revenue as well as lowering expenditure. Nine spent well over $100 million a year on its overseas output deals but each extra ratings point from a hit show like *CSI* added another $30 million or so to its bottom line. Gyngell, in fact, took a mauling from Park Street when he refused to let Channel 7's David Leckie outbid him in an attempt to pinch the *CSI* franchise. It meant paying millions more but, as he argued at the time, it would have cost Nine a lot more in the long run to have the program's devoted fans switch over to Channel 7.

Somewhere in David Gyngell's thinking, then, was the faint perception of a middle line that might have eased the network's traumatic transition from its former glory days – surrendering more nights to the competition than Kerry would like while stopping short of cutting expenses down to the bare bone, as James and J.A. insisted. That was not an easy vision to get across, however, especially coming from someone who had no previous experience in managing a business enterprise as large and complex as the network. By his own admission, Gyngell was not as proficient as he would have liked to be in putting his ideas down in black and white. In a strange coincidence, he had grown up suffering from dyslexia – the same learning disability that affected both Kerry and James – and had considerable trouble reading and writing. He felt, however, that he still had a pretty good grasp of numbers. It was a skill constantly on call as Kerry put him through his paces every morning, quizzing him on minute details of the business. What's the lowest budget we can get away with on that show? Why would you pay that much for so and so? How much longer has that output deal got to run? When is that renewal up? It was the kind of TV-speak that John Alexander had little interest in, and he was happy to leave the day-to-day running of the network to Gyngell.

In June, 2004, Alexander was named chief executive officer of PBL, taking over management of the entire organisation. While the promotion obviously represented an advancement in the overall amount of power he wielded, it also moved him a step further away from direct involvement in TV operations, which was exactly how Kerry would have wished it. The way became clear for David Gyngell, by then approaching his thirty-eighth birthday, to formally take on the managing director's job his father had once held with so much distinction. The two Packers enthusiastically endorsed the promotion, as did Alexander, presumably in the expectation that Gyngell would still be answerable to him within the normal chain of command. Their faith in the young CEO seemed well rewarded over the next few months as Channel 9 concluded the ratings season with a convincing lead over its opposition. Seven, despite its gains in the newscaff area, suffered an embarrassing dip in overall audience and its momentum appeared to falter. Before the year was out Gyngell would also be recognised for his hands-on role in an even more praiseworthy achievement for the network. Veteran news hands credited him with being the driving force behind Nine's unsurpassed coverage of the Boxing Day tsunami – a spare-no-expense effort that would carry a staggering price tag of $2 million in operational costs and another $3 million in charitable donations by the time it was over. 'We had twenty people in Aceh at one stage and that was all Gyngell driving that,' Ray Martin observed, noting how their new boss's willingness to have a go made everyone feel 'we were back to being number one again'. Gyngell won more kudos by authorising live, commercial-free coverage of the funeral of Pope John Paul II, well knowing the move was certain to cause a significant drop in ratings for the night, as well as revenue. He simply didn't care how badly that decision might go down among Alexander's circle at Park Street. As a CEO in his own right he was determined to return Nine to the high morale it enjoyed in the Golden Age, even if the network was inevitably forced to make do with fewer staff and resources.

'All I ask is to be proud when you drive through those gates,' he implored his beleaguered troops, hoping to imbue them with the same sentiment that had been drummed into him since early childhood. 'The culture of this company is everything that stands for biggest, best, fastest, strongest – and especially the network with the most integrity. That's what I was taught that Channel 9 was about – that's what my old man used to tell me, that's what Kerry Packer always told me.'

The fortunes of a television warrior, however, can change in an instant. If Gyngell finished his first eight months as CEO on an exhilarating high, by the start of the 2005 ratings season he was virtually a dead man walking. After years of struggling along with second-rate American product, Seven's overseas connections finally came good with two sure-fire hits, *Desperate Housewives* and *Lost*. The network had also taken up the licence to make a local version of *Dancing With the Stars*, a format that had proved a stunning success in Britain. Park Street was in for a shock with the loss of the first four rating weeks in a row. The press, of course, jumped on the story of mighty Goliath copping it on the chin from the underdog David – all the juicier a tale considering how Seven's David Leckie had been so ruthlessly dumped by Nine just three years earlier. The gloating coverage might not have stung so much if it had merely been confined to the success of Seven's new entertainment line-up. Cunningly, however, Seven's publicity department kept emphasising the gains being made by Seven's news, *Sunrise* and *Today Tonight*, knowing those advances into Nine's previously sacred newscaff territory would cause its rival all the more embarrassment. Gyngell himself remained cool, as did his chief programmer, Michael Healy, shuffling popular programs like *Super Nanny* and *Celebrity Overhaul* around the schedule to try to counter Seven's onslaught. Nine, in fact, would soon claw its way back to the lead, helped along by its sports coverage as well as its powerful array of one-off event programs like the Logies and Academy Awards. Still, the setback – if only temporary – would stir up further intrigues at Park Street, posing a far greater threat to Gyngell's tenure than anything Channel 7 could throw his way.

Around the time of Gyngell's appointment as CEO of the Nine Network, in the winter of 2004, two formidable new figures had been invited onto the board of PBL – each with qualifications that dwarfed Gyngell's own in terms of their experience in managing a large broadcasting organisation. Chris Anderson, though nudging 60, was hardly beyond running a network if called on to do so in a crisis. A former Fairfax CEO who served as mentor to John Alexander, he had gone on to take senior managerial positions at the ABC and Television New Zealand before a stint as head of Optus, the telecommunications company. Sam Chisholm was also new to the board although he had previously been called upon numerous times by his close contacts at Park Street to offer advice on specific issues. While in his mid-sixties, Chisholm had recently been given a new lease on life through a lung transplant and by his nature was someone who thrived on being in the heat of the action. Both men could be seen as likely prospects to take on a direct advisory role at the

The end of an era. James Packer passes Kerry's massive on-screen image after paying an emotional tribute at the State Memorial Service in February, 2006. (Andrew Meares/Fairfaxphotos)

Plenty to smile about. James Packer and John Alexander took PBL to a new dimension in corporate clout, but the Nine Network has suffered in the process. (Andrew Meares/Fairfaxphotos)

As a magazine executive J.A. was credited with doubling profits but Kerry Packer lived to regret letting him loose on television. (Kate Geraghty/Fairfaxphotos)

Nine's feisty boss of news and current affairs, Peter Meakin, quit in disgust and defected to Seven after calling Alexander 'a 24-carat c— '. (Newspix/Alan Pryke)

David Gyngell's sudden resignation as network CEO in May 2005 made headlines when he cited interference from Park Street. (Jim Rice/Fairfaxphotos)

Sam Chisholm led Nine to untold riches in the Golden Age. His return to the network in 2005 triggered fireworks. (Steven Siewert/Fairfaxphotos)

McLeod's Daughters at the Logies in 2004. The show's two senior producers, Susan Bower, centre left, and Posie Graeme-Evans, centre right, were each secretly wooed to become head of Nine drama. (Newspix/Cameron Tandy)

Mike Munro, as host of *A Current Affair,* was the first Channel 9 star to feel the heat after Alexander took command. (Newspix/Katrina Tepper)

Jim Waley, casualty of the fierce ratings war in news and current affairs.
(Newspix/Bob Barker)

Sunday's Jana Wendt found herself the target of vicious newspaper leaks.
(Newspix/Manuela Cifra)

Nine's celebrity CEO, Eddie McGuire. The network's sixth boss in just over four years, McGuire caused a sensation in more ways than one.
(Newspix/Graham Crouch)

They can laugh about it now. It wasn't so funny when *Today*'s Jessica Rowe first read claims that McGuire wanted to 'bone' her. (Newspix/Phil Hillyard)

Mark Llewellyn's sworn affidavit led to the biggest scandal in Nine's history. (Newspix/Bob Finlayson)

A tough negotiator. Jeff Browne hoped to cut Llewellyn's $750,000 salary by more than half – the infamous 'shit sandwich'. (Newspix/Cameron Tandy)

The dynamic duo: David Barbour, standing, and Julian Cress, creators of the smash hit *The Block*. The network refused to honour their handshake agreement for a share of overseas sales. (Courtesy David Hahn)

The Block at Bondi with contestants and fans. (Peter Rae/Fairfaxphotos)

Sunrise's Adam Boland, hailed as the creative genius spearheading Seven's victory over Nine in news and current affairs.
(Courtesy Seven Network)

The *Sunrise* family headed by its 'heartland' stars, Kochie, top centre, and Mel, front left. (Courtesy Seven Network)

Former Nine CEO David Leckie, now riding high at Seven. (Newspix/Graham Crouch)

Seven owner Kerry Stokes incurred Alexander's wrath. (Newspix/Chris Pavlich)

James Packer with Chris Anderson, a key figure in deciding the future of the Nine Network. (Newspix/Sam Mooy)

network – perhaps even a more powerful, supervisory function – if Gyngell showed signs of faltering under the immense pressures of the new survey season.

That possibility began to loom large in Kerry Packer's mind as the year progressed, and not only because of the stress of the ratings. He was genuinely worried that the young man he held so dear was endangering his health with the workload he was carrying. 'I hear it in your voice, it's killing you,' he warned Gyngell at one point. 'You are trying to run everything at the station at the moment – news, current affairs, sports, programming, and you just can't do it.' Packer, too, could see that the network's financial problems were multiplying at an alarming rate. Even if Nine managed to hold on to its number one ranking at the end of 2005 – as he was confident it would – its winning margin would no longer be big enough to maintain the one key commercial advantage that had made it the jewel in the crown.

During those decades when Nine remained so far in front, it had been able to extract a special premium of up to 15 per cent beyond the normal ad rates for any advertiser eager to use its precious air time. It was a bonus amounting to an extra $80 to $90 million a year, like so much icing on the cake. That premium, however, was destined to vanish virtually overnight if Seven managed to narrow Nine's lead. To add to the network's woes, Nine's financial experts were predicting its share of total advertising expenditure for 2005 could drop by 4 per cent or more, representing a further loss of income running into the tens of millions. By April even Kerry Packer had accepted the need to initiate large-scale retrenchments of staff and start shedding various overseas output deals, including paring down the network's multiple news feeds. His one caveat was that no cuts be made that adversely affected the network's on-air programming to the point of threatening its number one status. Even at that, it was clear he was beginning to move closer to James's position and the more he did, the more he began to worry whether David Gyngell had the skill or the stomach to enforce the rigorous efficiencies that were about to be imposed.

Despite his fearsome reputation as the man who never blinked, Packer could become quite jumpy in situations like this, prone to look for instant solutions. He still very much wanted to keep Gyngell at the network but began sounding out the various key players at PBL on whether they thought the CEO might need assistance to carry him through the year. While those conversations were carried on behind closed doors it is easy to imagine that almost all of them revolved around the most mischievous single word in the English language. *But.* Look, Kerry, I think David certainly has got a lot of potential, *but* . . . And then, out would come the list of his perceived weaknesses. He was reluctant to delegate, trying to do too much himself rather than using division heads to handle problems for him; his management meetings were more like pep rallies with dozens attending; he was spreading himself so thin, flitting from one issue to another, that he often failed to deliver the necessary follow-up. Always in the background was his age and relative inexperience. The fact that he once sold surfboards and beachwear was treated as a joke, prompting unkind accusations that he was trying to run Channel 9 like a hippy commune. The plain truth was, any number of people within Park Street were more than ready to point out David Gyngell's deficiencies in the guise of wanting to 'help' him. John Alexander was one of those, keen to see his former boss and good friend, Chris Anderson, appointed to a supervisory role at the network that would enable him to keep a close check on Gyngell's every move. The new position, in effect, would install Anderson as an intermediary between Gyngell and Packer senior, severing the hotline connection between the two. Their daily phone conversations had become a source of the PBL chief's growing antagonism toward his former deputy.

John Alexander, according to a former PBL colleague, would later come to think of his involvement in David Gyngell's appointment as Nine CEO as 'one of the worst mistakes I ever made'. Since their relationship had started off on such a positive note, it's worthwhile trying to pin down when things started going wrong between the two. At some point after Peter Meakin's sudden departure, Alexander must have picked up at least a whiff of Kerry Packer's loss of confidence in his ability to adapt to television. If so, that would have made him all the more concerned when he became aware that Gyngell was tending to leave him out of the loop in his dealings with the mogul. It was almost as if the two inhabited a secret little world of their own, speaking in their own private code, conniving to divert resources that rightfully belonged to the whole of PBL.

There was one particular incident that appeared to crystallise all of Alexander's suspicions about Gyngell's loyalty to him. In their newly announced capacities as PBL chief and head of Nine, respectively, the two men arranged to address a meeting of investment analysts to talk up the network's prospects for the coming year. Gyngell quickly sensed that the only thing these experts really cared about was whether or not Kerry Packer, with all his health problems, was still the man in charge. Those attending braced themselves for the usual dry statistics but were delighted when the young CEO regaled them instead with some hilarious anecdotes about the legendary businessman, followed by exactly what they wanted to hear. *It's still very definitely Kerry Packer who's running Channel 9. He's the one I report to. I speak to him every day.* With that, Alexander's mood visibly changed. He obviously didn't appreciate those words at all.

That session was held shortly after their joint promotions, when Gyngell's star was still on the rise. In fact, the recently installed Nine boss would finish 2004 not only ahead in the ratings but with the network's share of total TV advertising at an impressive 41.5 per cent, higher even than the target announced by James Packer after the sacking of David Leckie. In ordinary circumstances Alexander, as head of PBL, should have been delighted with Gyngell's achievements. With his political mindset, however, he was bound to see the younger man's closeness to Kerry as a threat to his own authority and he could hardly have been pleased to hear the head of the Nine Network publicly boasting to a group of financial experts about reporting not to him but directly to Packer every day.

When Alexander, with James's support, first told Gyngell about the plan to involve Chris Anderson in overseeing the network, he naturally tried to put the most positive spin on it. The move supposedly was meant to help take some of the pressure off Gyngell by using Anderson as an intermediary, shielding him from Kerry's hectoring phone calls. Gyngell was appalled. So long as he was CEO he was going to run the network to the best of his abilities and the last thing he needed was still another layer of management over his head. At any rate, the reasoning was preposterous. Was Kerry suddenly going to forget his phone number? What was he going to speak to Chris Anderson about – how this show or that show was rating? Kerry Packer was a programmer at heart. He wasn't interested in speaking about balance sheets all the time. He wanted to speak to people who knew their television.

The Anderson proposal was quickly aborted, although not because of Gyngell's objections. Someone had warned Kerry that Anderson's track record in television was not as impressive as it might look, with critics in New Zealand questioning a number of his programming decisions. With that, Alexander's favoured candidate was out of the running and Sam Chisholm emerged as a more likely contender to step in to steady the ship. In the meantime, however, Kerry had decided that there was one area where Gyngell definitely needed immediate help. He turned to Lynton Taylor, one of his most trusted lieutenants from the days of World Series Cricket, to join the network in the middle of April, 2005 as a senior consultant. His special brief was to oversee the negotiating and contracting of all sport, news and entertainment programming, including overseas output deals. Kerry also asked him to serve as a mentor to Nine's executive team, including Gyngell himself, attempting to rectify some of the problems that had shown up in the latter's management style. The CEO vigorously objected. He knew that Kerry was sincerely trying to help him, concerned that he was on the verge of burning out. He even acknowledged that Packer might be right but in his annoyance and frustration he still viewed Taylor as a 'spy' – one of Packer's henchmen from bygone days sent to find out every little detail of what was happening at the station. He was hurt all the more that the move was initiated not by James and Alexander but by Kerry himself, a sign that his patron had begun to lose faith in him. Still, out of respect for Kerry, he agreed to Taylor's suggestion that the two of them at least have a talk to see if the relationship had a chance of working. The meeting seemed cordial enough and Taylor took up his post at the network. He could hardly be aware, however, that for all Gyngell's outward appearance of calm acceptance, he was inwardly seething. Among the traits he had inherited from his father, it seems, was a short fuse when it came to defending his sense of dignity.

> It started to get at me. Here I was, running the most successful station in Australia, making [lots] more than Channel 7 up the road; and I thought, what the Christ, the more successful I am, the more everyone wants to know what's going on! Everyone wanted to get involved, come over and see what's happening in television. So that was pissing me off a bit. [Name deleted] particularly, was irritating me. Smart arse remarks suggesting great things, without any care or knowledge or understanding of what the business

was about; second guessing all the time. So I thought, I can't stand this.

That passage happens to be from an oral history recorded by Bruce Gyngell, David's father, describing the oppressive atmosphere that led to his stormy departure from the Nine Network in 1969. He quit after a furious row over constant interference from Sir Frank and his hangers-on. The smart arse he referred to, always making snide remarks about how much better the network should be doing, happened to be Clyde Packer, Kerry's brother, in that instance – but he could be looked upon as an early prototype of the Packer dynasty's modus operandi: hounding its senior managers with constant second-guessing.

On Thursday, 5 May, David Gyngell went into 54 Park Street to attend a regular meeting with James, Alexander and Lynton Taylor in his capacity as senior consultant. The network CEO was unusually subdued, even when informed of a change of policy that might normally have brought him to his feet in vigorous protest. The gist of it was this: *The days of spending the money needed to keep Nine at the top of the ratings are over. We are more interested in making significant revenue than we are in being number one. That must be your first priority from now on, profits before ratings.* He was simply too heartsick to bother raising an objection. Here was James, his oldest and dearest mate, asking him to do something Kerry could have only regarded as a heresy. They were the two most important men in his life and it had become impossible for him to stay true to one without betraying the other. He left that meeting giving no hint of the thoughts racing through his mind, but he had clearly reached the Rubicon. What would have been the hardest decision of his life only a few minutes before suddenly became the easiest.

Gyngell went back to the office that Thursday morning to pick up some personal belongings. He got James on the phone to tell him he was resigning. After giving some time for the shock of that announcement to wear off, he coolly went on to discuss some contractual and financial matters that required urgent attention. Then the 38-year-old walked out of the station and the job he had dreamed about from the time he was a child. His father, Bruce, had been just a year older when he quit the Packer network, also leaving in May, in the very middle of a ratings season.

James and Alexander agreed to hold off in saying anything to Kerry, hoping that over the weekend they could find some way to persuade Gyngell to change his mind There was nothing, however, that could change the hard facts of the situation. Kerry, James, Alexander, Anderson, Chisholm and Taylor – together they added up to one hell of a lot of opinions, a heavier psychological burden than Gyngell was willing or able to carry. Perhaps he was immature and supersensitive to criticism and a bit too cocky for his own good; but it was hard to disagree with his basic premise. 'You just can't run a business this way, guys,' he kept insisting. 'I've been given the opportunity to run this network. If I fail, sack me. Otherwise, let me get on with the job.'

On Sunday night James and Alexander called Sam Chisholm to an emergency meeting at James's apartment to ask his advice on how to handle the crisis. It was clear the sudden resignation would cause a sensation in the press, coming as it did when Nine had troubles enough. Whatever Gyngell's faults as a CEO – and in Chisholm's mind he had plenty – this was no time to be rocking the boat. 'Well, you've just got to try to invoke your relationship with David and see if you can hold all of this together,' he told them. He added, however, that if worst came to worst, he was prepared to return to the station on a temporary basis to do whatever he could to help.

On Monday, 9 May, Gyngell went back to Park Street to try to explain his decision to Kerry and bid him what he hoped would be a warm and affectionate goodbye. As he admitted to close friends afterwards, however, it unfortunately didn't work out that way. With so much emotion welling up in him, he just snapped, expressing his frustration – even his outrage – that the network they both loved with such a passion should be reduced to the lowly status of a mere commodity: an ATM machine inserted in the slot where there used to be a soul. His final words went along these lines: *I love you very much but I'm a better person than this and I don't want to put up with all this bullshit any longer. I'm out of here.* And so he was, slamming the door to Kerry Packer's office behind him with the bang of utter finality. Gyngell had offered his resignation twice before and as much as Packer adored him, he was far too proud a man to turn his cheek a third time.

The next day Packer was back making his usual morning phone calls to Nine's chief programmer, Michael Healy, when Healy asked how he felt about David's departure. 'Oh, well, what does it matter?' Kerry replied brusquely. 'We've got to get on with life.' And then his voice broke and he started crying.

The morning papers of Tuesday, 10 May, made the resignation front-page news and carried the full text of the brief statement Gyngell issued. It was surprisingly frank as such press releases go, though it barely scratched the surface of the real story.

I have today resigned from the post of chief executive officer of the Nine Network, effective forthwith. The decision was mine and mine alone. Not sought, nor pressured, nor otherwise influenced by any party. It was reached only after long and very careful consideration, and conveyed person- ally this morning with regret but clear intent to both Kerry and James Packer. I reached the determination that I was simply not prepared to allow my position to be rendered untenable by what I regard as increasingly unhelpful and multi-layered managing systems developing between Nine and PBL. Without the absolutely and unmistakably clear mandate required by all CEOs to properly run any major business, I believed it was in my best interests to move on. I do so without rancour or bitterness and express my genuine affection and support for the Packers, Nine, and its great people and its continuing excellent product and ratings dominance.

By the time that appeared he was already on the far north coast enjoying a surf.

Still, Gyngell's surprise departure from Channel 9 by no means set him free from the contaminating reach of Park Street politics. It was not long before ugly whispers began to circulate about last-minute payments he had authorised just before he left the station. Most involved contract extensions for key executives. There was one item, however, that was alleged to have come as a shock even to Kerry Packer. The ex-CEO was about to become the target of a smear of such proportions that it deserves the most thorough examination.

In March, 2005, a female newsreader, Kim Watkins, filed a complaint to the Human Rights and Equal Opportunity Commission in which she alleged Channel 9 had been guilty of discriminatory treatment towards her as a result of her having children. The great bulk of her evidence was devoted to citing various examples of her difficulty in obtaining the advancement and pay increases she thought were due her – the standard stuff of all such claims. In another part of her affidavit, however, Watkins went on to complain not just about sexual discrimination but harassment, accusing the network CEO, David Gyngell, of improper behaviour towards her. Since the two have different versions of the alleged incident, it's best to begin by stating the facts both would agree on. Watkins had returned to the station after maternity leave to begin a new season of the *Nightline* program. As she was going through rehearsal in the news studio,

Gyngell came in to welcome her back. The two had known each other over a number of years and their acquaintance up to then had always been most cordial. Gyngell congratulated her on having just given birth to twins and in the course of his greeting her, stepped forward to give her a kiss. From that point on their versions differ irreconcilably. Watkins insisted that Gyngell made indecent advances, touching her breast. He strongly denied any physical contact that could even remotely be construed in that way. A number of staff members who were present that night provided sworn statements saying that they saw nothing to suggest harassment. Despite such supporting testimony, however, Nine's lawyers proceeded to settle on her broader claim of being subjected to discriminatory treatment within the workplace. The terms were confidential but believed to involve a sum of around $200,000, taking into account her ten years of employment.

The Watkins case was thus resolved without ever being tested in court. Still very much alive, however, was an allegation that could be seen as far more damaging in the long run to the reputation of a high-profile corporate executive. Persistent rumours began to spread that David Gyngell had attempted to cover up the payment, authorising it on his own authority as CEO just before his resignation. According to the rumours – which are accepted as truth even to this day by a surprising number of old PBL hands – Gyngell did not even see fit to inform Kerry Packer of the Watkins settlement.

My own research has now established beyond doubt that David Gyngell kept Kerry Packer fully informed of the allegations at every stage of the legal progress. In fact, Kerry personally ordered that the case be settled immediately even though Gyngell was keen for a chance to establish his innocence in open court. 'You've just got to settle it,' Packer instructed his lawyers. 'Pay her whatever it takes to get rid of her. It can't get to court. A chief executive officer can't be seen to be involved in claims like this even if there's nothing to them.' The press, of course, would have gone into a feeding frenzy over such a story, coming as it did when the all-powerful Nine Network was already under siege.

A totally independent witness has told me that he discussed the Watkins case on several occasions with Kerry. 'Kerry was well and truly aware of what was happening,' this source assures me. 'He knew what the allegations were and knew of the payment.' This person is not a lawyer but someone Kerry trusted for his street-smart savvy. So why had Kerry raised the issue with him? 'The only thing he really asked was, did I reckon Gyng did it. I said to him, "Mate, all I can say is, everybody else in the room said it didn't happen. A couple of those people didn't even like Gyng that much, but they supported his version. So there's a fair chance it didn't happen and it seems to me we've got to give him the benefit of the doubt."'

Kerry could be capable of a wry sense of humour in such circumstances. 'Oh, I would have given it to him anyway,' he grinned. 'I'm just asking what you think.'

The confidential settlement was dated 15 April, almost three weeks before David Gyngell's resignation. Whatever else might be said about his time at Channel 9 he certainly didn't deserve the stink of poisonous innuendo that followed him out the door.

CHAPTER 10

Missing magic:
then and now

Publicity manager Vicki Jones was absolutely outraged and the young women who worked with her in one of the little white cottages surrounding Nine Network headquarters in Willoughby were close to tears. Not only were they already snowed under with too much work, but they were now being told they would have to mow the lawns themselves because Kerry Packer didn't want to foot the bill for a gardener. Jones stormed off to the main building and burst into the station manager's office without bothering to knock. 'You've got all the blood there is to get out of us, there is no more – my girls and I are not going to mow the fucking lawns, so just forget about it!' she remonstrated. The executive could only shake his head in wonder. 'What on earth are you talking about?' he asked. Jones realised in a flash that she had fallen prey to another 'gotcha' by Geoff Harvey, the station's musical director and self-appointed court jester, and slunk off in embarrassment to lick her wounds.

To fully appreciate what Channel 9 has lost in its transition to leaner times it's important to understand what it once had. There's no doubt Nine's glory years were tinged with a degree of extravagance that's almost embarrassing to look back upon from today's perspective. Yet the one attribute that made the network so unique cost absolutely nothing. Those of us who worked there in that era had different ways to describe it – spirit, morale, verve, zest, esprit – but they all boiled down to *fun*. The place was pervaded by a cheery togtherness that gave it the feel of an extended family. Where rival stations were often fragmented by petty jealousies, people at Nine shared in the excitement of each other's successes and offered comfort and advice in the down moments. When it came to creative differences they were quick to stand up for what they believed in but at the end of the day, they were always able to enjoy a good laugh together. A sure measure of their high morale was the practical jokes staff members frequently played on one another and there was no one better at it than Harvey, a black-belt master in the art of stirring. Nine's chief engineer, Bruce Robertson, fell victim to a Harvey sting when he found it almost impossible to get served a drink during a first-class Qantas flight to Los Angeles. What he couldn't have known, of course, was that Harvey had been on the phone to Qantas the night before. 'My boss is going overseas tomorrow,' he explained to a sympathetic official. 'I don't know how to put this to you, but he has a problem with alcohol. On long flights he tends to drink far too much, so anything you can do.'

Not surprisingly, some of the more memorable incidents from those glory days revolved around Kerry Packer himself. Of numerous anecdotes I collected for *Compulsive Viewing*, one in particular conveys the tangy flavour of pure adrenaline that once existed at the station. It involves an ill-fated experiment to intro-duce the first female cricket commentator to television in the early 1980s. David Hill, then Nine's director of sport, chose the vivacious actor Kate Fitzpatrick for the role because of her undoubted enthusiasm for the game. Unfortunately, press critics gave Fitzpatrick a merciless panning which, in turn, affected her self-confidence so that she performed at less than her best, judged out for a duck during the Pakistan test in Adelaide. Amid all the adverse publicity, Hill braced himself in anticipation of a mighty blast from Kerry, who normally was in contact every day to complain about the slightest hiccup in coverage. Surprisingly, there was not one call through the entire debacle – that is, until the exhausted producer arrived back home in Sydney to hear the phone ringing.

'It's Packer here,' came the gruff introduction. 'I don't have any comment whatsoever on your latest exploit. I just have a question. Is she a good fuck?'

Hill was almost too stunned to reply. 'Mr Packer, I really wouldn't know,' he protested.

'In that case, son,' Kerry advised him, 'you've missed out both ways.'

It was the kind of good-natured joshing that marked a true sense of camaraderie between Kerry and his producers, and a phone call like that was worth more than money can buy. With his spectacular sports coverage acclaimed around the world, David Hill was on many a network's wish list, both in Australia and overseas, but he would gladly have worked for Kerry for the rest of his life. He only agreed to join Rupert Murdoch after Packer, in effect, quit him, selling his stations to Alan Bond. Another world-class producer, Peter Faiman, was on the verge of leaving Nine to take up a tempting offer from Murdoch, when Kerry managed to win him back with just a few words and a single gesture. Faiman, known for his top-rating entertainment specials, went to Packer's office to try to explain that he was feeling a bit stale and needed to try something new. 'I can fix that,' Kerry told him. At every other point Faiman tried to raise – wanting to move from Melbourne to Sydney, hoping to work with different people, becoming more independent – Packer kept repeating the same line. 'I can fix that.' The producer felt himself visibly wilting under such relentless gamesmanship. 'Well, son, what are you going to do?' the mogul finally demanded. 'Oh, Kerry, please, I feel like shooting myself,' Faiman responded. With that Packer opened his top drawer, pulled out a giant old Texas six-gun and slammed it down on the desktop in front of him. 'Well, I can fix that, too,' Kerry grinned.

'I mean, quite seriously, how could you leave anybody who treats you that way?' Faiman later remarked of the encounter.

Kerry's notoriously bad temper, of course, was no fun at all; but whether he was in an awesome or amusing mode, his true motivational skill was in letting every one of his key producers know he cared enough to keep a close eye on whatever they were putting to air. David Hill found that out early in his career at Nine when Packer showed up at the Willoughby studios at 2.30 am during a live-by-satellite sports presentation from Europe that was being plagued by continuous technical failures. The mogul had obviously been watching from home, recognised that the problems occurring were out of Hill's control, and decided to drive across the Harbour Bridge to give him moral support. 'I felt this presence behind me,' Hill recalled, 'and I asked, "Mr Packer, what are you doing here?"' 'I thought this is arguably the greatest disaster in the history of television,' Kerry quipped. 'I just wanted to watch it up close.'

Presence – no word better explains Packer's profound influence in making Nine the outstanding creative force it once was. If he didn't turn up in person, the next ring on the studio phone might be from him, but in any case, he still loomed large in the minds of his program makers as the face pressed closest to the TV screen. It seemed natural enough that he should be in such close contact with David Hill considering his love for cricket, golf and other sports. Peter Faiman, however, remembered him ringing the control room one night to complain about the camera angles he was using during a song and dance routine featuring the buxom black singer, Delilah. Faiman had planned the sequence to feature tight close-ups of the visiting performer amid a series of artistic dissolves to the ballet in the background. 'She's a beautiful woman,' Packer challenged him, 'but why are we only seeing her face?' The producer immediately realised his boss was spot-on with that observation and ordered his cameras to pull back for wider shots that portrayed the star in all her curvaceous glory.

Kerry's keen interest in current affairs virtually guaranteed that any producer in that area could count on getting an earful from time to time. Just before the Falklands War he berated the *Sunday* program for a panel discussion raising the possibility that Britain might be about to launch an invasion. 'I'll tell you something, son,' Packer scoffed. 'If you think Margaret Thatcher is going to sail 12,000 fucking miles across the Atlantic in the middle of winter to recapture a pile of bird shit, you've lost your way over there.' Such comments, however, hardly fit into the pattern of a proprietor attempting to curb editorial freedom – they were more like a strongly opinionated viewer having a rant. The closest he came to imposing censorship was in his almost obsessional loathing of prison stories, especially those involving allegations of a convict receiving overly harsh treatment from his warders. 'They're lawbreakers, for fuck's sake, what are the warders supposed to be there for? I don't want to see any more of these cocksuckers on my channel – do you understand me?' To which a wise producer would nod obediently, knowing the next prison story he put to air had better be a case big enough to trigger a Royal Commission. The truth was that sports director

David Hill was bombarded by many more of Kerry's one-eyed views than any of us in current affairs. 'He wasn't out!' an indignant Packer would ring to tell the producer after a batsman's controversial dismissal. 'The umpires are incompetent. What's wrong with the commentators? Why aren't they saying that? He clearly missed the ball.' Hill's response would invariably be something along these lines: *Maybe, but out is how the scoreboard is still going to read.*

As executive producer of *60 Minutes* I certainly received more than my share of Kerry's phone calls, occasionally in praise of a story but more likely with a critical sting in the tail. I usually watched the program from home on Sunday nights, trying to see it through the eyes of our audience while having a few drinks before dinner. Kerry, like an impatient child, would often ring me even before the show was over to discuss the faults he found in a report. One night, unfortunately, I had had one too many drinks and he had one too many complaints. In response to his usual carping about a George Negus interview (Kerry Packer complaining about someone else being too opinionated!) I erupted in a temper tantrum that did me no honour, ending with this suicidal flourish: 'Anyway,' I shouted into the phone, 'what am I supposed to do? I've got 4 million viewers and you're only one of them.' There was a long, ominous silence. 'Oh,' Kerry replied at last, 'I would have thought I might at least count for two.'

And that he certainly did.

Packer happened to be an instinctive, if sometimes erratic, motivator but Sam Chisholm, as his managing director at Nine, found a way to turn the art of inspiration into everyday practice, like capturing lightning in a bottle. Chisholm stumbled into his television career through a most curious route, as a Johnson's Wax rep who convinced Graham Kennedy to plug a product called One Go by personally going to the entertainer's home to polish his kitchen floor. As Chisholm happily recalled for years to come, 'The floor was grey rubber and honestly, it came up like a mirror.' From there he went on to sell advertising time for Channel 9 with dazzling success, although Kerry actually fired him at one point for showing up at the office drunk after a long lunch with a client. He was immediately reinstated and it wasn't too long before he was rewarded with the top job at Nine, going on to negotiate contracts with Kennedy lucrative enough to keep him in One Go for several lifetimes. The comedy star recalled one such negotiation in which he responded to Sam's first offer by chiding: 'I would think it's worth three times that amount.' His former floor waxer immediately agreed without a blink. 'I really tried not to quibble with these people,' Sam would later explain. 'I was probably overly generous but the place was very successful and went on to have a position of great dominance.'

Chisholm is most frequently described as a James Cagney look-alike, short and pugnacious. That hardly comes close to encompassing the sharp mind and seemingly inexhaustible energy that added such an important dimension to his aggressive nature. He was exactly the type of CEO needed to push Nine to its full potential through the 1970s and 1980s. It was Sam who provided the pithy motto for those glory years, when Nine was likened to a Camelot of the TV medium, brimming over with vitality and enthusiasm. 'Winners have parties, losers have meetings,' he famously decreed. In Chisholm's reign, the ritual of Friday night drinks took on the semblance of group therapy sessions where executives, producers and stars felt free to let off steam, express pent-up grievances or even shed a tear to relieve the constant stress they were under. If the station became known for its fondness for internal frolicking, the lavish promotional parties it put on for the press reached almost mythological proportions. Vicki Jones, the publicity manager who once thought she might have to mow lawns to save the company a bit of money, would go on to spend $50,000 on just one lunch, using a fleet of helicopters to ferry TV reporters to a posh restaurant north of Sydney to mark the launch of a new season of the Mike Walsh show.

Chisholm was certainly never shy about spending his boss's money, but there was a lot more method to his munificence than he was ever given credit for at the time. If you could make your network personalities feel special by surprising them with a case of champagne or an expensive watch, you were likely to be repaid many times over in that little extra sparkle they turned on for the cameras. Better than any other executive of that era, Chisholm understood that the first step in creating a star is to make him or her feel like one.

'Self-belief is an enormous thing in a business that is so intangible,' he argued. 'It's not a business as in selling items off a shelf. It's not a factory and it has no warehouse, it has no stock. So you are dealing with something that at the end of the day relies on the creativity of the human mind.'

If he was adept at coaxing the best out of his stars, the Nine chief also gave constant encouragement to the production units working behind the scenes. 'They start off each day with a blank piece of paper and out of ingenuity and enterprise and energy and drive they create television programs,' he enthused. 'In order to do all that they need to be in an environment that stimulates everyone.'

Such was the philosophy that went into the making of an incredible array of new program formats introduced by Nine during the heyday of the Packer–Chisholm partnership. Leading the charge, of course, was a new form of cricket made for television – the day–night matches that revolutionised the game. It's often forgotten that when Packer first started World Series Cricket in 1977, no one had ever dreamed of lighting a metropolitan cricket ground, assumed to be a virtually impossible task. Unlike baseball or football, the game is in play from all 360 degrees of a circle, so there appeared to be too much risk of blinding anyone – player or fan – who inadvertently looked up into the half-dozen artificial suns needed to recreate daylight conditions. Kerry turned to the network's chief engineer, Bruce Robertson, to find a solution in time for the first one-day match at the Sydney Cricket Ground in November, 1978. The result couldn't have been more spectacular: those now-familiar bent-neck towers soaring twenty storeys above the stadium crowned by their shimmering jewels of light, a design later to be adopted around the cricketing world. It was a major technological breakthrough that marked Nine as the 'can-do' station, and that reputation just kept reinforcing itself through the years to come. *60 Minutes* followed in 1979, *Sunday* in 1981, *Today* in 1982, the evening edition of *Hey Hey It's Saturday* in 1984, *Burke's Backyard* in 1987 – local productions that each broke new ground in their own way, expanding the horizons of Australian television as no other network had ever attempted.

Though it's true that *60 Minutes* and *Sunday* were based on models first developed in the United States, that didn't detract from their unique impact within the local industry. Nine's *60 Minutes* changed the entire face of Australian TV journalism by pioneering the use of experienced producers to work with each on-camera reporter in contrast to the tradition of reporters having to carry the entire burden of research, scripting and editing on their own. From its inception the local *60 Minutes* also covered a much larger percentage of international stories than its US counterpart, giving viewers their first real taste of looking at the world through Australian eyes. Similarly, the idea for Nine's *Sunday* program may have been borrowed from the leisurely *Sunday Morning* arts program on America's CBS, but its special focus on in-depth political interviews and commentary set it well apart from the US version.

While Kerry and Chisholm deserve credit for giving their support to these new ventures at no small financial risk, it should be noted that in each case the programs developed in a way they had never foreseen, transformed by the practical realities of a local production team determined to make the cleverest possible use of the limited resources available to it. Only a few weeks before *60 Minutes*' shaky debut, Kerry demanded to know why I wasn't planning to cover the forthcoming British elections. I tried to explain that the *60 Minutes* format in the US was such a hit because it focused on fascinating people rather than general issues in the news, summed up in the dictum that very few viewers really give a shit about flood control but everyone's interested in the story of Noah. Packer, however, obviously thought he was about to get a more popular, Americanised version of the ABC's *Four Corners* and in his fury with me, he actually threatened to cancel the program. 'You're not serious,' I gasped, thinking of those I had persuaded to leave good jobs at the ABC and elsewhere to take a chance on this new project. 'Look at my face, son,' he replied in a voice that seemed to emanate from some cold, dark pit in the bowels of the earth. 'Does it look like I'm serious?' Needless to say, I did commission a hurried story linked to the British elections, though we made sure it stuck to the classic *60 Minutes* style, exposing the foibles of a hard-line 'I'm-all-right-Jack' British union leader, just the kind of character Margaret Thatcher was campaigning to get rid of.

Meanwhile, the founding producer of *Sunday*, Allan Hogan, would find himself in hot water with Sam Chisholm when he ran a segment on the performing arts featuring a young male dancer romping around on stage in a costume so flimsy that his backside could clearly be detected below the thin veils. In commercial TV terms it must have come across as a real shocker, adding a whole new meaning to *arty-farty*. Sam was immediately on the phone to Hogan, most definitely not amused. 'Do you realise you've just lost us our fucking licence?' Chisholm thundered, appalled that the new program would ever consider doing stories on such esoteric nonsense. Still, Kerry and Sam soon became very proud of the programs as they developed, despite the fact that they both turned out to be different in content and far more expensive than first conceived.

The lesson from those two Golden Age examples is simple enough. The creative flame burns best when given plenty of air to breathe. In suffocating surroundings, hemmed in by over-supervision and second-guessing, with constant emphasis on the price rather than the merit of a proposition, there's soon likely to be nothing left but ash.

Of course, it can be all too easy to try to justify wasteful spending in the name of furthering a station's 'creativity' or 'image'. If Sam Chisholm was known for his extraordinary generosity during his time with Kerry, he was hardly about to stint under Alan Bond, an employer prepared to splurge $54 million on an Impressionist painting to decorate his wall. With Bond's enthusiastic approval, Sam presided over a lavish $6 million refurbishment of the network headquarters at Willoughby. Set in a vast expanse of sea-green marble, it was an inexcusable extravagance considering the financial disaster soon to engulf the Bond Corporation. More outrageous still was a birthday bash that would come to be regarded within the industry as the single most damning symbol of Nine's propensity for excessive self-indulgence. In 1989 Chisholm's colleagues decided to buy him a spanking new Harley-Davidson motorcycle for his fiftieth birthday. The machine was hoisted to the third-floor corridors of power by crane and driven into the boardroom by his driver, John Bennett, with a beautiful model riding pillion. The fact that Chisholm's fellow executives had chipped in to cover much of the expense could hardly dampen the resentment under-standably felt by so many of Nine's production staff. The event happened to coincide with a wave of sackings as the Bond-owned network struggled to meet its huge interest bills. There could be no more telling example of how the network, on its way to dominance, had inevitably begun to sow the seeds of its self-destruction.

By the time Kerry Packer returned to Nine in 1990, buying it back for a fraction of what Alan Bond had paid for it, Sam Chisholm recognised it was clearly best for him to be off on some new adventure. His seven years at Rupert Murdoch's BSkyB Channel would see him go on to even more outstanding success, turning the pay TV station around from near bankruptcy to become a major force in British life. He returned to Australia as a veritable legend, renowned on two continents for his aggressive style of management. When he was eventually asked by Kerry to rush in to fill the gap left by David Gyngell, he would find a station that bore little resemblance to the Nine he had known during the glory years.

It was unlikely, of course, that John Alexander and his team at Park Street, as a new generation of media executives, should have any feeling of nostalgia whatsoever for the Golden Age. To them, the glamour and excitement of the era could only be seen as a smokescreen covering up the kind of inefficiencies and incompetence that allowed millions of dollars to be squandered on a whim. While it's hard to blame them for such an assessment, it would be a shame if it blinded them to Kerry Packer's true contribution to the development of one of the world's most successful television networks. Dollars and cents were only part of it. To encourage the best in his people, Kerry was always willing to give something back – not out of his pocket so much as out of his heart, a sign of his respect and appreciation for all their hard work. His close personal involvement with Channel 9 comes in sad contrast to the change of attitude in evidence just five months after his death.

In May, 2006, *60 Minutes* reporter Richard Carleton suffered a fatal heart attack while reporting on the Beaconsfield mine disaster in Tasmania. The tragedy occurred on a Sunday morning, yet the *60 Minutes* staff, stunned as they were, somehow managed to rush a story to air that same night featuring Carleton's classic grilling of a mine official. The emotional pressure was enormous, with people literally in tears as they went through their various writing and editing chores. Fellow reporter Liz Hayes had the painful duty of having to front camera to read the introduction to his final story. 'It was probably as dreadful as it gets having to announce the death of a colleague in that way,' she remembers. 'At one point I remember thinking, I'm not sure I can even do this. But in the studio all I wanted to do was to make the introduction as good as I possibly could, because Richard deserved that.'

It would be hard to imagine a more impressive display of total professionalism in the most heart-wrenching of circumstances than the story *60 Minutes* put to air the night of Richard Carleton's death, 7 May, 2006. Yet no one from Park Street thought of phoning the program to offer its staff a word of thanks, as Kerry had done so many times before.

Among the numerous background interviews I've done with Channel 9 people for this book, there was one stunningly insightful comment that served to inspire the theme of this chapter. *To fully appreciate what Nine has lost it's important to understand what it once had.* My informant, in this case, could hardly be described as having any authority whatsoever. She's simply one of the small army of skilled tradespeople needed to keep a TV station on air, employed at the station over many years. And this is what she had to tell me – not a lot, but still almost too much to bear.

'There's no joy here anymore.'

CHAPTER 11

Chisholm's second coming

Sam Chisholm's sensational return to Channel 9 could be described as a second coming in more ways than one. He had arrived back from Europe as a multimillionaire but desperately ill, afflicted with a genetic disorder that saw his breathing capacity steadily deteriorating. Considering the nature of the disease, the amount of energy he expended in pursuit of his career was all the more extraordinary – working late into the night, drinking with colleagues until the wee hours, then rising before the sun to start another day. Ultimately, though, he was on a rapid downhill run. No amount of money could buy the kind of operation he needed to save his life; not in Australia, at least. To qualify for a lung transplant, it's necessary to convince the surgeons you have what it takes to survive the ordeal. 'I'll tell you what gets you through this,' a doctor advised him. 'It's sheer bloody-mindedness and you seem to have plenty of that.' Truer words were never spoken. Chisholm spent two anxious years on a waiting list for compatible organs and was literally on the verge of death – two weeks away at most – when finally given the double lung transplant in April 2003. He bounced back like a clapped out Morris Minor with a new Ferrari engine. Everyone wished him well, of course, but it wouldn't be long before a sick joke began doing the rounds at Nine suggesting that he had been brought back to life by a doctor named Frankenstein.

Chisholm strode through the glass doors of the Willoughby headquarters late on the morning of Monday, 8 May, 2005. The lift he took to the third-floor executive offices might well have been a time machine, whisking him back to the era when he was the undisputed Lord of Australian TV. Fifteen years earlier he would have been walking on newly installed Italian marble but Kerry had ordered the exquisite stonework ripped out as a noxious symbol of Alan Bond decadence. Packer's trusty engineer, Bruce Robertson, wisely disobeyed him, realising the demolition cost would be enormous, and discreetly covered the gleaming floor with carpet instead.

A crowd quickly assembled in the corridors to offer Chisholm a warm welcome back – their fifth CEO in less than four years; but the message he had for them was hardly reassuring.

'This seems to me to be a business run by the staff for the staff,' he chided them. 'My idea of a business is that it is run by the managers for the shareholders.'

As Sam later remembered it, the place was 'a shambles.' Some of the executives pampered themselves with the equivalent of five-star room service, having snacks or meals brought up to their offices at all hours of the day. He was appalled by their casual dress standards and various idiosyncrasies, such as keeping exercise equipment by their desks. Drama head Posie Graeme-Evans came to his attention for her independent-minded tastes in decorating, having Kris Noble's old office repainted with jacaranda-coloured walls and a red door. 'A bit eccentric,' he thought. 'Not what you'd find in a properly disciplined company.' Doors, in fact, became a cause célèbre for the new network chief. One of the first things he noticed was that they were almost always closed – 'and that's not the way to run a business,' Chisholm bristled, 'not one that relies on communication.' He immediately decreed all doors remain open, unless there was proven need for confidentiality, and that no food be taken into the rooms. They were minor issues, perhaps, but a tangible demonstration of a new general taking command. If his various decrees weren't unsettling enough, Sam soon followed up with a wave of dismissals, retrenchments and forced resignations that would shed well over a hundred jobs, including some high-profile middle managers such as Max Uechtritz in News and veteran daytime TV director Steve Wood. While Sam himself was more than happy to accept responsibility for the purge, plans for such large-scale staff cuts were already in place well before he arrived on the scene. David Gyngell might have handled them a bit more sympathetically but he certainly would have been obliged to enforce them had he stayed.

Resentment at Chisholm's imperious style soon began bubbling up here and there like a Rotorua mud pool, ensnaring him in a nasty whispering campaign linked to the presumed side effects of the powerful cocktail of anti-resistance drugs he was required to take following his lung transplant. Steroids, in particular, were blamed for a host of perceived personality defects. His detractors accused him of being explosively temperamental and abusive, as well as erratic and impulsive in his decision making. 'With all those drugs in him, Sam's lost the plot,' was a common diagnosis. Such critics seemed oblivious to the fact that Chisholm had been using steroids much of his adult life to deal with his degenerative illness, actually having to cope with larger doses before the transplant than after. If he managed to put some noses out of joint during his reign at Nine, there could be an explanation a lot simpler than the biochemical one. Chisholm's natural combativeness and flamboyance had served him well through the 1980s and 1990s, turning him into a living legend. While at Nine he thought nothing of daring a star like Richard Carleton to flip for the extra $50,000 a year he was asking for in his new contract (Carleton lost). During his time at BSkyB he tested British stiff upper lips to their limits, once notoriously kicking the leg of a young female producer under the negotiating table to prod her to come up with a firm price for a promotional film ('Whatever it was it just doubled – and don't ever fucking kick me again!' she rebuked him). Those kinds of grand theatrical gestures might have been the hallmark of strong leadership in the past but they were about as unwelcome as Godzilla in the cosseted workplace of the twenty-first century, where harassment suits could be brought at the drop of a four-letter word and confrontation-wary executives preferred to exert their authority via e-mail.

Still, even old friends felt genuine concern that Sam had taken far too much pressure upon himself; and there were times when the stress showed in little ways he couldn't be aware of, making him seem insensitive and self-absorbed. To them the greatest mystery was why, after enjoying such huge success on the international stage, he should ever think of going back to the relatively parochial world of Australian TV with its notorious bitchery and badmouthing. He was approaching 66, with his body still struggling to adjust to the effects of massive trauma. With his various directorships and a beautiful grazing property on the Murrumbidgee to look after, he hardly lacked activities to occupy his time and he certainly had no need of the consultancy fees. Meanwhile, he enjoyed a professional reputation as high as any man could ever hope for, so there couldn't possibly be any upside to his return to Nine, only the risk of failure, whether real or portrayed as such by those he offended along the way. Chisholm, for his part, is adamant that he acted with only one thought in mind. 'I did it because Kerry asked me to do it. It's as simple as that,' he insists. 'At that stage his health clearly wasn't what it should be. He had that kidney transplant and I understood those things – I was happy to do it and couldn't care less what it might mean for my reputation.' In their conversation that Monday after Gyngell left, Packer gave him no particular brief on what he hoped Chisholm could accomplish. Their tacit agreement was that he would go to Willoughby to make his own evaluation of what needed to be done. Packer suggested he might need to be there a month. Chisholm thought perhaps three months, hoping by then PBL would find a suitable candidate to take charge of the network. It soon became clear, however, that he would have to hang in for a much longer haul and his caretaker's role would stretch on for nine months – a period filled with controversy and conflict, ending after a thunderous clash with Alexander that would soon see him gone not just from Nine but the PBL board as well.

By Chisholm's own standard, for a good chief executive to prove himself worthy it was essential for him to do two things. 'First, he decides and second – above all – he decides,' is the way he once explained it in a magazine profile. No doubt he could be shown to be mistaken in a number of his judgement calls during his turbulent tenure as interim CEO. It was far more important, however, that he was prepared to make decisions, right or wrong, at a time when the network was being subjected to such confusing signals from Park Street. One of his first moves was to settle what could have been a most damaging and embarrassing lawsuit brought by former anchor Jim Waley, removed from his anchor position in January with three years still to run on his contract. Here, by anyone's reckoning, was one of the hardest-working and longest-serving employees in the entire network – the very essence of what the term 'loyalty' was all about within the Packer empire – and yet for some unfathomable reason he had been singled out for a game of courtroom hardball. Chisholm brushed aside the legal fine points, arguing that it would be unconscionable to treat Waley so shabbily after all he had given to Nine. He invited the aggrieved newsreader to his home and offered a settlement on the spot. The figure remains confidential but is believed to be close to whatever Waley considered due to him. 'Thank God for Sam is all I can say,' Waley would later comment.

He also left his stamp on the network in a far more tangible way, making the kind of move few chief executives would ever dare attempt. To give the channel a more modern look he approved a simple but still radical change in the traditional Nine logo, dropping those nine dots so well known to Australians to produce a much cleaner, sharper image. It's difficult for an ordinary viewer to grasp the vast amount of money and effort that goes into such an exercise, adding up to many millions of dollars when one considers the network-wide change affecting everything from news sets to vehicles to stationery. There would be many a marketing expert to warn that tampering with a well-known logo in that way was a needless risk in its potential for alienating older viewers. Sam's response to such concerns is classic Chisholm. 'I'm not a status quo merchant.'

Amidst the large-scale staff reductions, the acting CEO set tongues wagging by bringing another handsomely paid celebrity into the line-up, and what a surprising choice it turned out to be: veteran entertainer Bert Newton called back to his old network in hopes of reviving the 5.30 pm time slot leading into the news. Sceptical commentators had a field day depicting Nine as a TV remake of the movie *Cocoon:* a retirement village for sprightly old show biz folk, or as some began referring to it, 'Channel Bert'. It proved a gamble well worth the taking, however, as Newton's new game show not only started cutting back into Seven's lead, but the ageing star also went on to prove himself a drawcard in prime time. Perhaps even more important, he was one of the few talking points Nine had going for it in a year when Seven dominated the entertainment and gossip columns.

Before the year was out, Chisholm had also set his sights on poaching a high-profile personality from another commercial network to serve as co-host in a major re-launch of *Today* for the 2006 ratings season. As the thinking went, the show was in desperate need of a lighter, brighter mood if it was to have any chance of surviving against Seven's *Sunrise*. Channel 10 in Sydney had a popular young female newsreader considered to be the ideal choice to team up with the personable Karl Stefanovic. So it was that Jessica Rowe would be introduced to the Nine line-up, soon to be caught up in a blaze of headlines.

There would be another Chisholm appointment, though, who was destined to become the central figure in a week of startling revelations about Park Street's secret meddling in Channel 9's editorial freedom. Mark Llewellyn was one of the network's most seasoned journalists, a former on-camera reporter who went on to become a field producer for *60 Minutes* and was then promoted to supervisory responsibilities as that program's managing editor. After the resignation of Jim Rudder in 2004, Nine had gone for more than a year without a director of news and current affairs. Indeed, some of Rudder's unkinder critics would say that the role hadn't been adequately filled with a universally respected newscaff chief since Peter Meakin left in February 2003. Chisholm began sounding Llewellyn out on how he would feel about taking on the job. 'You need to know I identify people and then I back them,' he assured the producer. 'You are great talent. I reckon you can be as good as Meakin or better than Meakin. If you play your cards right, you will be here as long as him.' The appointment, however, was highly sensitive and negotiations needed to be kept a closely guarded secret considering that there were others within the network who might have seen themselves as likely contenders. Kerry Packer would obviously need to give his blessing to whoever was chosen. 'Now don't worry, it's all on track, there's just a few more things I have to sort out,' Sam advised Llewellyn rather cryptically in early November. It would be another two weeks before the matter was finally settled – and then in the most dramatic fashion.

Llewellyn got a call from Chisholm one morning to say: 'There's a bit of chatter about you. We need to get this done. I want you to see the big fellow today. Do you have a suit?' Llewellyn, unfortunately, was caught without one but managed to pick something out from the wardrobe department. It was a stinking hot day and amid the heat and high tension he soon began sweating profusely, very much like the character in *Network News*, suddenly rushed into a try-out for the anchoring job, with fluid gushing uncontrollably from every pore. 'You're not handling this very well, are you?' Chisholm joshed him as they rode to Park Street in the CEO's chauffeured limousine. He had the driver turn up the air conditioning to as close to Arctic winter as it could get. While waiting in the anteroom to Packer's office, the two finally got around to their first serious discussion of remuneration and Llewellyn happily discovered what it must have been like to deal with Sam in the Golden Age. 'I figure I'm giving you between $650,000 and $750,000,' Chisholm announced. 'How about $750,000?' Llewellyn shot back. 'Yeah, you've caught me in a weak moment,' Sam replied. 'Let's sign off on $750,000.' It wasn't quite a 'Westy', as it was known around the station, referring to the $1 million salary given to John Westacott, executive producer of *60 Minutes*, after he temporarily took on the additional role of overseeing *A Current Affair* as well. Still, it wasn't bad for someone not yet 45 years old.

When Packer finally beckoned the two men into his office, Chisholm couldn't have been more supportive. 'Kerry, this is

Mark Llewellyn, the bloke I've been telling you about,' he began. 'I'd back him. He's brilliant.'

'Well, I hope so,' Packer responded cordially, holding out his hand. 'I know about you and I want to hear what you think about Channel 9.' Their conversation lasted for more than an hour and a half, touching on every aspect of newscaff operations, but Packer ended on an emotive note that Llewellyn would never forget. 'Son, I love Channel 9,' he told the producer. 'It's the only thing that's ever really made me proud – and I want you to make me proud.' After a poignant pause he went on to give the younger man a stern look in the eye. 'But don't you forget,' he added, 'I also want to get the ratings.' With that he turned to Chisholm. 'All right then, Sam, he's anointed.'

The meeting was notable for the absence of John Alexander, chief executive officer of PBL, Chisholm's direct superior and a man who clearly did not take kindly to being bypassed in decisions involving major network appointments. If Alexander had no qualms about setting out to humiliate an entrenched mandarin like Peter Meakin, he was hardly likely to be any easier on a new head of news and current affairs endorsed by Chisholm, a man he was beginning to see more and more as a political rival because of his direct access to Kerry Packer.

What a difference a few years could make in the relationship of two men who once considered themselves good friends, a bond firmly sealed in 1998 after Alexander had suddenly been dismissed as publisher and editor-in-chief of the *Sydney Morning Herald* in sensational circumstances. At that point he stood accused of stirring up trouble between the *SMH* and its Melbourne sister paper, the *Age*, by leaking confidential memos and otherwise creating political mischief within the Fairfax organisation, and he was being hounded for comment. He felt an urgent need to get out of the public spotlight and Chisholm graciously offered him secret refuge in one of the guest houses at

Bundarbo, his property in southern New South Wales. They continued on a friendly basis when Chisholm joined the PBL board in September, 2003. Almost inevitably though, their relationship began to cool after Sam agreed, at Kerry's urging, to become the networks's acting CEO, making decisions that Alexander saw as encroaching on his authority.

Mark Llewellyn's appointment was undoubtedly one of the most significant of those made by Sam Chisholm in his nine months at Willoughby – a chance to restore a sense of professional pride and stability that had been missing in the badly demoralised newscaff division since the loss of Peter Meakin three years earlier. What appeared to be such a promising development for the network, however, was not necessarily seen in that light by Alexander. Even before Sam Chisholm's departure, there could be little doubt that Mark Llewellyn was living on borrowed time.

CHAPTER 12

Licence to smear

In the heyday of Australia's powerful press barons, a senior journalist could find himself suddenly called into his proprietor's office to be told in no uncertain terms: *This bastard's causing us trouble – I want you to get everything you can on him so we can nail him to the wall!* When it came to protecting his company's vested interests no one was more adept at playing the spite card than the *Sydney Morning Herald*'s Rupert 'Rags' Henderson; and he wasn't even related to the ruling Fairfax dynasty. Instead he had started off as an enterprising young cadet who had worked his way up to managing director, from there going on to assume a position of such influence that at times he appeared to wield more authority than Sir Warwick Fairfax himself. 'Rags' didn't hesitate to use the columns of the Fairfax press to assist him in his battles with competing dynasties like the Packers, Nortons or Murdochs. In one notorious episode in 1956, he became particularly annoyed when a gossip columnist for Sir Frank Packer's *Sunday Telegraph* had a sarcastic dig at the *SMH* for publishing articles written by a visiting British playboy of dubious repute. Egged on by Rags, the *Herald*'s usually sedate Granny column soon hit back with a most unladylike response, accusing the Packer paper of 'a false, malicious and grossly dishonest [story] . . . written by people who do not hesitate to resort to threats of blackmail and to libel and to gross dishonesty'.

The next morning the *Telegraph* retaliated with an open letter from Sir Frank Packer to Warwick Fairfax declaring the Granny item to be a gross defamation and denouncing the 'COWARDS and LIARS' at the *SMH* responsible for perpetrating such an outrage.

Such a bizarre, tit-for-tat exchange was all too common in the world of print journalism, where there were virtually no restrictions on a publisher's right to be as biased as he liked in pursuit of his own financial interests. For better or worse, that remains a basic tenet of the democratic tradition: anyone willing and able to spend the money is free to print and distribute his particular views, no matter how one-eyed or offensive, subject only to the standard laws regarding indecency, racial vilification and so on.

When it comes to the electronic media, however, the number of frequencies that can be used for radio or TV broadcasts is severely limited. Governments quite properly reserve the right to issue licences for use of the airwaves within their jurisdiction and in so doing, they set forth certain 'community standards' that the applicant for a licence must meet in order to maintain his right to broadcast. In the licence hearings that preceded the introduction of television in 1956, transcripts are filled with sanctimonious testimony as to how the applicants hoped to serve up a steady diet of religious, artistic and other uplifting programs fit for a nation of saints and scholars. No one took such pretensions seriously, of course, but the one pledge that remained open to enforcement – as verified by the Soap Powder Inquiry referred to earlier in this book – was the duty to keep viewers properly informed with news of genuine public interest, undistorted by self-serving biases. Television stations not only paid a sizeable fee for their licences, they had the added responsibility of guaranteeing impartial and accurate reporting of any issue or event that could be seen as having significant impact on the community as a whole. If the corporation that controlled the TV station happened to get into trouble with stock exchange regulators, that fact was to be reported as comprehensively and scrupulously as any other. At the same time, if the owners hoped to build a new shopping mall in a controversial location, they would clearly be failing in their responsibilities by planting slanted news items favourable to their cause. The Soap Powder Inquiry was so important because it raised the very real possibility of a TV channel losing its licence for suppressing the news. Surely, then, the same threat was there for any licence holder who misused his company's television news and current affairs programs to obtain some secret benefit. It's within this context that we now examine a modern-day re-enactment of the scene depicted at the beginning of this chapter: a senior journalist called into his boss's office to be told, in effect: *We want you to get this guy.*

'On the evening of 9 January 2006 I received a telephone call from Mr John Alexander, the CEO and Managing Director of PBL. This was the first telephone call I had received from Mr Alexander since my appointment to the position [of Director of News and Current Affairs] on 17 November 2005.' So began Mark Llewellyn's sworn account of a worrying encounter he had with Alexander soon after assuming control of the Nine Network's formidable array of newscaff programs. He goes on:

In the course of the conversation Mr Alexander discussed a report that had appeared that evening on Channel 7's *Today Tonight* program which was critical of Mr James Packer. In the course of that conversation Mr Alexander said to me: 'Did you see *Today Tonight* and their report on James Packer?' I said: 'I saw the start of it.' Mr Alexander interrupted and said: 'The story is a piece of shit. It's about time we fought back.'

'It was a very brief conversation,' Llewellyn continues, 'at the end of which Mr Alexander said to me: "Just let me again say congratulations Mark on your appointment as head of news and current affairs at Channel 9. I think it would be a good idea for us to catch up. Are you free to meet this Wednesday?"'

Llewellyn's version of this exchange might seem surprisingly detailed – much more specific about the exact words used than most of us would be able to remember, thinking back to an unexpected phone call. As it turns out, on that Monday evening when Alexander contacted him on his mobile, Llewellyn was having a drink at the Coogee Palace with a small circle of friends that happened to include his solicitor, John Laxon. After he hung up, one of the friends told him that he looked upset. 'You've gone white,' he commented. Llewellyn noted that it was the first time the PBL chief had contacted him since his appointment and he had an uneasy feeling that he was going to be asked 'to do something that I don't want to do'. The friend remembers Laxon then advising Llewellyn along these lines: *If there's anything you don't feel comfortable with in a conversation like that it's important that you make a careful and accurate file note of what's said. You'll protect your own position if you do that.*

Llewellyn made sure to follow that advice, keeping a meticulous record of that night's conversation, as well as all subsequent discussions with Alexander. He would later include such file notes in a sworn affidavit, meaning that he was prepared to stand by his version of events, at risk of being prosecuted for perjury if any part of it was found to be untrue. Alexander has never challenged the accuracy of the Llewellyn affidavit, so even if there is a quibble over a word or two, it's reasonable to assume that the journalist's recollection of what followed next can be trusted as a reliable account.

At 9.30 am on Wednesday, 11 January 2006 I met with Mr Alexander in his Park Street office. We had an initial, general conversation about my plans for News and Current Affairs at Nine and then, after about 20 minutes, Mr Alexander turned the conversation to the story that appeared on Channel 7's *Today Tonight* which had been critical of James Packer.

A conversation then occurred as follows:

'What's your opinion on *Today Tonight*'s story on James Packer?' Alexander asked.

'Oh, I think it was a snide and cheap piece of journalism,' Llewellyn replied.

'What are you going to do about it?'

Llewellyn describes himself as being somewhat taken aback by the question. It's easy to see why because, on the surface at least, the *Today Tonight* report appeared to be so totally lacking in substance that it would be hard to find any reason for bothering to respond. It boiled down to a quick rehash of a well-worn tale: James's involvement with two pals, Lachlan Murdoch and Jodee Rich, in the failed telecommunications venture One.Tel. In keeping with the typical cheekiness of nightly current affairs, the program dwelled on the theme of three spoiled 'rich kids' born of wealthy parents – which would have made for an enticing promotion considering James had only recently come to inherit his father's billions. The commentary was certainly sarcastic, suggesting James may 'never rise above being a rich kid unable to grow out of his silver spoon'. However, as the new leader of the Packer dynasty, James could hardly expect to be immune from critical comment and there seemed little Channel 9 could do to prevent other networks cashing in on his notoriety. Still, as much as the newscaff chief was surprised by Alexander's question, he also would have spotted an opportunity to obtain a highly watchable exclusive for a show like *60 Minutes*.

'I think we should do a television profile on James Packer, given the genuine news interest in him now,' he suggested.

'Ah, that's just nonsense,' Alexander rebuffed him. 'That would look like a puff piece. If anybody was going to interview James Packer it should probably be on another network.'

'No, I don't agree,' Llewellyn persisted. 'I think the interview should be on Channel 9. If done properly a *60 Minutes* profile and interview with James Packer would be tough and fair. There's no point in making it a puff piece. As I said, there is a genuine news interest in James Packer after Kerry's death.'

Up to this stage in the conversation, John Alexander hadn't said anything that might be construed as a clear instruction to proceed on a certain course of action. Though he was the managing director of a major public company, he also happened to be a highly experienced newsman in his own right. His interest in discussing the *Today Tonight* profile on James could easily be explained as wanting to sound out Llewellyn in general terms on how he felt about retaliating against any competing network that decided to take a shot at Nine. As it turned out, Alexander had a more specific plan in mind – one that appeared to have little to do with the best interests of Channel 9, or even the interests of the audiences Nine was committed to serve under the terms of its broadcasting licence.

'Channel 9 is part of PBL,' Alexander confronted him. 'That

Today Tonight story was a direct attack on PBL interests and we should respond in kind with an attack on Stokes.' Kerry Stokes, of course, was the controlling shareholder in Seven. From what follows, one gets the impression that Llewellyn felt the need to frame his reply most carefully. He was, after all, being urged to use his network's current affairs assets to carry out what was known in the trade as a 'hatchet job' – purposely setting out to impugn the reputation of a prominent business rival for the dubious purpose of advancing the broader interests of PBL, the gaming, media and entertainment conglomerate.

'I am concerned,' Llewellyn began, 'that such a tit-for-tat attack response might be counterproductive. Aren't you concerned that's how it would be perceived?'

Alexander was not to be dissuaded. 'Nine has failed to go on the front foot previously with Seven and I am sick of that!'

Mark Llewellyn was certainly not averse to engaging in aggressive, hard-hitting journalism. At *ACA* he had proved his talents as an investigative reporter by tracking down and confronting the fugitive businessman Christopher Skase in Majorca. As a *60 Minutes* producer he was known for his relentless pursuit of high-profile drug cheats, porn peddlers and other elusive villains, both within Australia and internationally. To undertake such difficult and time-consuming exposés, however, there had to be at least some trace of suspicion credible enough to justify mounting an inquiry.

'If you or others have hard evidence of illegal or unethical conduct by Kerry Stokes, then of course that would be in the public interest to broadcast that in a story,' Llewellyn responded. 'But in the absence of any such evidence I do not want to run such a story and I do not believe it is journalistically appropriate to do so.'

Based on the printed word alone the conversation obviously bristled with underlying tension, but at this point, according to

Llewellyn's sworn file notes, Alexander raised his voice, suggesting he was getting more than a little annoyed at the Channel 9 executive's reluctance to do what he was being asked to do. 'The *Today Tonight* piece wasn't journalism,' he protested. 'What about a lot of stories on *A Current Affair* – they're not journalism!'

Here, then, was the head of PBL pressuring his network's newscaff chief to not only produce a story purely in the interests of PBL but a story patched together in a way that needn't necessarily meet the rigorous standards of fairness and accuracy expected of a professional journalist. Llewellyn, for his part, did not dispute that some of *ACA*'s shoddier efforts occasionally failed to meet such standards.

'If that is the case with *A Current Affair*, then that has to change,' he agreed. 'My view, John, in short, is that stories must be based on ethical journalistic principles.'

'Well, what are you going to do about this?' Alexander challenged. Llewellyn once again assured him that he would be willing to investigate any credible evidence of Kerry Stokes being involved in illegal conduct. At that point, Alexander went a step further, naming a specific Channel 9 journalist he thought would be well suited to the task of mounting the kind of 'attack' on Stokes that he was demanding. It was the same former newspaper colleague of Alexander who had so suddenly and unexpectedly been appointed executive producer of *Sunday* in 2003 despite his demonstrable lack of knowledge of the visual medium.

'There are plenty of journalists at Channel 9 who could do this, John Lyons among them,' Alexander insisted. 'Such a story should be put on *A Current Affair* or *Sunday*.'

Llewellyn simply repeated the question that had been his defence all along. 'Well, again, do you have some evidence that I don't know about that Mr Stokes is involved in something illegal or unethical?' John Alexander, whatever his other attributes, was known as a consummate networker, with useful contacts throughout the worlds of finance, politics and journalism. If there was the slightest whisper about some alleged misdeed by Kerry Stokes, he should have been among the first to hear about it; yet his reply, as quoted by Llewellyn, was not exactly a lot for an investigative reporter to go on.

'Stokes is a terrible man,' Alexander opined, 'and a terrible businessman. Everyone who has come into contact with him knows that he is an appalling human being.' On the Richter scale of wild, unsubstantiated assertions, that could have covered any or all of the seven deadly sins.

'I left this meeting feeling extremely uncomfortable about my conversation with Mr Alexander,' is the way Llewellyn sums up this part of his sworn affidavit.

> I formed the view that it was a deliberate attempt by him to interfere editorially with my position. I saw Mr Alexander's approach as being in stark contrast to how the late Mr Kerry Packer had in my experience approached editorial inde-pendence. In my experience working in News and Current Affairs in Channel 9 for many years, Mr Kerry Packer had gone to great lengths to support the editorial independence of News and Current Affairs at Nine.

As a former executive producer at Nine, I think it's important to add this qualification to Llewellyn's comments comparing Alexander to Kerry Packer in their attitudes towards editorial independence. Kerry was always full of advice about stories that needed to be told to 'make people wake up to themselves' or were 'bullshit' and should never have been shown. Some of those suggestions may well have coincided with Packer's own private interests in the sense of *what's good for business is good for Australia*; but it was impossible to tell because he never put them in such crude terms. Any producer subjected to Kerry's endless lectures on various pet topics had to have the strength and confidence to escape falling into the trap of self-censorship, either consciously avoiding stories bound to annoy him – or worse, choosing to do a story merely in the hope of pleasing him.

That being said, there could be no better testament to Kerry's intrinsic belief in editorial freedom than his hands-off attitude towards Channel 9 during the worst crisis of his life: the terrible days of the Goanna scandal, growing out of the Costigan Royal Commission. What many didn't realise at the time – and don't to this day – is that the episode came dangerously close to costing Packer his television licences in Sydney and Melbourne. When the Australian Broadcasting Tribunal opened its periodic renewal hearings in 1985, ABT investigators sought access to Costigan's secret files to determine if Packer was a 'fit and proper person' to hold such licences, as then required by the Broadcasting Act. (Subsequently, the Act's wording was changed to 'suitable'.) Here he was: publicly linked to large-scale tax evasion, drug smuggling, and even the death of a Queensland bank manager whose suicide was depicted as murder to stop him testifying against some of Kerry's supposedly shadowy associates. A criminal conviction might not automatically disqualify him, but then again, any grounds for serious suspicion about his character could be enough to do so. 'Without the quality of trustworthiness a person cannot be a fit and proper person to hold a licence,' the ABT ruled. Throughout this period the pressures on Packer personally and his media interests in general were enormous. Yet never once did he approach me, as executive producer of his network's most widely watched and influential current affairs program, to suggest doing a story critical of the Costigan investigators or otherwise pushing some point he wanted to make. In fact, in the midst of this great scandal, I assigned a producer and research team at *60 Minutes* to launch our own investigation into the allegedly suspicious death of bank manager Ian Coote. Needless to say it was a very tense time for us, with our boss accused of such grave misdeeds. This is how I summed up our situation in *Compulsive Viewing*.

> For the scores of us who worked within the Packer organisation during the Goanna revelations, this was a time of anxious soul-searching. Did we believe our boss could be capable of such evil doings? Would we be prepared to chase a follow-up to the Ian Coote case with even the faintest chance that it could lead back to our proprietor? I considered myself as loyal as anyone could possibly be to Kerry yet no one is above the law. If Packer had really done the criminal deeds attributed to him by Costigan then he sacrificed any claim to loyalty. I allowed my *60 Minutes* staff to go ahead with the follow-up inquiries they would make for any such breaking news story – not eagerly, I must admit, and not without the odd nervous twitch gripping my guts in the middle of the night.

Fortunately, the Federal Government itself would soon intervene in this travesty of justice, declaring its confidence in Packer's absolute innocence. By then, however, Kerry Packer's personal attitude on the issue of editorial independence had been established for all of us to see and cherish. Even in this darkest of hours for the Packer empire, Kerry did nothing to violate the sanctity of the Nine Network's news and current affairs.

Kerry Packer's Goanna 'crisis' versus James Packer's *Today Tonight* 'crisis'. The comparison does much to put the Alexander–Llewellyn confrontation in its true perspective. Could a pathetic little current affairs segment poking fun at James Packer really be deemed to be so threatening to the best interests of PBL as to warrant endangering the Nine Network's hard-won reputation for journalistic integrity? Indeed, was it worth risking the loss of a television licence, because that certainly was a very real possibility if Mark Llewellyn had caved in to the pressure being put on him by Alexander and assigned *Sunday*'s John Lyons to do a story aimed at smearing the reputation of Kerry Stokes. In any subsequent defamation action brought by Stokes, his lawyers would surely call Llewellyn to the stand to testify as to whether there was evidence of malicious intent behind the *Sunday* report. And of course, there was, plenty of it, because the object of the exercise was never to produce an objective and balanced profile of Stokes, good points as well as bad; it was to be – in Alexander's quoted words – an 'attack' on a 'terrible' and 'appalling' human being. In telling the truth, as Llewellyn would have been obliged to do, he could well have set in motion a formal investigation by the Australian Communications and Media Authority, successor to the ABT. Was PBL, as a corporate entity, a 'suitable' organisation to control a TV licence if it misused its news-gathering assets in such a blatant way?

The scenario I've drawn about the case ending up in a sensational libel suit is hardly an implausible one. James Packer himself subsequently initiated a defamation suit (since settled) against *Today Tonight* – which is exactly the way the matter should be dealt with if someone feels their reputation has been unfairly damaged. I have heard accounts of James, at various private functions, expressing his 'anger and frustration' at the failure of Channel 9 journalists to show any sense of loyalty to the broader interests of PBL. Such anecdotes, while seemingly credible, still boil down to mere hearsay. One insider's view that deserves to be taken seriously, however, speaks of the PBL hierarchy – post-Kerry – as being influenced by a 'newspaper mentality', claiming much the same right to impose editorial control over Channel 9 as a press lord like Rupert Murdoch is able to exert over his front pages. 'What they forget,' this insider tells me, 'is that if people don't like what they're reading in a newspaper, they turn the page. If they don't like what they're seeing on television, they change channels.'

At the very least then, the episode stands as further testament to the apparent inability of the Alexandrian regime at Park Street to understand the basic differences between print and TV journalism. The law simply doesn't permit the power of television to be used with the self-interested bias of a Rags Henderson striking back at one of his old newspaper foes. John Alexander's attempt to plant a story unfavourable to Kerry Stokes, as portrayed in the Llewellyn affidavit, could be summed up in a lot of different ways: inappropriate, ill-advised, impetuous. None of them come close to describing the true nature of his attempted intervention: so short-sighted and so very, very petty.

J.A. would at least try to end the tense conversation on a lighter note, albeit with a sting in the tail.

'Well, I wanted to congratulate you again on getting the job,' the PBL boss concluded, adding, 'I remind you that the financial markets will demand an improvement at Nine and you will be judged on this by the middle of the year.'

Mark Llewellyn, as it turned out, wouldn't quite make it to the middle of the year.

CHAPTER 13

Sunday blues, part I

N o program has more to tell us about the internal strife at Channel 9 than *Sunday*, once a breeding ground for gifted personalities like Jennifer Byrne and Andrew Olle, transformed into a Bermuda Triangle where distinguished careers can mysteriously sink overnight without warning or explanation. In a period of less than three years the once critically acclaimed show was to lose its most successful investigative reporter, Graham Davis, two top-ranking producers, Stephen Rice and Peter Hiscock, and a number of other highly valued behind-the-scenes personnel. *Sunday* would figure in the downfall of newscaff chief Mark Llewellyn and feature prominently in Sam Chisholm's less than amicable departure from the PBL board. Ultimately, the program's classy anchor, Jana Wendt, would prove to be the most high-profile victim of all, her character and professionalism smeared by a series of malicious leaks to the press while network executives plotted behind her back to introduce a new two-host 'happy chat' format that left her totally out of the equation despite having more than two years to go on her contract. Why would she want to stay there anyway considering the changes envisaged for the show? Segments dealing with weightier subjects were out. Sports commentary would begin to play an increasingly important role. Who could ever imagine Jana Wendt discussing the fortunes of a footy team like the Magpies or the Rabbitohs? An even more pertinent question, of course, was who could imagine *anyone* discussing the Magpies or the Rabbitohs in a program renowned for its commitment to more thought-provoking fare?

Since its inception in 1981 *Sunday* had established itself as a welcome sanctuary within the commercial TV landscape – a place of leisurely contemplation and enlightenment far removed from the crassness and hype of most mass audience programming. Its two-hour format offered a stimulating potpourri of news, political interviews and commentary, expertly crafted feature stories, in-depth investigations, movie reviews and an occasional sampling of the performing arts. No other commercial network would have ever dared to attempt a program like it, considering the limited audience for such cerebral content; and the ABC could never have afforded the cost of such a quality production even in prime time, let alone at the unlikely hour of 9 am. The program was there only because Kerry ordained it to be so, perhaps encouraged by Bruce Gyngell's dictum that broadcasting was all about appealing to 'a myriad of minorities', bringing together as many different segments of the audience as possible. The show went on to build a surprisingly large following for that time of the morning, and for much of its life even managed to rake in a modest profit from advertisers keen to reach an elite section of wealthier, better educated viewers.

For the regime settling into power after Kerry's death, however, prestige held far less interest than the practicalities of running a successful business in the toughest of economic climates. *Sunday* would prove to be a hotly contested battleground between the old philosophy – *whatever you do, make it the best you can* – and the new – *whatever you do, make sure it pays its way*. That might sound glib but it was simply a corollary to what James Packer and John Alexander had told David Gyngell just before his resignation: *profits before ratings*. Once profits are judged to be more important than ratings, it automatically follows that profits are more important than production quality as well: the less spent on achieving each rating point the better. In an era marked by a declining pool of viewers, it was simply deemed bad business to continue putting so much money and effort into a program catering to minority tastes, the fine arts in particular, since they often required more costly, time-consuming taping sessions. In any case, what were your two hosts supposed to chat about after seeing a report about an illustrious ballet company newly arrived from Moscow? 'Wow, Ross, that was some pas de deux, wouldn't you say?' 'Yes, Ellen. How do you think you'd go in one of those tutus?' Still, it would be some months before Jana Wendt gave way to the new team of Ellen Fanning and Ross Greenwood. The first leaks about her imminent demise didn't appear until July 2006, well after Sam Chisholm's departure. The seeds, though, had been planted much earlier, during a simmering feud with her newly installed executive producer.

At first glance, John Lyons would appear to be the perfect role model for all that John Alexander hoped to achieve in his reorganisation of the Nine Network. He was a hard-nosed print journalist recruited to *Sunday* from the *Bulletin* in mid-2000 because of his formidable reputation as an investigative reporter. Lyons let it be known from the start that he had nothing but contempt for the trumped-up mystique surrounding the visual medium – the technical jargon that TV professionals too often used to hide their self-indulgence and inefficiency. Indeed, he showed such little interest in adapting himself to the traditional rules for TV scripting and editing that a freelance producer was brought in as a special mentor to try to encourage him to learn at least a few basic principles of concise, attention-grabbing current affairs reportage. In compiling one of his reports, Lyons showed the producer a slab of commentary he had written containing 714 words. At a speaking rate of three words a second, that would have taken him almost four minutes to get through, a veritable Shakespearean soliloquy in TV terms, producing an absurdly long break in the pace of the action. The new recruit was less than pleased when told viewers wanted to be shown what was happening, not lectured to. 'Well what do you want me to do with it?' he demanded. 'Send it to the fucking *Herald*,' his mentor replied.

Still, that same John Lyons would go on to win a coveted Walkley award for Broadcast Interviewing in 2001 after being in television for little more than a year. In John Alexander's mind, as in Lyons's, there could be no sweeter proof that television was so much smoke and mirrors: all style and no substance. A disciplined print journalist had the news judgement to overshadow his TV counterpart any day. All he really needed to adapt to the small screen was a mere technician or two to help tidy up his reports.

The irony of the situation was that Alexander himself wasn't involved in hiring Lyons to work for Nine. He was recruited by newscaff head Peter Meakin and *Sunday*'s veteran executive producer Stephen Rice because they felt the program could use some meatier reporting. When Alexander took control of the network, though, he was swift to embrace Lyons as a key ally in helping to identify and clean out the station's deadwood. Lyons himself had been a senior editor at the *Sydney Morning Herald* during Alexander's time there and the two had enjoyed a long and amicable relationship. Meakin's departure cleared the way for

Alexander to make sure that his former colleague enjoyed rapid promotion to a position of influence within the network. In October, 2003, he organised Lyons's appointment as executive producer of *Sunday*, replacing the much-admired Rice, who had guided the program's fortunes for close to a decade. The move came as a shock to the great majority of the staff – a relative newcomer to TV put in charge of a show that prided itself on the grace and elegance of its scripting, camerawork and editing.

To appreciate their alarm, it's important to understand the pivotal role of an executive producer in ensuring the success of a current affairs program. His responsibilities go much further than assigning the stories to be covered each week. He is expected to know as much about every facet of the operation as a conductor knows about his orchestra. Like a conductor, he may not be able to play each instrument but he fully understands what each is capable of delivering – enough to coax and cajole the individual musicians into making beautiful music together. A conscientious EP can spend hours each week in the editing suites viewing the rough cuts, offering suggestions on how to improve the pacing and visual appeal of a segment or add a bit of explanation here and there for greater impact. He has the further logistical problem of juggling his journalists, camera crews and tape editors in such a way as to guarantee a smooth flow of stories into the system, avoiding backlogs where a field producer might have to wait for days to get near an editing suite. Like a good coach he must develop a close enough relationship with his staff members to encourage them along, while being quick to step in and mediate when conflicts arise, as they inevitably will – for example, a reporter blaming his camera team for dragging their feet or the crew protesting that they are being driven too hard.

It's certainly not all that difficult for a newspaper journalist to learn to cope with such intricate problems. In 1967 I joined the ABC's *This Day Tonight* as a reporter after ten years in print and adjusted to the new medium well enough to become a supervising producer within two years. My colleague, Peter Luck, also a newspaperman, did me one better, absorbing so much knowledge about filmmaking that he was soon creating well-crafted little movies to help illustrate his on-air reports. *Sunday* itself could boast outstanding success in converting any number of respected print journalists into celebrated on-air commentators or reporters, the late Robert Haupt being a notable example. However, the first step in learning about the special skills of TV journalism is *wanting* to learn. A complaint that comes through time and time again among the *Sunday* staff is that their new executive producer not only lacked any instinct for the visual medium, but showed no inclination to find out more about it. From his standpoint, why should he bother? Even his chief patron, John Alexander, agreed that much of what went on at Channel 9 was basically a giant con – a refuge for the mediocre and complacent seeking to use their supposed mastery of the medium to extort huge salaries for as little effort as possible.

It was easy enough, then, to understand why most of the *Sunday* staff should begin to develop a him-or-us mentality. According to Lyons's critics, they could see the program disintegrating under his control week by week in countless little ways, from sloppily restructured reports that never should have gone to air to a distinct falling-off in the arts and culture content that had made the program so unique. Lyons also came badly unstuck in trying to co-ordinate the complex elements of a television shoot so that cover stories too often missed their deadlines and rundowns had to be hurriedly reorganised at the last minute, not a good look for a leisurely-paced format. Lyons could hardly be unaware of such complaints by the TV professionals in his midst, so it's no wonder he should feel himself under siege and react accordingly. He sought out a few supportive staff members to treat as favourites, while plotting ways to rid himself of those on the program he identified as the more militant among his adversaries. Some days he simply locked himself behind his office door and refused to speak to anyone.

Networks, of course, have a perfect right to change formats any way they see fit to attract the kind of audiences they seek. That being said, those with the task of presenting and producing a program would at least like the comfort of knowing that the person appointed to lead them has a clear vision of what he hopes to accomplish and a good idea of how to achieve it. Without that, all trust is lost and disillusioned staff members are left with the choice of either opting out or defiantly making a stand in defence of a program they've come to love and believe in.

As the face of *Sunday* Jana Wendt found herself in a particularly invidious position, watching her program's standards steadily unravelling, yet with her executive producer apparently unable or unwilling to grasp that there was anything amiss. Wendt was hardly one of those presenters who shows up to read an auto-cue and collect her monthly pay without concern for the milieu in which she operates. Through her career she had been a meticulous professional, alert to every nuance in the studio lighting, every mistimed cue or clumsy wording in an introduction, but particularly sensitive to the quality of the segments she presented. If that made her 'difficult' in the eyes of some network executives she was prepared to wear the tag. She was never shy about speaking her mind to any of her executive producers and in most such cases the air could be quickly cleared with a good, healthy shouting match. Lyons, though, resented her criticisms and tended to retreat from any direct confrontation, leading to a kind of Cold War marked by long, icy silences or at most, a puff or two of frosty breath at times when they had no choice but to communicate.

Dissatisfied members of the *Sunday* team naturally looked to Wendt as the only one with enough clout to appeal to a higher authority over Lyons's perceived mishandling of the show. For many months, however, there was no one she could really go to in hopes of seeking reform. While John Alexander had personally wooed her back to Nine, he could hardly be expected to be sympathetic to her complaints against the EP he himself had put in place. The short-lived newscaff chief, Jim Rudder, was generally seen by those around him as lacking in decisiveness and hesitant to intervene in such conflicts. Though David Gyngell assumed the role of acting newscaff head after Rudder's departure, he had far too much on his plate to sort out *Sunday*'s squabbles. The truth was, he was not that big a fan of Jana in the first place, viewing her as overly demanding.

It was not until Sam Chisholm came on the scene, in May, 2005, that Wendt finally gained access to a sympathetic ear. Since *60 Minutes* days he had considered her to be one of the network's most valuable assets – a personality who summed up all that Channel 9 stood for in terms of polished performance. Whatever Jana told the newly arrived CEO about *Sunday*'s troubles would have carried significant weight but it wasn't long before Lyons found his own way to get Chisholm off side. The executive producer went to Sam's office one day to announce that he had just sacked Graham Davis as a result of a row in which the reporter had told him he was 'a fuckwit'. Davis was notorious for his short fuse but he also happened to be one of Australia's most respected TV journalists, the driving force behind many of *Sunday*'s hardest-hitting reports, including an acclaimed exposé of commercial infiltration within the ABC. 'You can't fire Graham Davis,' Chisholm told him succinctly. 'He doesn't work for you, he works for me.' Lyons attempted to raise a protest, pointing out that as a former *SMH* editor he had ample experience in hiring and firing. 'That doesn't give you some rite of passage here,' Chisholm persisted. 'Mr Davis is not an easy person to handle in the best of times, but in my view he's a very decent reporter. You have to go down and sort out your problems with him because that's what an executive producer is expected to do – establish a good working relationship with his talent.'

Chisholm, of course, was well aware of John Alexander's strong support for Lyons – there was no other way to explain why, with so little experience, he should be put in charge of a two-hour current affairs program. By the end of the 2005 ratings season, though, Sam had come to the conclusion that the show was on the verge of imploding if Lyons wasn't removed. In December, several weeks after he first took Mark Llewellyn to see Kerry Packer, the three men held another meeting to discuss a number of newscaff matters, including Chisholm's wish to bring Jessica Rowe over to Nine to co-host the *Today* show. Kerry gave his enthusiastic approval, describing the Ten newsreader as 'intelligent, likeable and bubbly'. When Sam raised another issue, however, Packer's reaction was more subdued, no doubt because he realised the possible repercussions when Alexander got wind of it. 'I'm thinking of removing John Lyons as EP of *Sunday*,' Chisholm ventured. 'He's not a protected species,' Kerry curtly replied. That was all that was needed for a swift execution but Chisholm decided on a course of action he would soon regret, delaying Lyons's dismissal until after the holiday period to save him and his family from having to cope with such bad news just before Christmas. Kerry's death that Boxing Day effectively changed the entire balance of power, but by then Sam was as fixed in his intentions as a guided missile and couldn't care less about the risk of Lyons's dismissal blowing up in his face.

On Wednesday, 18 January, 2006, newscaff chief Mark Llewellyn called the executive producer of *Sunday* to a special meeting. Also present was the Nine Network's chief operating officer, Ian Audsley. Quite clearly, this was not to be some informal chat. 'Prior to calling this meeting,' Llewellyn would later explain in his affidavit, 'I had had a discussion with

Mr Sam Chisholm, following complaints that had been made to me and to Mr Chisholm about Mr Lyons by various of the *Sunday* personnel.' There was no doubt in either of their minds that Lyons had effectively lost control of the program, not just in terms of its rock-bottom morale but, even more disturbing, in the show's ability to keep up with the basic essentials of week-to-week coverage. *Sunday* staff had returned from the summer break to find the place in an organisational mess. Instead of scheduling leave so that all his journalists were back in time to start preparing reports for the new season – the common-sense method followed by *60 Minutes* as well – Lyons had two reporters still away on holiday, leaving the program desperately short-handed. Similar poor planning affected the available camera teams. There was a very real possibility *Sunday* would begin 2006 in a frantic scramble to produce a reliable bank of cover stories. A nightly current affairs show might be able to recover from such mismanagement by rushing a flood of substandard stories to air but clearly those kinds of stopgap measures were unacceptable for the most prestigious newscaff show in the network's line-up.

The program's woes were compounded by a recently imposed cost-saving ban on the hiring of freelance personnel who might otherwise have been called in to help produce more stories. According to Llewellyn's account, Lyons was caught out trying to hire such people surreptitiously, taking creative licence with his administrative guidelines. One might assume that was a minor indiscretion compared to the havoc he was wreaking in production standards; yet in an era of complex industrial rules and regulations, it would be his managerial deficiencies rather than his lack of professional expertise that would be used to justify his sacking.

Before Wednesday's meeting Llewellyn and Audsley had consulted with Nine's legal advisers on how best to handle the delicate process of relieving an executive producer of his command. Llewellyn had nothing against Lyons personally. He fully appreciated his skills as an accomplished newspaper journalist and raised the possibility of trying to find him another position back at the PBL-owned *Bulletin*, to avoid the stigma of an outright dismissal. If that wasn't possible he hoped to at least soothe Lyons's feelings with the offer of a reasonable payout. The lawyer's advice, however, was that to reduce the possibility of expensive litigation, the meeting needed to be conducted strictly by the book, reading out a formal list of reasons to support a dismissal on grounds of due cause. Talk of a suitable payout could then come later.

Firing someone is never an easy task but in recent times it has tended to become an almost robotic ritual – the boss making sure to tick every box according to the relevant workplace legislation as he runs through a lengthy indictment prepared by the company lawyers. That's what Llewellyn proceeded to do: go through the EP's alleged administrative breaches one by one, though it was a process so very alien to his nature. He would have much preferred the more human approach of days gone by, sitting down over a drink at the pub to tell his colleague: 'So, John, I think we both know this isn't working out, and it's time you move back to the kind of things you do best.' Instead, we get a taste of the formality of the occasion in this concise summary, as it appears in his affidavit. 'In the course of my meeting with Messrs Lyons and Audsley, I advised Mr Lyons that I was removing him as executive producer of the *Sunday* show.' That fateful confrontation, as it happened, commenced at 12.45 pm – high noon in the incredible saga of the death and resurrection of John Lyons.

Llewellyn's first move after the meeting was to assemble the *Sunday* staff to tell them that Lyons was gone. His announcement was greeted with a spontaneous round of applause. With that totally unexpected ovation still echoing in his ears, however, he was about to receive a most unpleasant phone call. About an hour after Lyons's dismissal, John Alexander rang up.

'Why has John Lyons been removed from *Sunday*?' he demanded, according to Llewellyn's affidavit.

'There have been a number of serious performance issues that have been drawn to my attention in the previous 24 hours,' the newscaff chief responded.

'Did Sam tell you to do this?' Alexander pressed him.

'No. The decision was mine and was based upon information brought to my attention in the previous 24 hours which, on top of my other concerns to do with John Lyons's poor management of *Sunday* and of staffing issues, forced me to take action.'

'I'm going to ask the question again and think very carefully before you answer. Did Sam make you do this?'

'As I said,' Llewellyn replied, 'the decision was mine. I did not take this decision lightly but I genuinely believe it is in the best interests of the show. While I respect John as a person and a journalist, I believe the issues were serious enough to warrant his dismissal.'

'You need to be very careful here, very careful,' Alexander warned. 'Think about your answers. Think very carefully about what you do and say because I tell you, Sam is not going to be around for long. I'm telling you that now. James likes him but Sam's time is over. You need to protect your own backside so be very careful about what you say to me.'

He then ended the conversation on this ominous note. 'I want you to provide me with a written explanation of those matters which you say have come to light in the past 24 hours so that I can review it.' The director of news and current affairs did as he was told, preparing a report relating to Lyons's bungle in having two reporters still on holiday at the start of a new ratings season. Llewellyn had just discovered that fact in the last day through a tip-off from within the *Sunday* camp and felt the EP had purposely tried to cover up his mistake: requesting urgent free-lance help on the grounds that all staff reporters were simply 'unavailable' due to other activities.

When Llewellyn later told Chisholm about his encounter with Alexander, the acting CEO could hardly believe his ears. 'I am horrified and appalled by what Alexander has said to you. You should make a note of this for your own protection,' he advised.

It was time, now, for Sam himself to get a taste of Alexander's displeasure, with the PBL chief phoning him the next morning, 19 January. Chisholm was well used to dealing with withering outbursts from powerful moguls like Kerry Packer and Rupert Murdoch. No matter how furious they got, they still managed to retain an air of authority, keeping full command of the situation. What was coming down the line from Park Street, however, was something he had never heard before in his entire business career – a voice fraught with such high emotion as to border on hysteria. As far as I've been able to reconstruct it, their confrontation went along these rather bizarre lines, with Alexander arguing that the issue reached well beyond Lyons to threaten the stability of the Packer empire itself.

'James has just started his presidency,' he began.

'What the fuck has that got to do with it?' Chisholm shot back.

'This is all going to be too unsettling,' Alexander persisted. 'We just can't have it.'

As it unfolded, the case Alexander was trying to make would prove far different to the one he put to Peter Meakin three years earlier. Back then he had ordered the dismissal of Michael Pascoe, a popular and thoroughly proficient business reporter, for the vaguest of reasons – that *he's not taken seriously around the town.* Now, he was mounting a defence of John Lyons on the basis that he was a victim of wrongful dismissal – the elaborate procedure used to dismiss him was flawed because of a technical loophole. In accusing the EP of various instances of mismanagement,

Llewellyn had apparently overlooked an instance where he himself had reluctantly signed off on use of a freelancer, in the mistaken belief that all of *Sunday*'s staff reporters were fully occupied. It was an administrative oversight that didn't scratch the surface of Lyons's unsuitability as an executive producer but it was enough for Alexander's purposes.

To that point Alexander had mentioned nothing close to a directive, but Chisholm was too much of a pragmatist not to see where the conversation was headed. Of course, he could make a stand, even carry the matter to the PBL board; but what good could that possibly accomplish? As Alexander had told Llewellyn, Sam would soon enough be gone from Nine to make way for a permanent CEO. Once he stepped out the door there could be little doubt Alexander would rebound with a vengeance, 'making mincemeat' of Llewellyn and any others he suspected of conspiring to bring about Lyons's downfall. Meanwhile, Chisholm's longstanding loyalty to the Packers dictated that he should cut short this ugly confrontation as quickly and cleanly as possible. He knew what the gossip would be around the CBD next morning: 'Chisholm got into a joust with Alexander and Alexander won' – a humiliation to be sure but one that he was man enough to bear.

'Okay, what do you want me to do about it, John?' he broke in. 'Do you want me to reinstate him?'

'Yes,' was the relieved answer.

The sheer eagerness of that response grated in a way that made Chisholm bristle. He had no doubt that what he was being asked to do was to sacrifice the best interests of Channel 9 for whatever personal motives John Alexander might have in mind and it would have given him great delight to slam the phone down in his ear. But that impulse lasted only for a fleeting moment. 'Oh fuck it,' he said to himself and then went on to reassure the chief executive officer of PBL:

'Okay, done.'

As tough a nut as Chisholm was known to be, the next few hours would have been a real test of his mettle. First, he had to phone Llewellyn to break the news that Lyons would have to be reinstated. Then he made a similar call to Peter Hiscock, a highly regarded *Sunday* producer who was in line to take over as executive producer in Lyons's place. He arranged a hurried meeting with the two of them to discuss how Hiscock could continue to exert a controlling influence in the day-to-day operations at *Sunday*, even if Lyons nominally retained the title of EP. Before these talks commenced, Chisholm had also spoken to Lyons, ordering him to come up to the third floor and wait in an empty office until he was called into the discussion. 'I'm not reinstating you because you deserve it,' Sam informed him. 'I'm reinstating you because Alexander has asked me to do it. In my judgement that's the wrong thing to do, but you should know that's the only reason that you're being given another chance.'

Lyons would be kept waiting on his own for well over two hours, clearly part of a softening up process to make him agree to some sort of power-sharing arrangement with Hiscock. If he thought it was insulting to have to wait so long, he was about to find out what an insult really was. He was finally called into the conference to find Chisholm pacing around the room like an angry gorilla, pounding his fist into his open hand. He stepped up to Lyons virtually toe-to-toe to tell him what a 'fuckwit' he was, blasting him for his mishandling of the program, belittling him as someone totally lacking in the respect of his colleagues. All that, however, was merely the entree before the main serve. 'You're a fucking flea,' Chisholm sneered. 'You are fucking useless. Why don't you do yourself and all of us a favour and just fuck off!'

Even Llewellyn and Hiscock found themselves shifting uneasily in their seats to hear someone being subjected to such abuse. It was clear enough to them, though, that part of this routine was designed to make Lyons more amenable to accepting

Hiscock and another part of it, no doubt, was Sam releasing his pent-up fury over his humiliating back-down. At one stage Chisholm left the room to let the three journalists work out some practical formula for the power-sharing scheme. The idea was for Hiscock to be given the new title of 'Director', overseeing all story restructuring, rundowns and virtually anything else to do with the overall look of the program. He would also act as a kind of insulator, dealing directly with Jana Wendt and Graham Davis, the two personalities whom Lyons found the most difficult to deal with. None of these measures seemed to cause Lyons any concern and the three men looked to be getting along fine when Chisholm made a sudden reappearance, with the smoke almost coming out of his ears.

'I've just had a call from John Lehmann of the *Australian*,' he snarled, staring at Lyons accusingly, 'to ask me when I'm announcing the fact that I'm reinstating you. There's only the four of us here who would know anything about that. Have you been on the phone to John Lehmann telling him these things?' Without being asked, Lyons offered up his mobile phone as if to prove that he hadn't made any such phone calls. That didn't save him from another tongue-lashing but he simply let it wash over him, as he had all the other epithets hurled at him. Looking back over the entire ordeal, the one person in the room who reacted most calmly of all was John Lyons himself. Why should it be otherwise? He knew full well that from here on in, Sam Chisholm was a spent force, his power base shattered by the death of Kerry Packer. The newly reprieved executive producer could walk out of this room brushing Sam's spittle off his collar, assured that he had the protection and support of the only person who really mattered anymore: John Alexander.

Mark Llewellyn, on the other hand, was left to jot down this sombre entry in his file notes. 'I was concerned about John Alexander's behaviour in his telephone conversation with me. I felt a genuine fear that Mr Alexander would at some stage seek to undermine me in my role.' He had every reason to feel such concern considering events that Park Street would set in train less than two months later.

The *Australian*'s John Lehmann came out the next morning with an exclusive account of Lyons's return – the most noteworthy of all the leaks referred to in this book in the sense that the likely source could so easily be narrowed down to just two people. For that reason it's worth examining the report in some detail to identify the key words and phrases indicating who had most to gain by pushing such a line.

Nine Network owner James Packer and his lieutenant John Alexander have intervened to overturn the sacking of John Lyons, executive producer of the flagship *Sunday* program. Just 24 hours after Mr Lyons was axed, Nine Network boss Sam Chisholm reinstated him after talks involving Mr Packer and Mr Alexander, chief executive of the Nine owner Publishing & Broadcasting Ltd. Mr Lyons, a former *Sydney Morning Herald* editor-in-chief who has been producing *Sunday* for two years, was sacked from the role in a fiery meeting with Nine's newly appointed news and current affairs chief Mark Llewellyn. In a significant backdown, Mr Chisholm yesterday met with Mr Lyons and offered him his job back, surprising *Sunday* staffers who had already been told their new leader would be respected producer Peter Hiscock. The episode demonstrates that Mr Packer's executive team will exert greater influence at Nine following the death of his father, Kerry, on Boxing Day. It is understood Mr Chisholm wanted a more seasoned television producer at the helm of *Sunday*, a Kerry Packer favourite anchored by Jana Wendt. But Mr Llewellyn . . . botched the axing of Mr Lyons, who enjoys a reputation as a ferocious journalist. At the meeting, attended by Nine chief operating officer Ian Audsley, Mr Llewellyn read from a prepared script, criticising several decisions made by Mr Lyons. But Mr Lyons gained the upper hand by pointing out that Mr Llewellyn had signed off on some of the disputed decisions, including the recent hiring of a free-lance journalist despite budget cutbacks.

The mention of James Packer becoming personally involved in this dispute is especially intriguing since Sam Chisholm is adamant that he never spoke to James before agreeing to reinstate Lyons. It would certainly suit John Alexander's purposes, however, to see his fight to save Lyons publicly portrayed as having James's imprimatur. As for the revelations about the dismissal hearings, there could logically be only two people who had such inside information and reason to boast afterwards how Llewellyn 'botched the axing' – Lyons, who went through the ordeal, and Alexander, to whom he complained. While Lyons might appear to have the most to gain, it's difficult to believe he would dare give Lehmann such a sensitive story without seeking Alexander's approval. Nor was Lyons in a position to bandy about the name of James Packer. The only reasonable conclusion is that either Alexander alone or both men contributed to a leak that they knew would prove highly embarrassing to Sam Chisholm and Mark Llewellyn. The end result, of course, was bound to prove even more harmful to the already shaky public image of Channel 9. But perhaps that wasn't considered an issue worth worrying about. Llewellyn himself would later provide an inter-esting summation of the incident in his sworn affidavit.

'I was appalled by what I read in the article,' he wrote, 'as it was disparaging of my role in the whole affair and damaging to my reputation as well as to the reputation of Nine. I formed the view that the story had been leaked to the *Australian* by either

Mr Alexander or Mr Lyons. The reason for my view was that the only people with knowledge of what was said other than me were Ian Audsley and John Lyons. It was not in Mr Audley's interests to leak the story. I am aware that Mr Alexander is a friend of John Lyons.'

It was only Llewellyn's suspicion, of course, but contained within a well-publicised document and never denied.

Alexander, for his part, would have no trouble at all in defending his intervention to keep John Lyons at the helm of *Sunday*. Was he not a Walkley award-winning television reporter, testament to his mastery of the medium? He certainly was, but did he deserve to be? Therein lies quite a story.

CHAPTER 14

Sunday blues, part II

John Lyons's Walkley award-winning interview contains one of the worst examples of unfair reporting that I have seen in my 25 years in television. Appreciating the serious implications of that assessment, I am happy to offer Lyons his choice. If he intended to convey the wrongful impression that his report gave, then he is guilty at the very least of an egregious beat-up – making a sensational claim without the evidence to support it. If the error was unintentional, it demonstrates how utterly inexperienced he was in dealing with the highly sensitive tools of trade available to the television journalist.

His interview went to air on the edition of *Sunday* appearing on 11 March, 2001. It was part of a scathing analysis of the troubles besetting the NRMA at the time, in particular, political infighting that pitted the chairman of the board, Nicholas Whitlam, against a high-profile board member, Anne Keating. Their family connections – the son of a former prime minister, the sister of a former prime minister – made their well-publicised feud all the more intriguing. In the course of his story Lyons suggested that Whitlam treated the famous old motoring organisation and its insurance offshoot much like his personal fiefdom, rewarding those who supported him with jobs or other perks, punishing those who didn't by withdrawing patronage. Suspecting that Ms Keating had leaked unfavourable information about him to the press, Whitlam organised a special inquiry to look into the matter. It was in pursuit of this part of his report that Lyons came up with what must have seemed to the audience to be a truly startling revelation. This is what he told viewers in an introductory section of commentary.

> Lyons [commentary]: Tensions became war last year, after a series of newspaper articles which embarrassed Nicholas Whitlam by revealing his failed attempt to become Chief Executive. Whitlam was furious, and convinced the board that an internal investigation should be established. The board appointed Sydney QC Robert McDougall. Critics argued that McDougall was not independent, that he regularly earned other money from the NRMA, a fact that as late as this week, Mr Whitlam categorically denied.

> Whitlam: I know that was asserted by some people, but that is absolutely unfair and untrue and has no basis on any legal or proprietary basis that I am aware of. In fact, it is something that was asserted by someone that is simply – that is not fair.

Then followed another bit of Lyons commentary, making the bold assertion that Whitlam had been caught out in telling an untruth.

> Lyons [commentary]: But *Sunday* can reveal this morning that Mr Whitlam's statement is in fact false. A letter written by Robert McDougall himself admits only four weeks ago that [voice-over reading from letter]: 'I provided legal services to companies within the NRMA Group over the last 18 months.'

Lyons went on to cite more evidence of work McDougall had performed for the motoring organisation, as if to prove beyond doubt that Whitlam's answer to his question was a brazen attempt to evade the truth.

Whitlam would later claim to have been defamed by that section of the *Sunday* cover story as well as other parts. It's not my place to comment on the issue of defamation other than to note that it is very rare to hear any current affairs program publicly brand a prominent citizen as having told a falsehood – an allegation hardly meant to enhance his reputation. Normally, the reporter would limit himself to demonstrating point by point how the interviewee's response doesn't match the facts and let viewers make up their own minds. Lyons, as we'll see, gave the *Sunday* audience a most unwarranted interpretation of Whitlam's response. That will be easy enough to establish, but it's important, first, to understand the issues involved in ensuring ethical treatment of a TV interview.

In compiling a segment for a current affairs program of the standard of *Sunday* or *60 Minutes*, a reporter may conduct an interview lasting an hour or more to come up with five to ten minutes of material judged interesting and relevant enough to be put to air. That is a sizeable proportion to be consigned to the out-takes, especially if the interview involves allegations of wrongdoing in which an interviewee will naturally want to defend his position as thoroughly as possible. In order to justify such severe paring down of words, a television program accepts that it is bound by a duty of care to make sure the editing process leaves in the most important points that the interviewee seeks to make. The key word in this process, the sine qua non of ethical television journalism, is to always keep within the *context* of what someone is really trying to say. Here's just one hypothetical example of how a TV reporter is able to fiddle with a recorded question-and-answer exchange to give an impression that is clearly out of context. Let us assume this is the exchange as conducted in the uncut original.

Interviewer: You have shares in that company, don't you?
Interviewee: Well, a few, but they were bought years ago and I totally forgot about them.
Interviewer: Isn't there a conflict of interest?
Interviewee: No, none at all.

In the process of editing that videotaped sequence, it is possible, under the pretext of saving precious air time, to combine the first question with the second, in effect deleting the explanation beginning, 'Well, a few'. Viewers will then see an abbreviated exchange that casts the interviewee in the most unfavourable light, making him seem arrogant and uncaring about public opinion.

Interviewer: You have shares in that company, don't you? Isn't there a conflict of interest?
Interviewee: No, none at all.

Even worse, it is possible to reverse the order of the interviewer's first and second questions to give the impression the interviewee is telling an outright lie.

Interviewee: Isn't there a conflict of interest? You have shares in that company, don't you?
Interviewer: No, none at all.

That was roughly the technique used by John Lyons, framing a question that was in two distinct parts and then going on to give the impression that his interviewee's response was to one part of the question when it was really to the other part. In order to understand the context in which Whitlam was speaking, it's necessary to look at the line of questioning Lyons was pursuing in the raw, uncut interview just before his interviewee's allegedly spurious response. Up to that point, the reporter had been focusing on criticisms levelled at the QC chosen by the NRMA board to conduct its inquiry – in particular, a claim that his findings may not have been as impartial as publicly portrayed.

Lyons: Just on that McDougall Report, it very heavily talks about circumstantial evidence. 'There is evidence, although circumstantial, to enable me to identify Ms Keating as the source of one story.' He bases his findings on three things: one, she refused to speak to him; two, because a motive can be attributed to her; and three, there's no plausible alternative source. In the year 2001, is that enough to convict someone publicly as an untrustworthy board member in your view?

Whitlam: Well, John, you know I can't be drawn on the contents of the McDougall Report.

Lyons: But you can at least talk about the general justice or lack of justice . . .

Whitlam: No, that's not my domain.

Lyons: Do you give due regard to the circumstantial evidence?

Whitlam: Look, I am not a lawyer. Mr McDougall is a

Queen's Counsel, a most distinguished Queen's Counsel, and I am sure that Mr McDougall knows what weight can be attributed to circumstantial evidence. As best I understand it people have been found guilty of murder on circumstantial evidence so – that is not my domain, that is not my area of expertise.

Lyons: But given he does other work for the NRMA, was he independent enough to do the enquiry? He gets other income from the NRMA. Shouldn't he, in terms of conflict of interest, not be the person . . .

Whitlam: I know that was asserted by some people, but that is absolutely unfair and untrue and has no basis on any legal or proprietary basis that I am aware of. In fact, it is something that was asserted by someone that is simply – that is not fair. But in any event Mr McDougall – I have no doubt that Mr McDougall is totally independent and he can speak for himself.

It's difficult to imagine how any reasonable-minded person, hearing that exchange within its proper, unedited context, could come to the conclusion that Whitlam was attempting to deny that McDougall ever did any work for the NRMA. The question that was actually put to him – a question that was left out of the program as it went to air – specifically dealt with the issue of whether McDougall could truly be described as independent and followed several other questions challenging the fairness of his findings. It was to the issue of the senior counsel's impartiality that Whitlam was clearly directing his response. That interpretation is reinforced by Whitlam's concluding words, also left out of the program: *I have no doubt that Mr McDougall is totally independent and he can speak for himself.*

No wonder those final words were left out of the report as it was televised. They would have hardly suited Lyons's astounding conclusion: *But* Sunday *can reveal that Mr Whitlam's statement is in fact false* – an assertion followed by various examples of the legal work McDougall did in fact perform for the NRMA. Lyons's manipulative techniques become all the more apparent when we compare the actual question he posed in the uncut interview with his scripted commentary. Here, again, is the two-pronged question the audience never got to hear, but to which Whitlam gave his forceful denial. The key phrases are italicised to highlight the thrust of what was actually asked.

> Lyons [in uncut interview]: But given he does other work for the NRMA, *was he independent enough to do the enquiry?* He gets other income from the NRMA. *Shouldn't he, in terms of conflict of interest, not be the person* . . .

And here is the scripted commentary as it led into Whitlam's response, giving viewers the wrongful impression that his denial was to another issue altogether. Again, the italics indicate the thrust of the question as Lyons claimed to have presented it.

> Lyons [commentary]: Critics argued that McDougall was not independent, *that he regularly earned other money from the NRMA, a fact that as late as this week, Mr Whitlam categorically denied.*

In his reporter's commentary, then, Lyons reverses the order of emphasis to make McDougall's independence appear to be a peripheral matter and his NRMA income the main thrust of his interrogation. The end result, with a little tweaking, fits neatly into the corrupt pattern of the hypothetical exchange I cited earlier in the chapter.

Interviewer: Isn't there a conflict of interest? He did work for the NRMA, didn't he?

Interviewee: No, not at all.

Meanwhile, let's examine Lyons's sensational claim from an entirely different angle – the questions he never asked but certainly should have if he really wanted to establish that Whitlam was attempting to hide Robert McDougall's employment record with the NRMA group. Surely, a responsible investigative journalist would have gone on to confront Whitlam with example after example of McDougall's close links to the organisation to demonstrate how evasive he was being. I have examined the entire hour-long transcript of the raw, uncut interview. It contains only one brief exchange – not used in the program – where Whitlam is asked about a particular case in which McDougall is said to have worked for the NRMA. In that one instance he disputes whether the case actually involved NRMA Insurance, the company for which he carried out his inquiry, but openly agrees he could have worked for the motoring division of NRMA. 'He may have, I don't know,' is another Whitlam response that was edited out of Lyons's report. In no other specific instance could it be argued that Nicholas Whitlam attempted to deny McDougall ever having worked for the NRMA at all. Yet he is still accused on national television of trying to dupe the Australian public.

So in that shabby example of TV journalism we have the makings of the 2001 Walkley award for Broadcast Interviewing. More important for the purposes of this book, we have an apparently rational explanation for why a former print reporter with less than three years' experience in television should be chosen by John Alexander to become executive producer of commercial television's most widely respected current affairs program. If he was good enough to win a Walkley for his TV work, after all, surely that established his credentials for the top job? It could be argued that Alexander had no reason to suspect any possible flaw in Lyons's award-winning piece – but there was one significant development after the *Sunday* exposé went to air that should have set alarm bells ringing for the PBL Media chief, arousing at least some degree of concern.

Two days after his NRMA report, Lyons was invited onto the Graham Richardson show at radio station 2GB in Sydney to discuss the remarkable revelations he had brought to light. In the course of that radio interview Lyons repeated the allegations we have just examined.

'Nicholas Whitlam encouraged the board and the board agreed with him to set up this inquiry done by this Sydney QC,' Lyons explained to Richardson's listeners.

> Now I asked Nicholas Whitlam on camera, surely he wasn't the right person to do the inquiry, because he gets other income from the NRMA; and he flatly looked into the camera and looked at me and said, he doesn't . . . hasn't done other work for the NRMA, that is untrue. We then dug out two letters, two documents – one from their own legal counsel saying that I recommended him for this inquiry because he's done other work for us; and the QC, we got a letter from him, a private letter saying: I've basically been doing work for them for 18 months and I've been on a retainer. So what Nicholas Whitlam told us on camera was absolutely untrue.

Whitlam proceeded to sue 2GB over that broadcast. A Supreme Court jury subsequently found that he had in fact been defamed on three counts, the first one being the allegation that 'he lied on television when he said that a Sydney Queen's Counsel . . . had not done other work for the NRMA'. The radio station quickly moved to settle the case with an apology, with the result that

Lyons's credibility as a reporter was never tested under cross-examination, as it surely would have been if court proceedings had continued.

Nevertheless, the jury's decision in the 2GB case had obvious and worrying implications for Channel 9. If Nicholas Whitlam went on to sue the network, it was almost certain to find itself in the position of having to prove the truth of Lyons's assertion that the NRMA Chairman told a lie on air. Even a cursory attempt to match his script with the transcript of the full interview would have shown that to be a shaky defence at best. Despite the warning signs, however, there is no indication Alexander or his Park Street advisers followed through by asking a few pertinent questions. The settlement between 2GB and Whitlam was announced on 3 May, 2002. Alexander arranged to have Lyons replace Stephen Rice as *Sunday*'s executive producer in October, 2003.

By any journalistic standard, Lyons's treatment of Nicholas Whitlam could only be described as a 'hatchet job' – playing fast and loose with the facts to paint him in the worst possible light. That raises an intriguing question when one examines the section of the Llewellyn affidavit referring to Alexander's attempt to launch an attack against Kerry Stokes. 'There are plenty of journalists at Channel 9 who could do this,' the PBL boss is quoted as saying, 'John Lyons among them.'

Do what, exactly?

I have to confess that I myself have been guilty of authorising a story to be edited out of context. Though it's not directly relevant to the Whitlam episode it does illustrate the power of manipulation inherent in the editing process and how carefully that power must be wielded. While I was executive producer of *60 Minutes*, we sent Ray Martin to China to cover a much-talked-about tour there by the pop star and inveterate eccentric Elton John. Ray sent back a script and recorded narration that wasn't quite correct, suggesting that John had publicly admitted to being homosexual when, in fact, he had at that point only ever admitted to being bisexual. Ray was en route to another story and couldn't be contacted to change the line. It looked as if we might have to delay showing a well-promoted story or drop an important sequence in his report. Fortunately, I remembered that in Ray's audio tape there was reference to a scene we had decided not to use in which Elton goes off to 'buy' a Chinese lion sculpture. Our editor managed to take that 'buy' and intercut it with the word homosexual to produce 'bisexual', making the story 100 per cent correct. It was totally out of context but at least, in this case, used for a good cause. And that sums up the magic of television – much too potent a force to be put in the hands of those prepared to misuse it.

CHAPTER 15

McGuire and mates:
a whole new ball game

*W*e're picking our team now . . . really want you on our side
. . . all sing the same song . . . wear the same colours.

With that kind of locker room language to set the scene,
Channel 9 was about to write the most tumultuous chapter yet in
its 50-year history. Sure, the network had taken its hits, lost some
key players, blown its chances with some pretty iffy calls; but the
trick to winning was to pull together, re-energise, open the shoul-
ders and go for it. It was the dawning of the age of Eddie McGuire,
brimming over with hope that a badly demoralised network
could find new inspiration fired up by a celebrity CEO who knew
how to walk the walk and talk the talk, Nine's sixth boss in four
years of utter turmoil.

'What is needed is Eddie's personality, his creativity, his sales-manship and his charisma,' was the pitch adopted by Park Street at the time of McGuire's appointment in early February, 2006. 'It's no secret that the network is a bit shop-worn, it needs direction and a rallying point. We need to bring back its vitality.' Coming from within the PBL hierarchy (a highly placed source who demanded anonymity, according to the *Australian*) that evaluation was not without its irony, considering just how much of Nine's woes had been inflicted upon it by PBL itself.

Still, Eddie McGuire certainly did seem to have all the neces-sary qualifications. Not only was he a TV star in his own right, but the personification of a new generation of TV star, totally in tune with the rapidly changing tastes of twenty-first-century viewers. His *Footy Show* was James Packer's vision of a perfect TV program, costing virtually nothing compared to a *60 Minutes* or *McLeod's Daughters* yet attracting big ratings and plenty of water cooler gossip next morning. McGuire's *Who Wants to be a Millionaire* was a far more expensive format, of course, but a marvellous platform for him to show the full range of his chameleon-like abilities to relate to people in any type of mood or milieu.

For the production teams at Nine, struggling to maintain traditional standards amid drastic spending restrictions, he must have seemed a godsend: an on-camera pro who knew enough about their line of work to stand up on their behalf against the bean counters. While he lacked experience in large-scale corpo-rate management, there was no doubting his business acumen. As president of Collingwood AFL club, he was credited with tripling turnover within a few years. Nor could there be any question about his talents as a super-salesman considering the impressive list of big-name sponsors he had won over to the Magpie cause. While he was a household name across the nation, his close identification with Melbourne was considered a big plus, a demonstration that the network was not as Sydney-centric as some accused it of being. Meanwhile, his association with Australian Rules at the very top level of the game won him instant credibility as a mover and shaker within the wider world of sport that was so close to the hearts of most Australians. Both James Packer and Sam Chisholm pronounced themselves Eddie's avid admirers. John Alexander was reported to be less enthusiastic, concerned about his lack of managerial experience but prepared to accept that of all the potential candidates from within Australia and overseas, McGuire offered the most promising possibilities. Just the extraordinary amount of buzz he generated, filling the newspapers day after day with excited speculation about his prospects of becoming Nine CEO, seemed proof enough that he had the right stuff to turn the network's fortunes around.

There was only one problem, totally overlooked, that would prove to be his downfall. Eddie McGuire was appointed to a position that, in effect, no longer existed. Nine hardly needed its own chief executive officer when – as would soon become apparent – every significant decision affecting the network's future, from stars' contracts to the funds available for program purchases, would be in the hands of a PBL committee of four, including John Alexander; Alexander's offsider, Ian Law; board bigwig Chris Anderson; and chief operating officer Pat O'Sullivan.

McGuire had undoubtedly taken on his role in the best of faith, bursting with ideas on how to make the network more flexible and responsive to the needs of modern Australians. He couldn't have been long into the job, however, before detecting the first warning signs of how thin the line can be separating a leading national figure from a figurehead, reduced to defending decisions he had little or nothing to do with and in some cases, strongly disagreed with. Under such circumstances it's impossible to know what errors of judgement could be attributed to McGuire alone, compared to what was forced upon him by the

Alexandrian quartet. All that can be said is that under his new administration, the network was to plunge from one crisis to another, while the very last trace of Kerry Packer's enormous influence would be wiped out without a blink of regret.

As far as the general public is concerned, the most talked-about disaster to befall Channel 9 during Eddie McGuire's reign in 2006 would have to be the sensational headline coverage of the Mark Llewellyn affidavit in late June, with its stark disclosures of PBL meddling and memorable quote about *boning Jessica*. The fallout from the affidavit will be discussed a bit later. There was another controversial turn of events, however, that went virtually unnoticed in the press even though it was of far greater importance in terms of its symbolic impact, as well as its practical repercussions.

For all of Kerry Packer's whims and foibles, he had left Channel 9 with a truly precious legacy in the form of an absolute airtight code of honour that had once governed every aspect of the network's everyday dealings with its employees and program makers. From the day Kerry first took charge in 1974, a handshake had always been regarded to be as binding as any signed contract. Beyond an ethical principle, it happened to make good business sense, as well. Nine's reputation for having its word as its bond allowed the network to move far more quickly than its competitors in grabbing up the best people and the best deals without getting bogged down in prolonged legalistic quibbling over details and paperwork. Under the lash of Park Street's cost-cutting crusade that fine old tradition would be renounced without warning or even an apology. The two brilliant producers of *The Block*, Julian Cress and David Barbour, would be among the first to suffer the consequences. Their story tells us much about the difference between Channel 9 as it once was – a station that prided itself not only on doing the best for its audience but doing the best for its own people – and what has become of it in its struggle to adapt to the harsher realities of a new era.

After their dazzling success with the first year of *The Block*, Cress and Barbour had gone on to generate millions of dollars more for Nine in terms of both advertising revenue and royalties from overseas. In 2004 they produced a second *Block* series, still a clear winner though not by the extraordinary margins of the original version, due largely to overexposure from double the usual number of episodes. In 2005 they came up with two new formats, *Celebrity Overhaul* and *Celebrity Circus,* both of which helped Nine cling to number one position for the season despite Seven's formidable line-up of prime time hits like *Dancing with the Stars, Lost* and *Desperate Housewives.* Once again, revenue poured in not only from advertising built into the *Celebrity* concept but from the formats themselves being sold internationally. The two producers clearly had the golden touch but as they were soon to discover, that didn't necessarily guarantee them a bright and happy future.

In ordinary circumstances a creative team enjoying so much success would have been quick to strike out on their own, setting up their own independent production company and offering their ideas to the highest bidder. Cress and Barbour, however, were cursed with old-fashioned ideas of loyalty. They appreciated the opportunities Nine had offered them over the years to hone their production skills. They were thankful to David Gyngell for being so quick to grasp the potential for their *Block* concept and credited Nine's programmers for later giving them the seeds of an idea they went on to develop into the two *Celebrity* formats. They were more than happy to stick with Nine so long as they felt they were being treated fairly, not only paid well as producers but given a chance to share in any windfall profits from their original formats being sold abroad.

That issue had first come up at the end of the 2003 season when they were sent overseas to advise foreign producers on how best to adapt *The Block* concept to their own local audiences. A creative team from Belgium had flown to London to meet them for an eight-hour brainstorming session. At the end of it the group split up to go to their separate hotels. 'Where are you guys staying?' the Australians asked. 'The Covent Garden Hotel,' the Belgians replied, referring to a distinctly upmarket hostelry. 'Lucky bastards,' the Australians grumbled, knowing they would be spending the night in far less salubrious circumstances. 'But why not stay there too?' the Belgians inquired. 'You have the hottest format in the world. You could stay where you like.' If only.

Still, after mentioning that conversation to Gyngell he didn't hesitate to top up their share of overseas *Block* sales beyond what had been stipulated in their contracts. Similarly, as they plunged into work on the *Celebrity* series, the two producers had no hesitation in leaving fee arrangements aside for the moment, taking Gyngell at his word that, 'We'll look after you, you'll get your share at the back end'. When any Packer executive promised to do the best he could for you, you could trust that he really meant it.

Even when Gyngell got around to roughing out the actual terms of a new agreement, they felt no need to rush into signing it. They were simply too busy at the moment ploughing ahead, doing what they did best, which was translating the glimmer of an idea into a workable, ratings-winning format. What Gyngell had proposed meant a sizeable boost to their base salaries along with the prospect of weekly ratings bonuses and a healthy share of royalties and licensing fees for future formats. Was it fair and equitable? Who really knew? The fact was that Cress and Barbour had carved out a unique niche for themselves. Normally a TV channel simply bought a new program concept from an outside production house or otherwise commissioned a show to be produced to its specifications. It was most unusual to have a pair of staff producers capable of creating original programming, so no one really had any guide to the appropriate salaries and percentage of 'blue-sky' dividends to be awarded.

Gyngell's sudden departure came as a real blow for the talented twosome, who regarded him as a mentor and inspiration. They were a bit shaken at first when the incoming CEO, Sam Chisholm, looked at the agreement Gyngell had sketched out with them before he left and snapped: 'Nah, I wouldn't do it that way.' But then, he quickly reassured them: 'There's other ways to skin a cat, so we'll work out another deal.'

Sam, like Gyngell, was to prove true to his word. 'I believe that you two guys have been significantly underpaid,' he reassured them shortly after he had settled in. 'I want you to be with this network for a long time to come, so I want to work out a deal we're all satisfied with.' It was very much the sentiment that could have been heard time and time again throughout Nine's Golden Age, the glue that held the star system together. As much as you might already be working your guts out, you'd work even harder for someone who treated you like that. Sam followed through on that promise by putting the matter in the hands of a trusted outside legal adviser, David Gordon. 'I want to do a deal with these guys,' Chisholm told him. 'They're both very talented – the most talented we've got at Nine.' Gordon came up with a one-page term sheet listing the principal points for the deal. 'If I'm going to be able to put on one of your shows and can go out there and make a million dollars or maybe even ten million dollars selling the idea overseas, I should split it with you,' the interim CEO told the producers. 'Why not? It's money I wouldn't have had if you weren't here.'

Their agreement with Chisholm provided for about the same pay increase that Gyngell had offered, close to doubling their basic salaries, along with ratings bonuses if a show did better than expected. It went much further, though, in boosting their royalties on overseas sales from the 15 per cent built into *The Block* to an impressive 50 per cent for their two *Celebrity* formats – *Overhaul* and *Circus* – as well as all future foreign deals. The terms were agreed upon just before Christmas, 2005. 'Don't worry,' Sam told them. 'This new contract will start from the first of January. But go and have a great Christmas and we'll do the paperwork when you get back.' The three of them shook hands on it and Cress and Barbour were able to go off on their summer holidays with something special to celebrate. As far as they were concerned they had a firm agreement for a new contract that, in their view, gave fair recognition to their contribution as successful, internationally recognised program originators. They looked forward to coming back fresh and bursting with ideas for locally produced formats designed not only to appeal to Australian viewers but bring in extra returns from foreign networks hungry for new product.

The two went off on separate holiday destinations but both turned up at Channel 9 on Friday, 10 February, 2006 in response to an invitation to attend farewell drinks for Sam that evening. They not only wanted to thank him for his support but to assure themselves that everything was still on track for the signing of their agreement. 'We wish you well for the future,' Cress told the outgoing CEO. 'We just want to make sure our future is still secure.' Chisholm gave him a laser beam look that allowed for not the slightest misinterpretation. 'Of course it is,' he shot back. 'I'm the CEO of this network as of and up until today. I'm also still a member of the board of this fucking company, so the deal I did with you, that deal stands. No one can break it.' 'That's good to know, we appreciate that, Sam,' the producers responded, much relieved. They left Willoughby feeling able to enjoy a relaxing weekend – as it turned out, their last before being subjected to four aggravating months of high tension.

The two would go on, with the encouragement of their lawyer, to keep a diary of their repeated attempts to persuade Eddie McGuire to honour their handshake agreement with his predecessor. This is an excerpt from the first of Cress's entries relating to 8 March, when, after several weeks of pleading, the new CEO finally agreed to see them.

We arrived at his office at 9.30 am. Eddie is standing with his back to us, feet splayed apart and his hands placed firmly on the desk. 'From what I've heard about you guys, I guess I'm going to have to assume the position,' he says. Must be some kind of locker room humour from his football days. Not a good sign. I always suspect that someone who begins a business meeting trying to put you at ease with a man-joke is probably leading up to something less funny. And so it was.

We moved across to comfortable chairs – a massive sofa that you can sink so far into it's impossible to look serious. Typically, David and I perch on the edge of the seat to try to look like we mean business. The good news is that the e-mail I sent him the night before is sitting right on his coffee table between us. It outlines all of our claims – the money we are owed already for *Celebrity Overhaul* and *Celebrity Circus*, as well as details of our new Nine deal we concluded with Sam at the end of last year. Eddie glances at it like it contains Anthrax spores. Hmmm. Not a good sign.

'I just wanted to meet with you guys as soon as possible. I've heard nothing but good things about both of you,' McGuire assures them. 'You're very valuable to this organisation. I under-stand what you guys do. *The Block* was a fantastic show. There have only ever been two shows that have been true bona fide world-wide hits for this network – *The Block* and *The Footy Show*.'

In his diary notes, Cress admits that to that point he's found McGuire to be very impressive with his sales pitch. He's quite taken aback, however, by the CEO's description of *The Footy Show* as a world-wide hit. 'Huh?' he asks himself. But Eddie has yet to reach full stride.

> 'So I really want you guys with the new team. I've only been in the job a couple of weeks and frankly I'm still trying to find the dunny, but I can promise you one thing. I'm in this job now and things are going to change. We're all going to pull together as a team, everyone on the same side. You look after me and I'm going to look after you.' Oh shit!

'Well, Eddie,' Cress responds, as recorded in his notes. 'We're on board. We've got a deal already for three years which was signed off on by Sam in December. We just have to finalise the paper-work and get to work. Did you read through the e-mail we sent you last night?'

McGuire's reply makes their hearts sink.

> 'Yes, I read it. Look, fellas, I can tell you you're not alone in having a deal with Sam. A lot of deals were done by Sam. All I've been doing since I got here is trying to sort through all the shit with everybody and the deals they did. I've got meetings all day every day for the next two weeks with people wanting to talk about the deals they did with Sam. He's gone, fellas. We're going to start again. You're dealing with me, now.'

At that point David Barbour breaks in. 'But that deal was supposed to start from January the first,' he protests. 'Everybody agreed to the price and the back end. We've been working three months already on the basis of that deal.'

'Guys, I can understand how you feel,' their new CEO tries to assuage them. 'I got fucked over plenty of times trying to do deals here in my career. It's frustrating. But I'm in the job now, so you'll just have to forget about that deal and deal with me.'

'But the deal's already done,' Cress persists. 'Sam may not be CEO, but hey, he's still a director of the company, right? I mean, he's standing by the deal.'

Cress's file notes take on an increasingly sombre note from there on in.

> 'Look fellas,' Eddie continues. 'That deal with Sam was just lip service being paid to you by a guy who knew he wasn't going to be around for long.' Oh, no. We're fucked now. I joked with David after the meeting that I felt like we were on an episode of *Who Doesn't Want to be a Millionaire*. Everything we had negotiated for seven months had just gone out the window. But is that legal? Surely a promise from a departed CEO is still a promise. He was only here a few weeks ago. He's not dead. He's at our Park Street head-quarters, sitting on the damned board of the company.

As bad as the situation might have seemed to Cress and Barbour at that moment, it was destined to get a lot worse. McGuire urged the pair to delay further discussions for a couple of more weeks until the arrival of a new senior member of the McGuire admin-istration. 'The best negotiator I know,' McGuire assured them. 'He negotiated my deal for this place and he's who you'll be talking to. I promise you'll be at the top of his list.'

As Cress sums up in his diary notes:

> I couldn't understand why Eddie would think we would be pleased by this. I'm sure this new guy is a great negotiator and that's great for Eddie, but where's the upside for us? I mean he's going to be working for Eddie, not us. We already have a deal. Or at least we did until a couple of minutes ago.

My head's spinning. Did he just tear up our contract? What about all the money we're owed from last year?

Eddie's top gun *negotiator* would turn out to be Jeffrey Browne, as high-powered a lawyer as they come, renowned within AFL circles for his abilities to drive the hardest possible bargain for the code's multimillion-dollar broadcasting rights deals. He'd also been McGuire's long-time manager, responsible for negotiating Eddie's transformation from superstar to Nine managing director at the extraordinary CEO's salary of close to $5 million a year.

'Jeff is a leader in his field and will be key to the reinvigoration of Nine,' McGuire enthused in announcing Browne's appointment to the newly created position of executive director, effectively Eddie's deputy CEO.

Browne, for his part, couldn't have been more direct in revealing how he felt about assuming the job of second-in-command of Australia's number one television network. 'It will be a challenge,' he acknowledged to the press in mid-April, 'but a television network is just a bucket of contracts.' True enough, there had been buckets and buckets of contracts since Channel 9 first began broadcasting in 1956, introducing Australia to some of its best-loved and most influential personalities. In that light it was not the most sensitive of remarks. 'Buckets' would be Browne's nickname around the network from that time on. It's easy to imagine an enraged Kerry Packer threatening to sack him on the spot for such a public relations gaffe but the truth was, Browne's pragmatic opinion of the network was perfectly in keeping with the view from the Alexandrian perspective at Park Street, even if no one there was so gauche as to speak it aloud.

Cress and Barbour were to get their first taste of Browne's negotiating style at a meeting finally arranged by McGuire on Wednesday, 19 April, some five weeks after he first spoke to them in terms they had found so frustrating and disappointing. That delay might well have stretched on even longer were it not for an annoying little gossip item that McGuire spotted in the *Australian*'s media section a few days earlier. It referred to Browne's 'buckets' remark and then went on to offer this acerbic comment:

> One of the contracts in the bucket is the one negotiated by former boss Sam Chisholm with the dream team, Julian Cress and David Barbour. Barbour and Cress came up with *The Block*, which smashed all ratings records in 2003 with its clever mix of renovation and reality. It was Nine's last blockbuster hit. The two also delivered reasonable successes with *Celebrity Overhaul* and *Celebrity Circus*, and all their formats have been sold overseas. They expected to produce some much-needed ideas for Nine this year but have been left in limbo as their contracts are about to expire and McGuire has not got around to renegotiating them. We hear if they're allowed to leave they may consider joining former chief executive David Gyngell in the US. Together the producers have been at Nine for 25 years and losing them would be a serious blow to a network so bereft of ideas.

McGuire hit the roof when he read that, phoning to accuse the producers of being the source of the leak and admonishing them for their cheek. 'I don't want to be reading about this shit in the paper,' he warned them. 'I said I would look after you blokes and that I was waiting for Jeff to get into his office here. So let's not see this sort of thing in the papers again.'

The auspices for this next conference, then, are not looking all that promising, even though, according to Cress's notes, it starts off cordially enough. 'We walk into Eddie's office and finally meet Jeff Browne. He's all smiles. So's Eddie. So who's this, they ask?

Our lawyer, Bryan [Belling]. "Oh, right. Well, come in anyway."'

The amiable mood quickly changes, however, as McGuire interrupts proceedings to complain about another press article that's upset him, quoting former *Today* host Steven Liebmann as bemoaning the decline of the once-respected program since he's left. 'They have just become a poor imitation of *Sunrise*,' he's reported as saying. 'It's very sad . . . they have caused almost irreparable damage to it.'

'By the time we sit down, Eddie is apoplectic,' Cress observes in his notes. 'But it's not us that's upset him this time. It's Steve Liebmann. "I'm gonna fucking get that guy. I'm going to rain hell down on him so hard he'll never know what hit him. Who the fuck does he think he is?" Etc. etc. He nearly runs out of breath. "I'm so fucking angry I can hardly speak."'

At that point McGuire, though, apologises for the interruption, explaining: 'I just needed to get that off my chest.' In what appears to be a conciliatory gesture, he goes on to commiserate with the two producers, acknowledging how badly burnt they must feel if they genuinely believe there is money owing to them that hasn't been paid. If they can establish there is, he assures them, they'll be compensated accordingly. Cress and Barbour remain sceptical. There's been no sign of the pay increase that was due in their salaries from 1 January, let alone money owed on licence fees and royalties from the previous year.

'Well this is certainly going to be an interesting meeting,' Cress continues in his notes of the meeting. 'Now it's Jeff's turn to speak.' To that point Browne has been the picture of civility; but what he says next, though spoken in the politest of tones, strikes the producers as 'outrageously profane'.

I just want to say right up front that the deal you have with Sam . . . well, we don't recognise that, okay? We're going to forget that and start over. We're not going to be doing things like they were done in the past. This man sitting right here beside me is going to do remarkable things with this network. This is a business about ideas and this man here has a thousand great ideas. This is the place you want to be boys, so what's it going to be?

Barbour is first to react. 'Thanks, but we're not sure that starting the whole process over is what we want to do at this point. This has been an incredibly frustrating time for us and starting to work out a new deal doesn't seem fair.'

The two producers, by this time, feel themselves being pushed past the psychological point of no return. As devastated as they are by Nine's treatment of them, however, they still want to leave the network with enough goodwill to keep it as a potential client if and when they set themselves up as independents. Jeff Browne, consummate negotiator that he is, is quick to recognise their quandary and doesn't hesitate to rub their noses in it.

'Look, if you guys stay with us we can work out a good deal. We'll look after you,' David Barbour's diary notes quote Browne as saying. But then he goes on to warn: 'Free to air is where the big money is at and being outside is probably not the place to be.'

Barbour finds that line hard to swallow. 'We already have a deal, the same deal that was supposed to have commenced from 1 January, four months ago.' When Barbour goes on to reaffirm their intention not to re-sign under such conditions, Browne doesn't bat an eye. Their refusal to enter into a new agreement, he warns, will make it 'difficult' for Nine to find its way clear to pay any of the moneys they claim to be owed. That's a giant step backwards from McGuire's conciliatory gesture when the meeting first started.

The next day their lawyer, Bryan Belling, sends Eddie and Jeff a letter expressing his clients' disappointment in Nine's refusal to honour their agreement with Sam Chisholm and confirming their intention to leave the network because of that. He proposes, however, that Nine at least agree to negotiate in good faith on a settlement of all fees and entitlements due to the two producers upon their departure so they can leave on fair and equitable terms. Browne doesn't bother to reply to Belling's suggestion. It's only when he happens to run into a very hung-over Julian Cress at Sydney Airport on Monday, 8 May, the day after the 2006 Logies, that the negotiator cheerfully breaks the news.

> I'm standing at the carousel and I run right into Jeff Browne. 'Hello, Julian, I just wanted to let you know that . . . we will be letting you go, but not on the terms you have proposed to us.'
>
> 'That's very disappointing to hear, Jeff. David and I have not even had an opportunity to explain any of the promises that were made to us. You should at least be fully informed before making a decision like this.'
>
> 'Okay, call my office and set something up.'

On Wednesday, 17 May, Cress and Barbour enter Browne's office for what will prove to be the negotiation from hell, two relatively naive young program makers nose to nose with an expert deal broker capable of playing take-it-or-leave-it hard ball with the likes of Kerry Packer. Browne has promised that all they have to do is give him evidence of the moneys due them and he will write out a cheque on the spot. He seems so genuine they even agree to his condition to bring no lawyer with them. Cress and Barbour have no qualms about complying, since they're convinced that justice is so clearly on their side. They not only can cite witnesses to their handshake agreement with Sam Chisholm but they have brought along various e-mails from the program and finance departments referring to money approved for payment due to them for *Celebrity Overhaul* and *Celebrity Circus*. To top off their case they present Browne with an actual program production budget showing specific provision for their various fee and royalty arrangements. 'Well, it's hardly a legal document, is it?' Jeff Browne's icy observation – technically correct, perhaps, but totally without compassion – brings them crashing back to earth, face to face with the harsh reality of what it is like to do business with Channel 9 less than five months after the death of Kerry Packer. The diary notes of both Cress and Barbour fairly quiver with exasperation and disbelief. This is Julian's bitter summation.

> To say that we're unbelievably angry would barely hint at how we're feeling. We've just been completely fucked over. We showed all of this to Jeff. His response: So what? That hardly constitutes a contract. 'Jeff, we never had time to draw up a contract. We always worked on the assumption that if everybody here makes you a promise, that it's worth something. If we deliver, you'll deliver.'
>
> 'Well,' says Jeff, 'that's not how we're doing things around here anymore. Maybe next time you'll know better.'

This, indeed, would have been a sobering lesson for anyone, let alone two of the most innovative and successful creators of light entertainment programming ever to come out of the Australian television industry. Next to Reg Grundy's efforts, perhaps, it's hard to think of another local TV production team that had proved such a consistent ability to attract so much international interest in their reality show formats – and the export dollars to go with it. Tough as he sounded, Browne must have recognised that, too, because what he said next, as quoted in Cress's diary notes, left them gobsmacked.

> 'But if you guys are willing to stay with the network, then maybe we can sort something out. Are you willing?'

'Are you fucking kidding?' I very nearly said. David looked like he was going to leap across the table and strangle him. He's completely speechless, which is incredibly rare for David. What do I say? 'No, Jeff, we've decided to move on. But we believe we're making a considerable offer here in good faith. We're willing to part ways amicably, despite all the shit that's gone down, and to continue to consult on *The Block* for you – because you're going to need it. The only way that show is going to get up in the time frame for next year is if we're around to work with the sponsors and the cast to help finalise the location.'

Once again, another stony rebuff from Browne.

'We don't need you guys to make *The Block*. If you leave right now, we'll simply do it in house. We've got plenty of people here to make shows and that's the way it's going to be in the future. We'll be doing the programs in here. And you'll be out there.' Out there in the freezing fucking cold – he didn't need to add.

Cress goes on to reply:

'Jeff, the only reason we're leaving, is that you're not honouring the deal we already had. We were fully signed up for another three years starting in January.'
    Jeff says: 'And because you two have decided you no longer want to work here, there really isn't any way we will be paying you anything for these other shows.'
    'But it's all there in black and white,' I say lamely.

It should be stressed, at this point, that this is one side's version of what must have been a very intense and at times heated discussion – a debate revolving around complex issues of financial liability looked at from two distinctive perspectives, legal and ethical. Cress is a seasoned journalist, a former *60 Minutes* producer, trained to report other people's statements in a fair and responsible manner, though in this case his impartiality is obviously not beyond question. On the other hand Browne, up to this stage, has not been quoted as saying anything beyond what a lawyer might be expected to say in defending a position that boils down to *no payment without proof of a legally binding agreement*.

What follows next, however, might well turn out to be a matter of contention should this dispute ever come before the courts. During the course of their meeting with Browne, Cress and Barbour insist that one or more of the senior executives within the McGuire administration not only knew about the 'term sheet' drawn up by David Gordon at the behest of Sam Chisholm but had actually discussed it with Gordon himself. This is how their diary notes record Browne's responses in the following exchange.

Barbour: But the deal with Sam has been confirmed, right?
Browne: No, no one from this network has confirmed the deal with Sam.
Barbour: Yes, they have, as we understand it. [He mentions the names of several executives.]
Browne: I'm telling you, no one from this network has ever spoken to David Gordon about the deal. No one has ever confirmed any deal.

My own inquiries suggest that at least one senior executive at Channel 9 was definitely aware of Gordon's term sheet setting out the principal terms for a deal. It is possible, of course, that Browne is not being accurately quoted in his alleged assertion that *no one from this network has ever spoken to David Gordon about the deal.*

It is also possible that no one within the Nine hierarchy ever informed him of having done so. There is a third possibility that he is equivocating, refusing to accept that a term sheet falls within the definition of a 'deal'.

The one fact beyond dispute is the historical significance of that meeting with Julian Cress and David Barbour on 17 May, 2006. It does more than mark the death of the handshake, a fine Nine tradition honouring the human imprint above the legalistic fine print. In all of the forensic evidence gathered for this book, it most clearly establishes the exact time of death for Channel 9 itself in terms of what generations of Australians knew as the old Kerry Packer station.

CHAPTER 16

A letter to Eddie

Predictably, the relationship between the network and its two most prolific producers could only continue to degenerate after their split, like a messy divorce. At one stage, amid the legal jousting, Jeff Browne went so far as to declare that Cress and Barbour had sacrificed all further claims to any entitlements because they had dishonoured the one written contract that was in existence – a three-year agreement they had signed during David Gyngell's time, expiring on 30 June 2006. The network alleged that because the two had physically departed from Willoughby one week before the official expiration date (they had been left in limbo, with no work to do) they had effectively invalidated the entire contract. Writing from Los Angeles, where the two producers had joined David Gyngell, head of Granada in the United States, Julian Cress sent this impassioned plea to Eddie McGuire. I asked Cress's permission to quote it at length. I think it speaks volumes about the pain of losing a genuine Australian cultural institution that once meant so much to so many.

Dear Eddie,

In our last meeting you said that even if we decided to leave the network we could work something out that would allow us all to have a positive and continuing relationship.

What happened?

Now we have letters from your lawyers threatening to take away not only any of the money we believe we are owed from our most recent productions but even to withhold our future royalties from *The Block*.

What did we do to you?

Yes, we did ultimately decide to leave, but let's take a look at the circumstances. Both you and Jeff were crystal clear that you would not be willing to honour the contract we had negotiated with Sam. You offered nothing in return except for the vague promise of starting the whole process over again to negotiate a different contract – a process that had already taken us most of a year – and here we were, right back at square one.

So what did we do?

It turns out there were many other people who were interested in employing us. We could have gone to another network in Australia, which I might point out, would have been far more damaging for you. Instead we very carefully considered our options – and then grabbed an opportunity, which was impossible to pass up.

I ask you – wouldn't you?

You're a man who knows better than most when a good opportunity presents itself and you have taken them when they came along. If you hadn't taken chances you wouldn't be sitting where you are today. So if anyone can understand us taking the chance to work overseas in the world's biggest television market, it's you.

We're all going to be in this business a long time. I've always known that, which is why I've always tried to conduct my professional affairs with a high degree of honesty and loyalty. I'm sure you have always tried to do the same. In my fourteen years at the Nine Network I never expected it to end with a complete lack of communication, then a flood of threatening legal letters.

I'm writing to you in the hope that we can solve this issue without going down a path that will damage opportunities to do good business together in the future. Hopefully we've all got another twenty years or more of television left in us. To me, it looks like your lawyers are looking at short term gain instead of the long term benefits of us having a mutually respectful and beneficial relationship.

David and I have created some very profitable shows for Nine. They have earned tens of millions of dollars for the network. Our share of these is comparatively small. The lawyers believe that by taking this away from us they can win. But win what? The game – or the premiership.

You want Nine to be a powerhouse of creative thinking, a place that will draw in people with good ideas. It's an ideal strategy and one which will reap rewards for Nine. But you cannot do that if you don't reward them in return. Or if you treat them with contempt when they do. The writer Hunter S. Thomson once said: 'television is a long plastic hallway, a cheap and shallow money trench where thieves and pimps run free and weak men die like dogs'. Funny guy certainly. But is that the sort of television network you want? I don't believe so.

Eddie, I would like to leave you with a speech made a couple of years ago by Roy Disney to the shareholders. A passionate man speaking in hope for a once great company. The sort of company Nine has been and can certainly become again:

'My dad was quoted once as saying, "It's easy to make decisions, once you know what your values are." Unfortunately, our corporate values have been compromised in recent years. In large part, this is the result of a cynical management's belief that, in the absence of ideas, the road to success is to cut back on everyone and everything that once made you successful ... that creativity and originality are luxuries you can no longer afford ... that art and artists are commodities to be bought and sold like any other office supply.

'To me, the wrong-headedness of these beliefs is self-evident.

'Creativity is a funny thing – difficult to quantify, but obvious when it's missing. It's a living, breathing force with a life of its own ... It doesn't always show up on demand ... or at convenient times or places. And it often gets killed by committees or by something called strategic planning. So we need to always be on the lookout for ways to nurture it, and not let it be trampled by a lowest-common-denominator mentality.

'How did the Disney Company create enormous shareholder value in the past? Two ways: first by trusting the talents and imagination of its creative people – and then by supporting them with the resources they required. The plain fact is, you can't ... succeed in our business by trying to get by on the cheap. Consumers know when they are getting value for their money, and they know when you're trying to sell them second-hand goods.

'It is my firm belief that we are not a commodity. As long as we continue to believe in the power of creative ideas, then our best years still lie ahead.'

Eddie, thank you for your attention. I wish you well in your difficult job – and hope, as you said, that we will be able to work something out. Might I suggest we begin by putting a leash back on the lawyers and settling this in a more amicable fashion. Person to person. It is a people business after all.

Yours sincerely,

Julian Cress

CHAPTER 17

Scandals galore: the Llewellyn saga

If two tried-and-true money-spinning producers like Cress and Barbour could be dealt with in such an arbitrary manner, what chance was there for someone like Mark Llewellyn? Llewellyn, of course, had been well aware that his position as director of news and current affairs was shaky, to say the least, after his two nasty run-ins with John Alexander. Bad enough that he should stubbornly refuse to commission the kind of critical profile Alexander wanted carried out on Kerry Stokes. Worse still, he had dared to try to sack John Lyons, one of the PBL chief's most trusted apparatchiks, a man obviously positioned to play an important role in the future of Park Street's new-look Channel 9. Before Sam Chisholm left the network he had cautioned Llewellyn on several occasions to be on his guard. 'You're okay while I'm around, I'll look after you, but when I'm gone Alexander will move against you,' he advised in late January, 2006. On 9 February, the day before he left the station, Sam phoned the newscaff chief using a much scarier turn of phrase. 'Your life is going to be a nightmare. You are going to have to watch your back. The truth is, they will want to bump you off and stick Lyons in.'

There was little Llewellyn could do in such a precarious situation but to let his achievements speak for themselves, working as hard as he could to get news and current affairs back on a winning track and attempt to earn a reprieve from Alexander's enmity. Like Cress and Barbour, he was naive enough to believe that Channel 9 was still a place where talent was regarded as a precious asset, too valuable to be squandered because of some personal grudge. Just three weeks after Chisholm's departure Llewellyn got his first inkling of how very wrong he was. As in the kind of nightmarish scenario Sam had predicted, Llewellyn suddenly found himself under attack by a swarm of stinging e-mails emanating from within the PBL hierarchy all the way up the line to Alexander himself.

The occasion for this bizarre episode was Nine's presentation of the 2006 Academy Awards, broadcast in this country on Monday, 6 March. Oscar night, of course, is viewed by audiences around the world as the Hollywood Olympics, a sure-fire ratings winner. Nine is believed to pay a whopping $800,000 a year to America's ABC for exclusive Australian broadcasting rights. To take advantage of their network's special access to the awards, the news and current affairs division naturally tries to milk such a prestigious event for all it's worth, sending reporters to secure numerous feature stories and exclusive interviews with big name celebrities. Nine, in fact, had cleverly extended the ratings appeal of the night by adding the *Red Carpet Special*, an introductory program revelling in the stars' glamorous gowns as they make their way to the main arena. *Today*'s entertainment reporter, Richard Wilkins, hosted that program as well as doing pieces for the *Today* show itself and Kerri-Anne Kennerley's popular morning program. *A Current Affair* had also sent a reporter to Los Angeles to help boost ratings with some Oscar sidebars and hopefully score an interview with Australia's Heath Ledger, should he happen to win the best actor category. Channel 9 news also had two journalists resident in LA, their reports adding to the buzz surrounding the event. As far as any television professional was concerned, there was nothing at all unusual about mounting such blanket coverage of one of the year's most avidly watched spectacles. Indeed, to do anything less would have been seen by envious rival networks as an inexcusable waste of a golden opportunity. Not so, however, in the sceptical eyes of Park Street.

> From: O'Sullivan, Pat [chief operating officer, PBL]
> To: Backwell, Andrew [head of Channel 9 production]
> Cc: Audsley, Ian [Channel 9 chief operating officer]; Healy, Michael [head of programming]
> Subject: OSCARS
>
> Andrew I understand that we may have had 4 reporters at the awards last night compared to only 1 from [Channel] 7. I know we ran a show last night and to my knowledge 7 didn't but can you please provide me with some insights as to the size of the team we had versus competitors.
> Appreciate your help. Rgds
> Pat

What is remarkable about that query is that it shows no understanding whatsoever of Nine's exclusive access to the Academy Awards venue, with the extra opportunities that offered for news and current affairs coverage. Meanwhile, why would Channel 7 be interested in promoting a Channel 9-owned blockbuster, other than by a cursory mention in its news?

In a return e-mail, Andrew Backwell tried to explain to O'Sullivan 'that as Seven did not have the rights to broadcast the awards, I imagine they only used their local news reporter to file a story'. He added that the reporter for *ACA* had flown to Los Angeles to cover 'a number of *ACA* stories' in addition to the Academy Awards. So it was that 'Richard Wilkins was the only Nine presenter to travel to LA specifically to cover the awards, with the cost covered in the *Today* show budget'.

That, obviously, was still not good enough for O'Sullivan, who sent his next e-mail directly to Mark Llewellyn, along with a copy to Ian Audsley.

> Mark/Ian, please see below Andrew's response to a question I asked him about reporters at the Academy Awards the other night. As this is a recent event I want to ensure I get my head around what appears on face value to be a double up of costs so I can understand if we can be more efficient in this type of instance going forward and if so how.
>
> The obvious 'dumb' questions this begs are:
> 1) Why couldn't we use a common resource for both [Channel] 9 programs?
> 2) How does our LA office come into play here?
> 3) Can we be more efficient going across the [network] if we are covering the same stories?
>
> Don't want to waste your time on small issues but also trying to see if systemic issues that can be removed to help costs going forward.
> Cheers
> Pat

Llewellyn got back to O'Sullivan a few hours later with this explanation.

Dear Pat,
Tried to reach you. Please feel free to call when you have the time.

The explanation given is that Richard Wilkins was simply too busy to cover every base. On the day he filed live crosses and packages for the *Today* show and KAK [Kerri-Anne Kennerley] before doing a series of pre-interviews for the *Red Carpet Special*. As it was he worked 15 hours straight for these commitments. In addition he is currently recording a series of interviews which will be run over the next few weeks in *Today* and Ninemsn.

LA News files for the 11 am, 4.30 pm and 6 pm bulletins as well as *Nightline*. Wilkins didn't have time to do this.

Re *ACA*, they decided a presence was needed in the event that Heath Ledger won and because previously Oscar has helped ratings. The Academy Awards gave them a preview story including a Nicole Kidman update, a set-up story on the Australian animator who won an Oscar, a live cross to Hollywood for red carpet fashions – plus two other separate stories [on a *CSI* star and plastic surgery exposé]. In short five stories in five days.

As to going forward, I would propose that if Leila McKinnon becomes a 9 presence in LA that she have a wider role than just News which would solve some of the concerns expressed – this will be part of my proposal.
Regards
Mark L.

O'Sullivan's reply to that seemed straightforward enough, if a bit niggling.

Many thanks for that response. Clearly an opportunity to be tighter on this going forward.

The next morning, however, on 9 March, O'Sullivan was to send another e-mail to Chris Anderson, deputy executive chairman of the PBL board, putting the correspondence to that point in a much more sinister light.

From: O'Sullivan, Pat
To: Anderson, Chris
Subject: OSCARS – FYI

Chris, a brief summary of the 'double up' on Oscars. Clearly a good example of some bad behaviour that I have on my radar to remove.
Rgrds
Pat

Chris Anderson, for his part, would paint a blacker picture still in his e-mail to O'Sullivan, making sure to copy in John Alexander.

From: Anderson, Chris
To: O'Sullivan, Pat
Cc: Alexander, John
Subject: Re: OSCARS – FYI

Pat
Tks [thanks] – a small matter – but clearly nonsense. See Backwell's response below. *ACA* 'just happened' to have a reporter/crew in the area covering a 'number of stories' (in LA???) so they covered the Academy Awards??? And Llewellyn contradicts this by saying they were there for Heath Ledger! They clearly think we're idiots – and presume (as happened in the past) we'll just go away.
Tks
CJA

From John Alexander comes the most scathing response of all, sending an e-mail directly to Llewellyn that fairly resonates with his disgust. The note contains a reference to the Packer estate at Ellerston, where a conference had recently been held to stress the need for greater efficiencies.

From: Alexander, John
To: Llewellyn, Mark
Cc: Anderson, Chris; O'Sullivan, Pat
Subject: FW: OSCARS – FYI

This sounds like something from the wizard of OZ . . . is this true? If it is it is very disappointing . . . is this your idea of running news and current affairs efficiently? was Ellerston a waste of time?

As much as he had been warned to watch his back, Llewellyn could only have been stunned by the extraordinary vehemence of such a response. Within an hour he sent the PBL boss a carefully worded response, remarkably calm and level-headed under the circumstances.

Dear John,
In short, Ellerston was not a waste of time. My primary focus these past ten days has been preparing a proposal to be presented to Eddie McGuire tomorrow which will outline efficiencies that have to be made in News and Current Affairs to 1/ slash the News Caff budget and 2/ reinvigorate our shows and reinvent the way Nine does news and current affairs 3/ vastly improve the linkage between Nine, Ninemsn, PBL and ACP and 4/ increase the opportunity for reporters/presenters to appear widely across network programming.

If approved and if implemented, Nine News and Current

Affairs will not only be substantially cheaper but more progressive – in line with the views that have been expressed.

I clearly do not think you are idiots nor do I presume that you 'will just go away'. In fact I would much prefer a more regular line of communication. For the record, the old ways are not my way – I am very much onboard with the ideas that have been communicated by you, Chris and James. However, if you have doubts about my ability to do this then we should clear the air.

The report I sent to Pat was not an attempt to whitewash or 'spin'. I went to the various EP's and asked for their explanations which I reported. As I mentioned to Pat yesterday, part of my proposal will be for increased pollination of reporters/presenters on various shows – with the express purpose of eliminating unnecessary duplication.
Kind regards,
Mark Llewellyn

That was to be the end of the e-mail trail, at least until it surfaced again as an attachment in Llewellyn's affidavit. His appeal to 'clear the air' was met by stony silence from Alexander – no phone call, no further contact of any kind. He would later hear that even Pat O'Sullivan and Chris Anderson were taken aback by the PBL chief's vitriolic reprimand. Llewellyn's sense of hurt and disillusionment comes through clearly enough in his affidavit.

I have no difficulty with robust e-mail exchanges. However, I found the tone of John Alexander's e-mail of 9 March at 9.07 am to be extremely aggressive and deliberately disparaging. I perceived Mr Alexander's e-mail (on top of my earlier discussions with him) as a further attempt to prepare grounds to get rid of me from the position. I inter-

preted the e-mails as an attempt to create the means to question and criticise my competence. Of particular concern to me was the fact that neither John Alexander nor Chris Anderson had telephoned me prior to sending the e-mails to discuss the matter with me first.

Just two months after that intimidating episode, another print journalist in Alexander's favoured circle was to be secretly offered Mark Llewellyn's job. Garry Linnell, then editor-in-chief of the PBL-owned *Bulletin* magazine was, by any standard, an outstanding newsman, rising through the ranks of the Melbourne *Age* as reporter and deputy editor before going on to become a feature writer for Fairfax's *Good Weekend* magazine. Though he had no television experience, Linnell would at least have the good sense to understand the importance of learning the techniques of TV journalism as quickly and thoroughly as possible. The details about how he was approached to take over as Nine's newscaff boss would only be revealed when he was required to file an affidavit for the Llewellyn court case. (Linnell would later tell me that he made an inadvertent error in that hastily prepared sworn statement, confusing a brief chat he had with Eddie McGuire in March to a more formal approach from McGuire and Jeff Browne in early May.)

In or about early March [May, as amended] I was approached by Jeffrey Browne and Eddie McGuire to join Nine as Head of News and Current Affairs. I had a series of discussions [with them]. When I first considered this position one of my immediate concerns related to Mark Llewellyn. I was concerned because I thought Mark Llewellyn was a strong performer, a long-standing employee of Nine and someone who had a lot to offer. I also understood that Mr Llewellyn was well liked and I did not want to lose him. During my discussions with them I had been informed by Mr McGuire that: 'I had a chat with Mark and I don't think he is adverse to changing roles.' Mr McGuire said words to the effect: 'We need to become news breakers and to do this we need someone in this role who can make quick and firm decisions.'

Llewellyn, of course, knew nothing about the approach to Linnell when he was called into conference with McGuire and Browne. His sworn accounts of this and subsequent meetings are described by Channel 9 lawyers as 'untested allegations' and a passage here or there specifically contested as lacking in accuracy. My own assessment, however, is that the general tone of these discussions can be taken to be very much as Llewellyn depicts it, although the first part, in particular, is disputed.

At 3.30 pm on 31 May, 2006 I was called to a meeting with Eddie McGuire and Mr Jeffrey Browne, Executive Director at Nine. After some initial conversation about general news and current affairs topics a conversation took place as follows. Mr McGuire said: 'What are we gonna do about Jessica? When should we bone her? I reckon it should be next week.' [McGuire denies using the word bone in the context suggested.]

By Jessica, McGuire was referring to Jessica Rowe, the presenter of the *Today* program.

I said: 'Are you sure you want to get rid of her?'

Mr Browne said: 'She's a laughing stock and if we keep her on air we will be the laughing stock.'

I said: 'Have you thought through what might happen if she goes? We went to all that trouble to get her from Ten and they copped the bad publicity and now we'll cop it. Secondly, Peter Overton [Rowe's husband and a *60 Minutes* reporter] will be really upset and we run the risk of losing him from the network. That might be a real problem, because he might end up at Channel 7.'

Mr McGuire said: 'Well, maybe we have to take that risk.'

After another brief exchange on the issue, McGuire gets to the point of the meeting. The quotes to follow are drawn from the sworn affidavit but in slightly edited form to preserve the natural flow of the conversation.

'Look, mate, I'll think about it,' McGuire begins. 'Now, let's talk about you.'

'This is not going to be a pleasant conversation,' Browne forewarns, 'but you've got to know that you're a gun, a real talent.'

'Absolutely,' Eddie agrees.

'We've got big plans for you at the network,' Browne continues, 'and Eddie and I think you are one of the real talents at Nine. This is therefore a difficult chat, because there is a shit sandwich you're going to be asked to swallow. We want to cut your pay to $400,000 and we want you to consider taking on one of two new positions.'

'That's some shit sandwich,' Llewellyn responds.

McGuire goes on to explain that John Westacott, executive producer of the ratings powerhouse *60 Minutes*, is also being asked to take 'a massive haircut'. If Westacott chooses to leave, 'we want you to run the program because there's nobody else on this network other than you who can do it'. McGuire then mentions a number of other opportunities, including producing major one-off special events for the network and initiating other new programs, as well as implementing changes to existing programs such as *Today* and *Sunday*. 'I want you to be the network's storm trooper answering only to me,' he adds.

Llewellyn is obviously unimpressed. 'I don't want to go back to *60 Minutes*. Is the $400,000 negotiable?'

'We are being squeezed by Park Street,' Browne replies, 'and this is the best deal we can offer. If we pay you more it means someone else is losing a job.'

'I want someone to come in and oversee Nine News,' McGuire then reveals.

'Who's that?'

'Garry Linnell, the editor of the *Bulletin*. I want the two of you to work hand in glove and together you can turn the network around. The excellent work you've done on Beaconsfield [the Tasmanian mine collapse] and the [Kerry] Packer Special shows me that you are one of the people I need on my team.'

'You've got to realise, Mark,' Browne encourages him, 'that Eddie and I not only like you enormously but we think you are an absolute talent.'

'Your creative skills are second to none,' Eddie reaffirms, 'and that's why I want you to consider the new role so you will be playing to your forehand.'

Browne adds, reassuringly: 'We do not want to be having this conversation about money, but you will be paid at the top echelon of executive salaries at Nine; and others as well will have to take pay cuts. You can choose your title and for that matter have an input on Linnell's. This is not a demotion for you and it won't be sold that way if you agree to take on the new role.'

'Do you think Linnell could do a better job than me?' Llewellyn asks.

'Look me in the eye,' McGuire responds, 'because I'm going to give it to you straight. I don't know whether Linnell will be better or worse but I think you are being played out of position. I regard you as a mate and hopefully a friend and I want you to be part of my team. I want you to be making television.'

Browne returns to the issue of salary. 'Those who stay loyal, even if they got a pay cut, will be rewarded when the good economic times come back to Nine. I can't give you an absolute promise, but I will do my best to make sure you will be looked after and rewarded when the good times return. You know what type of man I am and you should trust me on this.'

'There might be a bit more in the kick regarding the $400,000 but not much more,' McGuire adds hopefully.

That clearly is enough information for Llewellyn to have to take in for one afternoon. Browne sums up his options as follows. 'There are three ways you can play this. You can tell us to fuck off, which is not a helpful answer; or you can say yes, and be part of our team, going forward; or you can say you'll think about it, which isn't the greatest answer for us either.'

Llewellyn, in his own words, is by then feeling shocked and threatened with the loss of entitlements guaranteed to him by a written contract signed less than six months earlier. He takes the third option. 'I will think about it. I will consider everything you said and I will get back to you. Understand that I like you both and have been tremendously loyal to you and to the network. But this is a bitter pill you have asked me to swallow.'

The next day, Llewellyn is called into another meeting. According to his affidavit, it begins this way.

'My lawyer's advice is that what happened yesterday was repudiation of my contract. I don't want to change my contract because I would lose my rights under it and I also think a contract is a contract.' That announcement brings a stern warning from Browne.

'Mate, you've got to know I like you,' he says, 'but if you want to choose the legal route it's gonna get really nasty and it will be your word against mine and Eddie's. Let's just look how we can sweeten the deal.'

McGuire moves quickly to cool down the situation. 'Look we came on a bit hard and a bit low yesterday. I think I can get you a bit more. I tell you, we wouldn't be trying this hard with some other people in the network.'

Llewellyn, once again, asks for more time to consider his

position. On Friday, 2 June, he's called to the third meeting in three days. As much stress as he feels within himself, he can't possibly know that the pressure is also building up on the other side. It appears Park Street has set a deadline for an important announcement of a major upheaval within the news and current affairs division.

'Well, Mark,' Eddie greets him, 'are you going to tell us to fuck off?'

'If it wasn't for the fact that I respected you both that probably would have been my answer,' Llewellyn tells them. 'This is really disappointing for me. I've been working my guts out for the network not just for the last few months but for the last few years.' With that he raises the possibility of a compromise. 'Without prejudice, I want to put a proposal. You pay me out what you owe me on the rest of the contract and we will negotiate a new one.'

'Mate, we're not gonna do that and you know that,' Browne rebuffs him. 'We really like you, we really want you to stay, ours is a good offer.'

'Come on, Mark,' McGuire encourages him, 'let's shake hands and do the deal now. I'm not gonna let you out of the office until we've done the deal.'

Once again, however, Llewellyn insists he needs more time to discuss the situation with his lawyer, as well as his partner, Margie. Like many couples they have a mortgage and car lease repayments to consider. The following Monday afternoon, 5 June, there is a fourth meeting at which Llewellyn makes this heartfelt plea.

'I'm sure Garry Linnell is a fantastic bloke, but he's got no experience in television. Are you sure you want to get rid of me? This is exactly what happened to Peter Meakin when Alexander got rid of him. It was a huge blow to the network. We lost all that knowledge and experience. The damage has been enormous.'

According to Llewellyn, his appeal was met with silence.

'McGuire and Browne just looked at me.' As he gets up to leave, however, Browne steps in with another offer based on a starting salary of $425,000 and topped up with bonuses, but still considerably below the $750,000 a year Llewellyn was already earning.

'Mark we can do it a bit better. I could pay you a $50,000 bonus in the first year and a $25,000 bonus in the second year to bring it up to $500,000.' Llewellyn has his own solicitor, John Laxon, waiting for him downstairs on this occasion and Browne agrees to meet him. That would ordinarily mark the beginning of a classic lawyers' wrangle over the terms under which Nine's director of news and current affairs might – just might – agree to surrender his title and accept a lower level of salary. Incredible as it seems, however, Park Street has already approved a press release timed for the next morning announcing Linnell's appointment and a new title for Llewellyn that will be total news to him. At about 9.30 on the morning of 6 June, Llewellyn is called into Jeff Browne's office and a conversation takes place as follows.

'We've got to make this announcement today,' Browne tells him. 'I've got your current contract here and it's within our rights to ask you to do these duties.'

Llewellyn has obviously been well briefed by his solicitor and responds with due caution. 'Mate, I haven't seen your new proposal but I'm happy to look at it. But until there is an agreement, there's no agreement.' Browne escorts him next door to McGuire's office, where he tells Eddie the same thing: 'There is simply no agreement until we have an agreement.' McGuire then shows him the press release, urging: 'Come on, mate, let's just do it.' Llewellyn's affidavit, describing his immediate reaction to the document shoved in front of him, gives but a faint idea of what he must have really felt.

'I read the press release headed "Nine Unveils Vision for Future of News and Current Affairs – Garry Linnell Appointed Head of News and Current Affairs". I was upset and shocked by this and as a result was not able to make any comment on its contents.' Who could blame him? On the first day of discussions Browne had assured him of his right to have input into the changeover, yet he was not even given the courtesy of having the slightest say in the press release that mentions him by name.

Nine's press release of 6 June, 2006, would turn out to be an example of public relations spin so out of control as to be almost Monty Pythonesque in its patent absurdity – an announcement met by howls of ridicule from media circles throughout the nation. It speaks volumes about the Park Street mentality that it could ever imagine journalists being distracted by such glitzy nonsense.

'Nine Network CEO Eddie McGuire today appointed *Bulletin* Editor Garry Linnell as Head of News and Current Affairs to lead the development of a new, cutting edge blueprint for news and current affairs broadcasting in Australia,' the announcement began. It then went on to read in part:

> 'Around the world, the way news is gathered and presented is changing rapidly and I want Nine to lead the evolution in this country,' Mr McGuire said. 'We regard Garry Linnell as one of the best news people in Australia, and he is the right person to lead, innovate and invigorate our news and current affairs programming. I am delighted to announce that Mark Llewellyn will move to Executive Producer of News and Current Affairs and will have the prime responsibility of overseeing our leadership in news production. Garry and Mark have highly complementary skills sets. Garry as head of News and Current Affairs will drive the new vision. Mark makes great news and current affairs television. It's a powerhouse combination.'

Only then comes the real news of the day, almost as a footnote.

Mr McGuire said the new strategy would mean that up to 100 redundancies would occur at the network, the majority of which will affect news and current affairs in Sydney.

Nine was about to give the chop to close to one in five of its news and current affairs staff in the face of a steady decline in audience over the previous four years. That, presumably, was Park Street's idea of *cutting-edge* TV journalism.

Llewellyn would suffer the added indignity of having to join the parade into the Channel 9 boardroom to confront the curious glances of his long-time colleagues as his fate was revealed to them. True, he could have stormed off in protest but it's easy to understand his dilemma. Llewellyn, at that stage, had no sure prospect of finding another job if he left Nine. If he chose to fight for his rightful entitlements under his existing contract he faced the prospect of piling up crushing personal debts in a lengthy court battle with no certainty of what amount he might be awarded in the end. It was a daunting prospect for someone not yet 45. Even if he emerged from the legal meat grinder with the settlement of a million dollars or more, he would still have to try to find work in a relatively small industry whose bosses were inherently suspicious of anyone with a reputation as a troublemaker.

For the next two weeks, then, he appeared to be resigned to staying on, at least long enough to help Linnell adapt to his new environment. They met on several occasions to discuss various changes the new newscaff chief intended to introduce, including the redundancy process which Park Street had ordered. No doubt Llewellyn was still hoping that Nine would show good faith by proposing a more realistic settlement of his existing contract. Just the opposite: two incidents occurred in quick succession to leave him almost totally shattered.

'On 9 June I was at lunch when I received a phone call from my personal assistant. She said to me: "You don't have an office to

come back to. They reckon they've got a new office for you upstairs." No one had bothered to warn Llewellyn in advance of such a move and indeed, there would not even be a word of apology until it became obvious a few days later that he was on the verge of leaving. According to his legal adviser, his contract had in fact already been repudiated by the network. On that basis he felt free to contact his long-time friend and mentor, Peter Meakin, to seek his counsel on what other opportunities might be open to him within the industry. The two met for what they hoped to be a strictly confidential lunch together on Wednesday, 14 June. The next day, however, Llewellyn was surprised by Eddie McGuire walking into his office.

'I know you had lunch with Meakin yesterday,' McGuire told him.

'Eddie,' he replied, 'a lot of my colleagues are concerned about my personal and professional wellbeing.'

'That's okay, but you've got to realise that here at Nine we're also concerned about your wellbeing,' Eddie assured him. 'I really want you to stay. It's like a footy team. If you're on the team you'll be looked after for life. We'll be blood brothers. I want you on my team.'

Llewellyn answered as honestly as he could, telling the Nine CEO how upset he had been by all that had happened, topped off by his office being taken away without anyone having the courtesy to inform him.

'Oh, mate, that was Audsley,' McGuire tried to laugh off the incident. 'We all know he was born without a compassion gene. Don't worry, these things can be fixed.' Before McGuire left he tried to reassure him once again: 'Stick with us, we'll make sure you're looked after', while adding: 'Mate, we've got to do this soon.'

That same day, however, there would be another distressing incident – also to be lightly dismissed by Jeff Browne as a simple mistake. Llewellyn checked his monthly bank statement to see that in place of the usual deposit of $24,947, Nine's payment had been reduced without warning to $16,087. 34 – $8860 short.

'This represented the final straw for me,' Llewellyn says. 'I formed the view that Nine would do whatever it wanted to do, regardless of the terms of my contract.' On Monday, 19 June he instructed his solicitor to formally notify Nine that Mark Llewellyn accepted Nine's repudiation of his contract and considered his employment with the network at an end. With that decision made, he accepted an offer put to him by Channel 7 on terms that were actually below what McGuire and Browne had finally ended up offering him. He began working with his new boss Peter Meakin the next morning, Tuesday 20 June.

For all the headlines to follow, many people still have a mistaken idea about what the Llewellyn court case was all about. They assume that he was taking action against Channel 9 for wrongful dismissal. The truth – as hard as it is to believe under the circumstances – is that Nine launched the lawsuit against him, claiming breach of contract and naming the Seven Network as a co-defendant. Not only did Nine's lawyers initiate the action, but they did so playing as ruthless a game of hard ball as the law allows – applying for an injunction in the New South Wales Supreme Court at 3 pm on Thursday, 22 June, after giving Llewellyn's solicitor notice of their intentions in a fax sent at 2.33 pm, leaving less than half an hour to get to court. From that point on it became the kind of legal battle that movies are made of – the prestigious CBD law firm Deacons against the small inner-city practice of Hillman Laxon Tobias based, symbolically enough, atop the quirky old Verona cinema in Oxford Street, Paddington. Deacons had a small army of lawyers, clerks and secretaries on call to start compiling the bundles of documents needed to mount such a case. John Laxon had only a few extra hands to help him. He called an industrial law barrister, Arthur

Moses, to rush to the court in time to oppose Nine's motion for a restraining order to stop Llewellyn's defection. The presiding judge, Justice Campbell, refused to grant the injunction but set the matter down for further hearing at 2 pm the next day and ordered the parties to exchange affidavits.

For Llewellyn it must have been like setting off on the equivalent of a legal marathon, working with Laxon late into the night and through the next morning to start putting together a substantial sworn affidavit in time for the next court appearance. Because he had been keeping extensive file notes ever since that night at the Coogee Palace when John Alexander first phoned him, they made good progress. There was no doubt of the relevance of such explosive material. For Nine to sustain its claim of breach of contract, it would have to try to explain away ample evidence of pre-existing malice towards Llewellyn traceable to the chief executive officer of PBL himself. In preparing his sworn statement, there must have been a point when Llewellyn suddenly realised the inherent irony of McGuire's question about Jessica Rowe – the seamless segue from being asked how he felt about the destruction of her career to discussing the destruction of his own.

With time rapidly running out for their 2 pm court appearance that Friday, Laxon must have still had a mountain of formalities to get through. Loaded down with bundles of paperwork, he raced into court just seconds before Justice Campbell arrived at the bench – first handing a copy of the affidavit to his barrister, Arthur Moses, to brief himself as fast as he could. Then he presented more copies to the high-powered legal teams representing Seven and Nine, Tom Hughes, QC in the case of of Channel 7 and Tony Bannon, SC for Nine. The room, of course, was packed with journalists. They couldn't help but notice the faces of Nine's lawyers as they flipped from one page to the next of Mark Llewellyn's sworn statement – their expressions running the gamut of emotion from looks of studied disdain, to disbelief, to utter dismay.

The hearing lasted no more than an hour. By 6.25 that evening Deacons had raised the white flag, sending notice that Nine's legal action was to be withdrawn and costs paid to both Llewellyn and Seven. That, however, was only the beginning of the network's embarrassing backdown. Even before McGuire and Browne set their lawyers on Llewellyn, he himself had told friends he was seriously considering mounting a case against Nine for breach of contract somewhere down the line. Nine's bullish aggressiveness left him little choice but to proceed to defend his interests. His solicitor, John Laxon, was quick to file a statement of claim on behalf of his client in the Federal Court that same evening.

Park Street now intervened to ensure damage control, taking negotiations out of Nine's hands. Desperate to avoid any further court action that might see the affidavit formally introduced as evidence – thus making it a privileged document freely available to the press – PBL lawyers signalled their intention for an immediate settlement. At a conference called for Sunday afternoon, the two sides agreed on terms that were strictly confidential but believed to be close to what Llewellyn was seeking. Ironically, just around the time that deal was being finalised, the media world came alive with rumours of a major story about to break – details of the Llewellyn affidavit had somehow leaked into the public domain. The *Australian*'s John Lehmann, the same reporter who had published the leak about John Lyons's reinstatement, was known to have a copy of the affidavit in his hands by that Sunday. For some reason, however, he didn't proceed to file a story for his paper that night. Meanwhile, at 4 pm on Sunday the Internet newsletter *Crikey* received the following message on its computer system.

As a former Nine employee (for over 15 years) I'm hardly surprised that Mark Llewellyn was treated like he was, it was

only a matter of time before they turned against one of
the only decent people left in executive ranks. The PBL/
Alexander/McGuire regime is the most oppressive in the
network's history. But it is only half the story. See the affidavit filed in the case Nine brought against Mark last week.
Is it any wonder Nine fell on its sword and will be left with
a huge legal bill for themselves as well as Mark's and Sevens.

The message carried a name that was most likely a pseudonym
but to ensure protection of identity – as the sender requested of
Crikey – I will only mention the initials: J.Y. What followed was a
virtually complete copy of Llewellyn's sworn statement. *Crikey*
had no hesitation in publishing highlights of the sensational
affidavit. PBL, in full panic mode, hurled itself into a week of
intensive court action trying to prevent the story from spreading
throughout the mainstream press. The power of the Internet,
however, would prove all conquering. To try to stop information
flowing from it is tantamount to fanning the flames of a bushfire.
The press in Victoria and other states, for a start, were not necessarily bound by any edict issued by a court in New South Wales
and the *Age* was delighted to pounce on the story. Newspapers in
New South Wales soon overflowed with hints and whispers that
appeared more titillating than the actual allegations themselves.

By Friday, 30 June, Park Street had once again admitted defeat,
withdrawing attempts to suppress documents tendered in the
federal and state courts, as well as another widely ridiculed bid to
force Fairfax and News Ltd newspapers to disclose the sources of
their reports. The QCs' picnic would have ended up costing
Channel 9 a small fortune. Whatever the cost in dollar terms,
however, it was negligible compared to the toll inflicted by the
public relations disaster to follow. If Mark Llewellyn hadn't been
hounded with a senseless law suit, his account of John Alexander's
attempt to misuse his network's current affairs resources against

Kerry Stokes might never have come to light. As it was, the Stokes allegation not only captured the keen attention of the press but of Federal Court Judge Steven Rares, who pointed out its serious implications in his order of Thursday, 30 June, dismissing Nine's attempt to prevent details of the affidavit being reported. 'In my opinion,' he ruled, 'the way in which public broadcasting licences are conducted and the responsibility of those in senior positions within them as to their conduct is a matter . . . capable of being of genuine public interest.'

Alexander's vigorous intervention in the Lyons affair, for reasons known only to himself, might also have passed virtually unnoticed. Those were both issues of potentially explosive signif- icance, though for the general public the scandal could be summed up in a single phrase. 'Bone Jessica' was suddenly on everyone's lips, an instant talking point, likely to become a lively part of the Aussie vernacular, perhaps even granted a hallowed place in the Macquarie Dictionary. Its definition: *to betray someone one publicly pretends to hold in high esteem.*

Ten days of litigious madness had turned Australia's most influential television network into a national laughing stock.

CHAPTER 18

Kerry who?

There was a fleeting moment when a faint ray of hope appeared – a slim possibility that the troubled network might yet find a way to hold fast to the values that had once given it such a special place in the homes and hearts of so many Australian viewers. In October, 2005, amidst all the purges and politicking, Sam Chisholm recruited one of the nation's best-known television executives to try to revive Nine's fortunes with her fresh ideas and strategic vision. Sandra Levy's special brief was to develop programs that could satisfy Park Street's budgetary demands, yet still offer an exciting new range of viewing options to Nine's dwindling share of prime time audience.

Levy, up to then, had held the most prestigious job in TV programming – director of television for the ABC. What would some sequestered high priestess of public broadcasting know about life in the savage jungle of commercial television? It may have been an obvious question for anyone outside the industry, but hilarious to those who knew Levy's formidable track record. For a start, she had spent much of her career in the tooth-and-claw environment of independent production, proving herself as tough and wily a survivor as they come. Having been through the infamous Jonathan Shier era at the ABC, she had no qualms about facing up to the political infighting raging at Nine during the last months of Kerry Packer.

Packer himself greeted her warmly as a most promising acquisition to the management team and he obviously knew a lot about her achievements. He made a point of congratulating her on the original programming she had introduced to the ABC and her success in growing the public broadcaster's audiences by a remarkable 24 per cent. Levy, for her part, had her own firm opinions of where Packer's precious network was going wrong, running out of the 'creative energy' that had made it such a formidable competitor in the past. That kind of mental electricity can only be generated within the grinding mill of artistic freedom – allowing your people to take whatever risks necessary to produce the best programs possible, subject to the resources they have to work with. As to the need to take risks, no one disagreed – not Kerry, not John Alexander. It wasn't long, however, before Levy began to realise they might as well have been speaking different languages. Their meaning of *risk* – unlike hers – most definitely did not include the possibility of making mistakes or failing. But that was only one of any number of disillusioning discoveries awaiting her when she walked through the impressive glass doors at Willoughby. Sam had offered her the position of director of development, with the prospect of having control of tens of millions of dollars in funding for locally made productions.

'When I got there,' Levy recalls with a wry smile, 'I didn't know there was somebody there who already had that title, director of development and production, so that was shock number one.

Shock number two: there really wasn't a job, there really wasn't a budget and there really wasn't much interest in anything I wanted to say or do.'

Under the circumstances, being the positive, alpha-type female she was, she set out to carve a useful place for herself as best she could. There was no doubt in her mind that the network was in urgent need of local content. Its traditional overseas output deals had failed to come up with a new generation of hits to match Seven's and apart from news and current affairs, some of its domestic offerings were beginning to look decidedly stale and old-fashioned. Drawing on her lengthy experience in production, she attempted to establish her own development group, only to find no real support from within Nine's programming department. There was no one to report to her and none of the research facilities she had been used to at the ABC. Still, she put forward some intriguing new program concepts, including the idea for a crime drama to be performed live on air, a touch of pure theatre meant to coincide with the fiftieth anniversary of television in Australia, taking the medium back to its seat-of-the-pants beginnings. The show could have been made for a rock-bottom price and fitted perfectly into the theory that in the days of pay TV and the Internet, modern free-to-air television needed to be driven by unique events to give it that special buzz. Those around her went through the motions of nodding 'good idea', only to let it sink without trace. She also tried to interest the network in an ambitious strategy for large-scale production of weekly tele-movies – up to 90 over three years – allowing it to meet its compulsory drama quotas in a distinctly innovative, yet cost effective way. No one could see any merit in such long-range planning, let alone be bothered trying to find out more.

'I just felt like I was moonwalking,' is her vivid metaphor, 'not knowing how to get anyone to commit to anything, they were all so busy being terrified. What drove me mad was the passivity, the dysfunction of the place, the inability to get anyone to stick their head up above the trenches and make decisions.'

The situation got no better for her even after Posie Graeme-Evans decided to resign as head of drama in November, 2005, to get back to what she loved best, producing series and writing historical novels. Like Levy, Posie herself felt at times as if she were walking through jelly. Under the pressure of cost-cutting it was a tribute to her that she could still get widely acclaimed block-busters like *Little Oberon, The Alice* and *Two Twisted* off the deck, designed as high-quality pilots with a built-in potential for future series spin-offs. The gossip columns made up stories about a supposed rivalry between her and Levy; but the truth was, they both had nothing but respect for each other and the last thing Levy had wanted, in joining Nine, was to involve herself in drama. Upon Posie's departure, Sandra's high-sounding title of director of development was extended to director of development and drama, but even that led to a dead-end amid the crackdown on expenditure. As she sums up: 'I was given enormous seniority in that place, and absolutely nothing to do.'

Levy first thought of resigning in mid-December, only a couple of months after she arrived. It was clear, however, that with Kerry's health rapidly fading, there would soon be another regime in place under James. She decided to wait a little longer in the hope that the network might yet be given a chance to introduce the creative thinking so desperately needed. After Kerry's death, James called together all of PBL's various divisions to a meeting at Ellerston to outline his corporation's broad goals for the future. Levy attended and took to heart the message that came out of the conference: that Nine was but a small part of a very powerful empire and needed to prove its worth by becoming a more prof-itable operation.

Far from disagreeing, she had a clear vision of how that goal could best be accomplished. Here was a network built on the fundamental principle that winning the ratings was all that mattered and profits were sure to follow. For more than a quarter of a century, Kerry Packer's hard-line message had been hammered into every brain – there was no excuse for being second best. Now, under James Packer, the guidelines had changed to put the focus on profitability before ratings; yet the old mentality at Nine still persisted. People were afraid to take chances, to attempt new solutions because they still lived in a climate where losing a time slot was synonymous with failing. Anyone who dared to try something different and didn't succeed knew he was putting his job on the line: left out on his own to suffer the consequences.

What was required, Levy decided, was to call a kind of psychological moratorium for a year or two to break the vicious cycle of blame and shame. Nine needed a leader strong enough to take the heat of coming second or third, as nerve-wracking as that could be – a boss able to guarantee his program makers that their jobs were secure even if they took a risk and failed. 'They need to feel their CEO is there to protect them in that phasing-out period and say, "This is a shift in policy. I'm accountable. I'll wear the damage, you don't have to."'

To an old Packer man, that might sound like heresy – accepting the idea that second place is good enough.

'It's not saying its okay to come in second,' Levy insists. 'It's a CEO saying to his people, "You should make the best program you can, with the budget that you've got, with the deficiencies that we've put forward to you – and I will take the rap if the ratings go down." That's what seniority is all about.'

Sandra Levy would never get the chance to put that common sense proposition to Park Street. By March she had endured all she could take. She told Eddie McGuire she intended to resign. He made at least a gesture of trying to get her to stay, calling a meeting for the next evening with his chief programmer, Michael

Healy, to see if there was some way the network could define a more meaningful role for her. The three of them enjoyed a lively discussion over a scratch meal of pizzas in the office and spoke of various issues, but never quite got around to addressing the specific problem.

If Levy had any thoughts next morning of reconsidering, the decision had already been taken completely out of her hands. Someone had given the press a leaked report about her intentions to quit the network. Management decided it had no choice but to put out a statement confirming it was true, though with the usual sop about her keeping in touch in a consultancy role – which was quite untrue.

It's interesting to think what Sandra Levy might have achieved under a more supportive and sympathetic CEO like David Gyngell, who happened to be one of her great fans. Instead, that fleeting glimmer of hope she brought to the network would soon vanish in the prevailing gloom. The former director of ABC Television walked out of Nine with nothing more than three days' holiday pay and 'immense relief'. Her fate reveals a great deal about the sterile mindset that had taken hold at Park Street in terms of the running of the network, the kind of dead-end thinking that automatically favours negative decisions over those that have any chance of bearing fruit. It's easy enough to get rid of people to save a little money, as Channel 9 would do with its large-scale retrenchments; but if you fail to recognise and nurture your most valuable talent, you lose more than money can buy.

The idea of Eddie McGuire, on an extraordinary CEO salary exceeding $4.7 million a year, setting out to slash contract fees and staff numbers is not without a certain irony. His base remuneration was more than four times that of Seven's David Leckie, who was in the process of steering his network to unparalleled success. Jeff Browne, McGuire's alter ego, would not have come cheap either. Still, their two salaries together were dwarfed by

John Alexander's $7.7 million, much of which was earned over-
seeing the 'efficient' running of Channel 9. He wasn't the only
one at PBL headquarters with that brief. If we take, as a useful
guide, just the three names appearing on those notorious Oscar
emails to Mark Llewellyn – Alexander, Pat O'Sullivan and
Chris Anderson – the total annual wage bill exceeds $10 million,
largely representing their reward for holding down spending at
Channel 9.

In times of shrinking revenues, of course, painful decisions
have to be made and large-scale staff cuts are likely to be one of
them. Several years earlier the Seven Network reduced its staff
levels by even more, some 300 employees, and yet the news caused
barely a ripple by comparison. Nine's status as industry leader no
doubt added to the attention given to the job cuts – another sign
of its fading glory. Even then, however, the network seems to have
gone out of its way to handle an unpleasant task in the most
controversial way possible by pompously linking its retrenchments to a 'cutting-edge blueprint' for news and current affairs.

Before the finish of the 2006 ratings season, viewers would be
treated to their first glimpse of this new-look, cutting-edge journalism in a remodelled version of *Sunday* under the command of
the Walkley award-winning John Lyons. Lyons had been riding on
a high since his good friend and sponsor John Alexander ordered
his reinstatement as executive producer. The two men who dared
to try to remove him from his job – witnesses to his ritual humiliation – had left the network with their reputations scarred by
rumour and innuendo. Sam Chisholm retired in February. Mark
Llewellyn's career with Nine had effectively been scuttled at the
end of May. By late June, *Sunday*'s Peter Hiscock, considered
among the best producers at Willoughby, had also been sent
packing on the grounds 'there's no longer a place for you'. Management at first baulked at the prospect of having to compensate him
for the two years still to run on his contract but quickly caved in

after the furore stirred up by its treatment of Llewellyn.

Among those Lyons regarded as the chief conspirators against him, Jana Wendt was the only one still at the station – though not for much longer if he had his way. He and newscaff chief Garry Linnell had secretly begun to plot out a new *Sunday* format featuring Ellen Fanning and Ross Greenwood as co-hosts of a faster-paced, chattier show in the style of Seven's *Weekend Sunrise*. Clearly there would be no place for Jana, but no one was game to publicly admit as much since she still had more than two years to run on her contract and Park Street would have been furious to see the network paying out a million dollars or so without anything to show for it.

Of all Nine's programs, *Sunday* had been hardest hit by the recent wave of retrenchments and budget cuts. Wendt was forced to watch the 25-year-old institution – like some grand old castle – literally being dismantled around her piece by piece as she sat in her host's chair trying to exude a dignified presence. Bound by contract as she was, that's all she could do until management either came up with an acceptable alternative to using her services or made her a reasonable offer to terminate her agreement.

So began a tense stand-off as the star stood her ground, waiting for the network to openly declare its intentions. John Lyons, however, had no intention of seeing the game drag out, having to bear the presence of someone he regarded with growing resentment as the last of his arch-enemies still at the network.

On Friday, 28 July, the *Daily Telegraph* published a leaked report as vicious as one could be. It read in part:

AXE OVER JANA AS NINE TUNES TO ELLEN

Jana Wendt's position at Channel 9 is officially under review, with the star tipped to be axed as host of the flagship *Sunday* program. The *Daily Telegraph* can reveal Wendt's future will be decided in the next month ahead of a revamped *Sunday* to be unveiled on September 3. Former *60 Minutes* journalist Ellen Fanning is a front-runner to replace Wendt, who according to Nine insiders earns $600,000 a year and rarely comes into the office. It is understood Nine chief executive Eddie McGuire – who was accused of trying to 'bone' struggling *Today* co-host Jessica Rowe – is unimpressed with Wendt.'

Jana would naturally have expected the normally loquacious McGuire to immediately rush to her defence with a stinging denunciation of such an unwarranted attack on her character. For a start, she was renowned among her colleagues for her obsessive work ethic. If she had recently gone missing from the office for a day or two it was only because she had taken on the added task of writing feature pieces for the *Bulletin,* a PBL publication. The salary quoted in the article appeared to include not just her TV salary but her projected earnings from the magazine as well – a private arrangement that would have been known only to a few. Despite such distorted reporting, McGuire refused all attempts to elicit a meaningful comment and his silence spoke volumes. Jana's only logical choice was to speak out in her own defence, while seeking legal advice to make sure her contractual rights were being properly protected.

It makes little sense to speculate on who might have actually planted such a poisonous leak, but one fact can be established easily enough. As hurtful as the article must have been to Jana, it was also highly damaging to a network only just beginning to recover from the public relations disaster triggered by the 'boning Jessica' scandal. The one person most likely to derive any personal satisfaction from seeing such a vindictive piece in print was John Lyons. Perhaps, like good King Henry II, he, too, had sycophantic followers more than eager to help rid him of a troublesome presence. Unlike Henry, he didn't even attempt to deny revelling in the results of their dirty work.

For Wendt there was worse, much worse, to come. On 23 August, the *Telegraph*'s daily gossip section claimed to have the inside running on further developments involving Jana and Channel 9. Noting that three weeks had passed without McGuire issuing a supportive statement on the star's behalf, the piece went on:

> *Confidential* can also reveal that two of Wendt's own colleagues have lodged letters of no confidence in the *Sunday* host. In a brave mood in the current climate, two *Sunday* reporters made the official complaints about Wendt this week, lodging letters describing their dislike of Wendt with Executive Producer John Lyons. The reporters hoped their show of unity would influence Nine CEO Eddie McGuire's decision to remove the highly paid presenter and replace her with *Nightline*'s Ellen Fanning.

Together, the two leaks could only be described as an orchestrated smear against the reputation of one of the best-known names in Australian television, painting her in effect as a pampered, lazy ogre, detested by her workmates. If McGuire and other senior executives at Nine couldn't foresee the possible repercussions, the legal advisers at Park Street certainly could. The poisonous outpourings emanating from the *Sunday* cottage may have begun as a personal vendetta against Jana Wendt but they were now so clearly out of control as to threaten to engulf the entire network. To allow such invective to go unanswered could end up costing PBL a fortune in aggravated damages.

On 23 August, the same day as the *Telegraph*'s story about John Lyons having to put up with an anti-Wendt rebellion among his staff, Nine issued the following press release:

The Nine Network said today it had been in discussions with Jana Wendt in relation to . . . the possibility of a wider and more prominent role within the network's news and current affairs division. Nine said reports that Jana had been forced to leave the hosting role on *Sunday* were unfounded. Further, press reports to the effect that Jana had been the subject of official complaints from *Sunday* staff – or anyone else at the network – were untrue. Nine Network CEO Eddie McGuire said: 'Jana is one of Australia's most respected television journalists and the Network holds her in highest esteem. I am determined to see her remain in a prominent role with Nine.'

It was much too little and much too late. As Brad Norrington, a media writer for the *Australian*, astutely observed:

Kerry Packer would never have allowed the shenanigans evident at Nine to run out of control. The media mogul would not have permitted his plans to be communicated through press leaks and humiliation. He would not have tolerated the reputation of one of his brand-name stars getting trashed week after week, at a cost to Nine's standing, even if he happened to have misgivings about the person concerned. The treatment of Wendt is symptomatic of the turmoil that has taken hold across the board at Nine since Packer's death.

The legal jousting over Jana's contract entitlements would continue for a few days more. There had been speculation at one point that she might still agree to stay on at Channel 9 to do occasional reports for *60 Minutes* as well as take on the role of special correspondent covering major stories in the news. The truth was, though, the leaks had done the damage they were calculated to do – pushing her relationship with the network beyond any possibility of reconciliation. The terms of her settlement, like the others, were strictly confidential but believed to involve a substantial sum.

The revised program, with its two beaming hosts and breezier style, made its debut in the first week of September, reportedly bringing rave reviews from James Packer and Eddie McGuire who phoned John Lyons to congratulate him on a job well done. Well they should, because his show was destined to emerge as the perfect metaphor for the transformation of the entire network – its transition now complete from the old era to the new. A week after Jana left, it was still called *Sunday,* yet bore no relationship to the thought-provoking program of the same name that had given its devoted viewers so much pleasure and enlightenment for a quarter of a century. So it was with the network as a whole. It was still referred to in the TV guides by the same number but there was no doubting the difference.

Once there was Kerry Packer's Channel 9. Now there's a Channel 9 that bears no trace of anything he stood for. When I look at the network these days I imagine those solid old golden dots replaced by a minus sign. Minus Nine, to symbolise all that's missing.

Epilogue: a tale of two channels

Grandfather, father, son: three generations of Packer men called upon to steer Channel 9 through three distinctively different eras of Australian television. For Frank Packer, in the grey dawn of an exciting new industry, that meant infusing those around him with the raw energy needed to be first on air, rushing a studio complex to completion and transmitting the first magical images well before his competition. The promotional impact of such a feat was priceless, giving Channel 9 the aura of a winner – if not always the ratings to match – for decades to come.

For Kerry it meant forging ahead of his competitors, whatever the cost, to seize the dominant portion of the advertising bonanza that defined the Golden Age. As self-interested as that might sound, his pioneering efforts paved the way for commercial television as a whole to enjoy an unequalled period of prosperity when one considers the unique circumstances: a market restricted to just three licensed commercial networks, gorging themselves on one of the world's highest per capita levels of advertising expenditure.

To James has been left the far more complex task of finding a way to keep free-to-air television viable during the transition through its third and most precarious phase – the period commonly known as the sunset years. In his grandfather's time, when television enjoyed a virtual monopoly on home entertainment, Channel 9 could count on an astounding 75 per cent of all families with TV sets tuning into a favourite like *I Love Lucy*. That's three times the audience share that defines a hit show in today's terms, when attention is split among a variety of electronic diversions. Meanwhile, an information resource which his grandfather could never have imagined – the World Wide Web – is overtaking TV ad revenues at a furious rate.

James has been quick to grasp the implications of this tidal change, not just for Channel 9 but for broadcasting organisations world-wide. With the coming of the Internet as a universal distributor of audio-visual content, it no longer makes sense to think of free-to-air television as a stand-alone business. Reduced to basics, a TV station is merely a launching pad for one form of information among many and the future value of a network like Nine will be wholly dependent on the other activities to which it becomes aligned. Less than ten months after Kerry's death, James put that kind of forward thinking into practice with a deal hailed by business analysts as a major coup. In October, 2006, he sold 50 per cent of PBL's media assets to a foreign-owned investment company while still maintaining, temporarily at least, the controlling interest, giving him a multi-billion dollar war chest with which to finance future acquisitions both in the gaming and communication divisions. PBL itself would soon be split into separate corporations to reap a share market bonanza.

One can only guess what his father might have thought about such bold moves, producing figures that dwarfed his own billion dollar 'once in a lifetime' sale to Alan Bond. Since Kerry's passing his son has gone out of his way to defend his father's image as an astute and far-sighted businessman. Nevertheless, there's evidence to suggest that even if the late magnate recognised a new era looming, he was hesitant to do much about it, regarding it as a threat to all that he had achieved over 30 years. He needed someone else's more objective eye to point out the many opportunities just begging to be exploited.

In 1997 PBL joined forces with Bill Gates' Microsoft Corporation to launch ninemsn, destined to become Australia's most successful online content provider. It's generally been assumed that Kerry Packer himself initiated the necessary negotiations through his friendship with Gates – James was still in his late twenties and caught up in the hectic beginnings of the One.Tel saga. Harold Mitchell, the prominent media buyer, is happy to admit that he was among those who gave Kerry all the credit until a casual chat with James triggered a flash of insight into the true situation.

'PBL was there [with an Internet tie-in] right at the beginning, ten years ago, before any other media company started climbing aboard,' Mitchell enthuses. 'I can remember saying to James only recently, "It was pretty smart of Kerry to do that." It's not all that easy to slightly raise one eyebrow, but that's exactly what James did. And I suddenly realised it wasn't Kerry. James was just being appropriately fond and protective of his father, but it was really James.'

At the time ninemsn began operating, the amount of online advertising in this country was minuscule. By April 2007 it had passed the $1 billion mark. PBL, under James Packer's leadership, could claim almost one in every four dollars spent, most of it generated by the inspired cross-promotional link between the

Nine Network and Microsoft. That income is bound to grow exponentially. Before Channel 9 reaches its 55th anniversary in 2011, television industry revenues will almost certainly have been overtaken by online in terms of advertising share.

Amidst the starburst of revolutionary new media forms, then, was an old-style broadcaster like Nine doomed to shrivel and die in any case? Instead of asking *who* killed Channel 9, should we have been looking for a more natural cause for its demise – a dinosaur suffocating amid the heat and dust of a cataclysmic change of economic climate? The problem with that explanation is that it's so easily refuted by simply looking at how the Seven Network appears to be thriving in the same oxygen-deprived conditions, enjoying healthy profits, its people happy, self-confident and abuzz with creative excitement. That assessment has nothing to do with the ratings situation, which can always change in an instant based on the success or failure of one or two programs. Nine, as it turned out, still managed to scrape by to win the 2006 ratings season. Never, though, did a victory ring more hollow considering that Seven ended the year so far ahead by every other significant measure.

In fact, 2006 would mark an historic turning point in the 50-year history of Australian television – the first time ever that a second-ranking network actually ended up raking in the biggest share of available advertising revenue. Obviously, businesses anxious to publicise their wares saw Seven as where the action really was and were willing to pay premium prices to secure a spot within the network's formidable array of blockbuster hits. Nine, technically, was still number one, but no longer the dominant force in the industry.

The lesson seems clear enough. Nine's troubles since 2002, when a new management under John Alexander took control, go well beyond the repercussions to be expected from the pure economics of the situation – the squeeze on revenues inflicted by pay TV, online and other interactive media. Seven has had to run the same gauntlet, yet its morale has never been higher – seen by its staff as the most stimulating place to be, a mecca for men and women of talent just as Nine was regarded in its glory days. A prominent sports promoter and talent agent who has worked closely with both networks over many years finds himself amazed at the turnaround in attitude. 'You go to Seven and it's buzzing – people coming in and saying, "What about this? Can we do this?" At Nine, now, that's gone. People are frightened of making mistakes. Once you get like that, if you're worried about trying to keep your job or someone looking over your shoulder, you're behind the eight ball already, aren't you?'

The bitter twist to this tale is that of all networks, Nine should have been in the best position to take on the challenge of a new era in mass communications. James Packer, as we've just seen, understood the need to forge an alliance between TV and online services well before his father or, for that matter, any of his father's competitors. With that strategic vision in place even before the turn of the century, PBL should have been able to make the most of a giant head start. Channel 9 at that time could still boast the best creative brains in the business, led by the industry's most highly experienced executives. With the right encouragement they could have easily adapted their talents to developing content suitable for cross-promotion and presentation across multiple media platforms. That advantage, however, was frittered away in the five chaotic years when Kerry Packer stubbornly insisted on clinging to power despite his failing health.

Perhaps Kerry's obsessive attachment to his network helped to give him something to live for in those pain-wracked final years but, if that were the case, he could well be found guilty of having loved Channel 9 to death. During that critical period the issue of strategic vision, how to use a precious resource to best advantage, inevitably got lost in the rush to deal with more practical priorities, stopping the haemorrhage from rising costs and shrinking revenues. Even then, what should have been a calm, straight-forward exercise in proper management – trimming staff levels, reducing overseas program purchases, introducing efficiencies in local production – somehow became politicised, quickly degener-ating into open hostilities. Some of the network's most valuable people were driven away, not because they were unproductive but rather because they were arbitrarily branded as part of the 'old guard' and too difficult to control.

It's worthwhile noting where some of the casualties of the new-look Channel 9 have ended up. At the start of 2007, David Leckie, Peter Meakin, Mark Llewellyn and John Stephens were all busily helping to steer Channel 7 from one success to another. Kris Noble continued as the guiding force behind the top-rating *Big Brother* series. Julian Cress and David Barbour have been working with David Gyngell at Granada in Los Angeles, with one of their program concepts eagerly snapped up by America's ABC network and other ideas gaining considerable notice.

Among the on-air personalities caught up in the turbulent reign of Eddie McGuire, Jana Wendt would move on to a productive life outside the box, using her much admired interviewing skills to write a book featuring influential characters from around the world. Jessica Rowe found herself back in the headlines when news broke, just before the 2007 Logies, that Nine had decided to pay her out of her contract as *Today* show co-host in a settlement report-edly approaching the million dollar mark – despite McGuire's repeated public assurances that when Jessica returned from mater-nity leave she would be free from the shadow of the 'bone'.

Meanwhile, harsh reality finally caught up with Eddie himself. After barely 15 months in his largely titular role as Nine's top decision maker, he made the long-expected announcement that he was resigning to return to full-time stardom. Can one really quit a job that isn't actually there? 'The existing Nine Network management team headed up by Jeffrey Browne will take the network forward,' PBL Media's Ian Law enthused, adding almost as a throwaway line that under a new executive structure there would be no need to appoint anyone to replace McGuire. Spin to the end.

There's still every chance, of course, that the Nine Network, in its new incarnation, will prove to be a far more efficient broad-caster in terms of cost per ratings point than any of its competitors, delivering profits to twenty-first century investors that Kerry Packer would never have dreamed possible. Then again, as fond as Kerry was of making money, it's doubtful he would like much of what he would find at Channel 9 today. Perhaps he wouldn't notice a great deal of difference in its on-air look but he might well be stunned at the change in attitude of its hardworking creative staff – once so confident and even cocky, recognised throughout the industry for their resourcefulness and daring.

Guts, initiative, chutzpah – whatever one chooses to call it, it was certainly missing from the Channel 9 news on the morning of Monday, 20 March, 2006. That's when Cyclone Larry crossed the North Queensland coast to inflict one of the greatest natural disasters in modern Australian history. Seven's *Sunrise* was filled with dramatic coverage. It included live crosses to its weather reporter, Grant Denyer, who had been rushed to Townsville the night before, as well as emotion-packed eyewitness accounts phoned in by terrified storm victims huddled in their shelters in hard-hit Innisfail. Seven's programmers immediately approved Adam Boland's request for *Sunrise* to stay on air well past its normal 9 am sign-off to keep flashing continuous updates.

In stark contrast, Nine's *Today*, broadcasting from Melbourne to help promote the network's coverage of the Commonwealth Games, had its weather reporter in the studio pointing to a weather map. 'Strong winds and storms for Townsville today,' his patter went, or something like it. The Games remained the main topic of the program even while North Queenslanders slowly picked themselves out of the rubble and the state's devastated banana industry began counting losses adding up to hundreds of millions of dollars. Then, incredible as it seems, the *Today* show signed off promptly at 9 am as scheduled. Staff members had to suffer the indignity of going back to their hotel rooms to watch the rest of the special edition of *Sunrise*.

To be sure, Nine's news had suffered its share of bad luck. The network's regional affiliate in North Queensland had closed down its facilities for live broadcasting, whereas Seven's regional partner still maintained a live broadcast capability. Nine's Brisbane studios owned a satellite dish that could easily have been sent north to deal with the emergency but that, by sheer mischance, had been flown down to Sydney earlier in the week to fill in temporarily during some technical glitch. No one saw any great hurry to get it back until the first reports began streaming in of an ominous low off the Queensland coast. By Sunday afternoon, it had become clear that a monster storm threatened, but even then there was hesitation to authorise the chartering of a special wide-bodied jet transport needed to fly the bulky equipment up to Cairns to service the danger zone.

'That was the point of thinking, well, do you spend what would have been $50,000 chartering it now, not knowing before-hand [if there's going to be damage],' the news director at the time, Tony Ritchie, remembers agonising. The pressures on a senior news executive in such a situation – weighing the odds of a cyclone hitting a populated area or fizzling out – would be diffi-cult to bear in any circumstances. They can only be multiplied enormously when working under a management that has shown itself quick to punish anyone suspected of wasting money.

Punish? Is that an exaggeration? One need only recall those abusive e-mails from Park Street blasting the news and current affairs division for using four reporters to highlight its exclusive coverage of the Academy Awards when Channel 7 had used only one. The fact is, Channel 9's poor showing on its Cyclone Larry coverage came a little more than a week after that unsettling reprimand.

'This sounds like something from the Wizard of Oz,' John Alexander admonished. 'Is this your idea of running news and current affairs efficiently?' It would be hard not to be cowed with that kind of scornful message from senior management ringing in your ears.

Granted, working for Nine in its glory years was hardly for the faint-hearted. Some of us thrived, but many wilted in the blast furnace atmosphere generated by Kerry Packer in his driving ambition to make his cherished network the best it could possibly be. Still, for all his bullying and ill-tempered antics, he recognised the creative spirit of his dedicated staff as the precious but highly vulnerable resource that it is.

So easy to inspire with just the right word. With the wrong one, so easy to kill.

Bibliography

Anderson, Chris, *The Long Tail: Why the future of business is selling less for more*, Hyperion, New York, 2006

Barry, Paul, *The Rise and Rise of Kerry Packer*, Bantam/ABC Books, Sydney, 1993

Boyer, Peter J., *Who Killed CBS? The Undoing of America's Number One News Network*, St. Martins Press, New York, 1988

Dunlap, Albert J., *Mean Business*, Fireside, Simon and Schuster, New York, 1996

McHugh, Siobhan, *Shelter From the Storm*, Allen & Unwin, St Leonards, New South Wales, 1999

Munro, Mike, *A Pasty-Faced Nothing*, Random House, Sydney, 2003

Schwartz, Tony, *The Responsive Chord*, Anchor Press, Doubleday, New York, 1973

Souter, Gavin, *Company of Heralds: A century and a half of Australian publishing by John Fairfax Ltd. and predecessors*, Melbourne University Press, Melbourne, 1981

Stewart, James B., *Disney War*, Simon and Schuster, New York, 2005

Stone, Gerald, *Compulsive Viewing*, Penguin Books, Ringwood, Victoria, 2000

Index